CANADIAN ANNUAL REVIEW OF POLITICS AND PUBLIC AFFAIRS 2004

Canadian Annual Review
of politics and public affairs
2004

EDITED BY DAVID MUTIMER

Published with the support of York University by
University of Toronto Press
Toronto Buffalo London

ISBN 978-1-4426-4228-7

A cataloguing record for this publication is available from Library and
Archives Canada.

University of Toronto Press acknowledges the financial assistance to its
publishing program of the Canada Council for the Arts and the Ontario
Arts Council.

 **Canada Council
for the Arts**   **Conseil des Arts
du Canada**   **ONTARIO ARTS COUNCIL
CONSEIL DES ARTS DE L'ONTARIO**

University of Toronto Press acknowledges the financial support of the
Government of Canada through the Canada Book Fund for its publishing
activities.

This book was published with the support of York University.

Copies of the *Canadian Annual Review* published annually for 1989 and
1991–2003 are available.

Contents

Contributors

MELVIN BAKER, Archivist/Historian, President's Office, Memorial University of Newfoundland

EMMANUEL BRUNET-JAILLY, Assistant Professor, School of Public Administration, University of Victoria

PETER E. BUKER, Assistant Professor, Department of Political Studies, University of Prince Edward Island

KRISTIN BURNETT, Assistant Professor, History Department, Lakehead University

KEN COATES, Adjunct Professor of Political Studies, University of Saskatchewan

ROBERT DRUMMOND, Associate Professor, Department of Political Science, York University

ROBERT EVERETT, University Secretariat, York University

ROBERT G. FINBOW, Associate Professor, Department of Political Science, Dalhousie University

JOSEPH GARCEA, Associate Professor, Department of Political Science, University of Saskatchewan

CHRIS HENDERSHOT, doctoral candidate in the Department of Political Science at York University, and compiler of the Calendar and Obituaries

CAREY HILL, Independent Researcher, Ottawa, Ontario

HAROLD JANSEN, Assistant Professor, Department of Political Science, University of Lethbridge

GEOFFREY LAMBERT, Professor, Department of Political Studies, University of Manitoba

WARREN MAGNUSSON, Professor, Department of Political Science, University of Victoria

DAVID MUTIMER, editor of the *Canadian Annual Review of Politics and Public Affairs* (carppa@yorku.ca), Associate Professor of Political Science at York University, and Deputy Director of the York Centre for International and Security Studies

PETER NEARY, Professor, Department of History, University of Western Ontario

GREG POELZER, Associate Professor, Department of Political Studies, University of Saskatchewan

DANIEL SALÉE, Professor of Political Science and Principal of the School of Community and Public Affairs, Concordia University

CHRISTOPHER SPEARIN, Assistant Professor, Department of Defence Studies at the Canadian Forces College, Toronto

SHANNON STETTNER, managing editor of the *Canadian Annual Review of Politics and Public Affairs* (carppa@yorku.ca)

RICHARD WILBUR, Fundy Promotions, St Andrews, New Brunswick

Canadian calendar 2004

1   Montreal's Dorval Airport is renamed Montreal-Pierre Elliott Trudeau International Airport.

–   Governor General Adrienne Clarkson spends New Year's in Kabul with Canadian peacekeepers.

–   At least thirty-six landed immigrants are barred from re-entering Canada because they were not carrying the new permanent resident cards that came into effect 31 December.

4   Pay increases for public servants are frozen by Prime Minister Paul Martin. However, salaries for senior political staff, such as chiefs of staff to cabinet ministers, are increased by $32,000 a year.

–   Workers who pay into employment insurance are now entitled to six weeks' compassionate leave, with EI benefits.

5   Canadian dollar rises above US$0.78 for first time in over a decade.

7   Prime Minister Paul Martin announces a review of the federal gun-registry program.

–   DNA tests confirm that a BSE-positive cow in Washington State was born in Canada.

9   Statistic Canada reports that employment increased by an estimated 53,000 in December 2003. Employment gains from September to December 2003 totalled 219,000, which was four times the gain of 52,000 made over the first eight months of 2003. Full-time work accounted for most of the employment increases in 2003.

–   Statistics Canada reports that the unemployment rate decreased 0.1 percentage points to 7.4 per cent in December 2003.

12   Prime Minister Paul Martin and U.S. President George W. Bush reach an agreement that will allow Canadian companies to bid on a second round of contracts to rebuild Iraq.

- Stephen Harper enters the Conservative leadership race, while Jim Prentice withdraws from contention.
- What is believed to be Canada's largest and most sophisticated marijuana grow-op to date is discovered and dismantled by police in Barrie, Ont.

13 Peter MacKay declares that he will not enter the Conservative leadership race.

- Statistics Canada reports that the national debt stood at $526.5 billion on 31 March 2003, down $8.2 billion from the previous year. As a percentage of gross domestic product, the national debt fell from 47.6 per cent in 2002 to 43.5 per cent in 2003, which is the largest percentage drop since 1984.

15 Belinda Stronach and Tony Clement enter the Conservative Party leadership race.

21 Statistics Canada reports that between 1992 and 1999, on average, people who move into a low-income neigbourbood will live there for 3.8 years. A low-income neigbourhood is one where at least 40 per cent of residents live below the poverty line.

- Maher Arar sues the government of the United States, seeking financial compensation and a declaration that the United States acted illegally in sending him to Syria.

23 Statistics Canada reports that the employment rate in 2003 increased 2.2 per cent, or 334,000 jobs, to a total of 15.7 million people employed.

- Prime Minister Paul Martin confirms that Canada will cancel the $750-million debt owed by Iraq.

- Ernie Eves, former premier of Ontario, announces that he will be stepping down as leader of the Progressive Conservative Party of Ontario.

28 The federal government seeks clarification from the Supreme Court of Canada regarding the constitutionality of limiting common-law marriages to opposite-sex couples.

- Bank of Canada introduces new $100 bill in an effort to thwart counterfeiting.

29 Canadian Steelmaker Stelco files for and is granted creditor protection.

- Jaap de Hoop Scheffer, NATO secretary general, requests that Canada keep its soldiers in Afghanistan after the scheduled return of troops in August.

30 The Supreme Court of Canada rules that parents, and in some cases teachers, can discipline children with 'reasonable' use of force.

31 An extra $2 billion for health care is promised by Prime Minister Paul Martin after a First Ministers Conference in Ottawa.

FEBRUARY

4 Prime Minister Paul Martin announces that 500 soldiers will remain in Afghanistan after the completion of the Canadian Forces' mission in Kabul in August.

5 The 'Commission of Inquiry into the Actions of Canadian Officials in Relation to Maher Arar' is established by the federal government.

6 Statistics Canada reports that employment numbers demonstrated little change in January as an increase of 47,000 full-time jobs was offset by a decrease in part-time work.

7 In his first Speech from the Throne, Prime Minister Paul Martin promises cities a full rebate on the GST. The rebate is estimated to be worth $7 billion over the next decade.

9 Canadian Lieutenant-General Rick Hillier assumes command of the International Security Assistance Force in Afghanistan.

10 Auditor General Sheila Fraser releases a report that finds that millions of dollars were mishandled on federal government advertising and sponsorship contracts in Quebec.

13 The CBC's French news service releases a document that reveals that close to $2 billion has been spent on Canada's gun registry since its inception.

– Jane Stewart, former minister of human resources development, retires from politics to become an executive director of the International Labour Organization.

16 Elsie Wayne announces her retirement from public service. In the 1993 federal election, Wayne was one of only two Conservative Party members to win a seat in the House of Commons.

– Second general election is held in Nunavut.

17 John Bryden announces that he is leaving the Liberal Party and says he might run as a Conservative. He is the eighth MP to change party allegiance since December 2003.

18 British Columbia Finance Minister Gary Collins unveils the provincial Liberal government's first balanced budget, which includes an estimated surplus of $100 million.

19 Statistics Canada reports that in 2003 consumers paid an average of 2.8 per cent more for goods and services. This is a slight increase from the 2.2 per cent average increase in the 2002 Consumer Price Index.

20 CN rail workers go on strike.

– Nova Scotia and Prince Edward Island declare states of emergency after an estimated ninety cm. of snow falls over a two-day period.

– Justice Louise Arbour announces she is leaving the Supreme Court of Canada to become the new UN high commissioner for human rights. She will replace Brazilian Sergio Vieira de Mello, who was killed in a bomb attack on the UN headquarters in Baghdad.

– The federal government reaffirms that North Korean defector Song Dae Ri is a war criminal and thus not entitled to Canada's protection, despite a lengthy government report stating that Dae Ri be allowed to stay since he will be executed for treason if returned to North Korea.

23 Statistics Canada reports that, as of 2002, the drug-crime rate has risen an estimated 42 per cent since the early 1990s and now stands at a twenty-year high. The majority of incidents in 2002 involved possession of cannabis.

25 Statistics Canada reports that in 2001 more seniors remained in the workforce than in the five years previous. According to data collected, an estimated 305,000 seniors were employed in 2001, which represented a 19.6 per cent increase from the 255,000 employed in 1996.

24 Prime Minister Paul Martin suspends the heads of three crown corporations: Michel Vennat, president of the Business Development Bank of Canada, Via Rail president Marc LeFrançois, and Canada Post president André Ouellet.

27 Statistics Canada reports that real GDP grew 1.7 per cent in 2003, which is almost half the pace of the 3.3 per cent growth in 2002. However, GDP was up 0.5 per cent for December 2003, capping a total increase of 0.9 per cent for the final quarter of 2003.

MARCH

1 Jean Pelletier, chairperson of Via Rail, is fired after making belittling comments about Olympic champion Myriam Bédard, a whistleblower who questioned how Via handled federal sponsorship money.

3 Despite calls for him to step down, Premier Dalton McGuinty allows Greg Sorbara to continue to serve as Ontario's finance minister.

4   Nine Quebec Hells Angels are found guilty of gangsterism, drug trafficking, and conspiracy to murder in the first successful jury conviction under new federal anti-gang laws.

5   Paul Okalik is returned as premier of Nunavut, following the 16 February general election.

–   A Statistics Canada report reveals that interprovincial exports have represented a primary source of economic growth for Canada's provincial and territorial economies since 2000.

–   Canadian Forces will send 450 troops to Haiti for a ninety-day mission.

8   A new constitution is signed in Iraq.

9   Sheila Copps asks the Liberal Party of Canada to overturn the result of her loss to Tony Valeri, alleging voting irregularities in the Hamilton East nomination contest.

–   Belinda Stronach secures the Conservative Party of Canada nomination for the riding of Newmarket-Aurora.

11   A series of coordinated bombings target the commuter train system in Madrid, Spain. The final number of casualties total 191 people killed and 1,755 wounded.

12   Statistics Canada reports that business productivity grew only 0.1 per cent in 2003, which is smallest annual increase in close to a decade.

–   Michel Vennat, the president of the Business Development Bank of Canada, is fired as a result of the ongoing investigation into the sponsorship scandal.

18   Alfonso Gagliano, former public works minister, begins his testimony before the Public Accounts Committee. Gagliano maintains that he is an innocent victim of the sponsorship scandal.

19   The Quebec Court of Appeal rules in favour of same-sex marriage. The ruling upholds a lower-court decision and follows similar decisions in Ontario and British Columbia.

20   With 55.5 per cent of the vote, Stephen Harper secures a first-ballot victory to become the first leader of the Conservative Party of Canada.

22   Prime Minister Paul Martin announces a farm-aid package worth almost $1 billion in response to losses caused by the mad cow crisis.

–   Frank Iacobucci announces his retirement from the Supreme Court of Canada – effective in June.

–   The federal government announces legislation that will protect public-sector whistleblowers.

- Statistics Canada reports that Canada's population as of 1 January 2004 is 31,752,842.
23 The federal budget is tabled in Parliament.
- The federal government announces plans to sell its remaining stake in Petro-Canada – worth over $2 billion.
25 Statistics Canada reports that Canada's national net worth grew to $4.0 trillion by the end of the fourth quarter in 2003.
- Statistics Canada reports that, despite popular belief, Canadians were no more likely to lose their jobs during the 1990s than they were during the 1980s.
26 Statistics Canada reports that, in 2003, one in twenty-five people worked for or below the minimum wage in their province of residence. Although numbers varied widely by province, nationally 547,000 people worked for minimum wage in 2003.
29 According to a new study of Canadian vital statistics, immigrants are less likely than native-born Canadians to commit suicide.
- Ottawa resident Mohammad Momin Khawaja is arrested on terrorism charges. Khawaja is the first person arrested under Canada's new anti-terrorism laws.
30 Statistics Canada reports that tourism spending fell 2.7 per cent in 2003. However, spending did increase 3.2 per cent during the fourth quarter of 2003.

APRIL

1 The number of seats in the House of Commons increases from 301 to 308 as redistribution of federal ridings goes into effect.
- Over 20,000 civil-service employees go on strike in Newfoundland. The province responds with plans to lay off as many as 4,000 because of an $840-million deficit.
- Michael Hendricks and René Leboeuf are married in Montreal and become the first legally recognized same-sex marriage in Canada.
6 In a measure aimed at stopping the spread of avian flu, the federal government orders the slaughter of about nineteen million chickens and turkeys.
8 Statistics Canada reports that 13,000 jobs were lost in March, which led to a 0.1 per cent increase in the rate of unemployment to 7.5 per cent.
- Monia Mazigh, the wife of Maher Arar, wins the NDP nomination in Ottawa South.

14   Statistics Canada reports that the value of the Canadian dollar
      grew 21.7 per cent in 2003 from US$0.6339 to US$0.7713. This
      is the largest single-year movement in Canada's history.
15   New Democratic Party MP Svend Robinson announces he is tak-
      ing medical leave after admitting he stole a ring.
16   Statistics Canada reports that e-commerce posted a big gain
      in 2003; however, online sales continue to account for less than 1
      per cent of overall operating revenues for private businesses.
19   Statistics Canada reports that the national crude birth rate
      dropped to 10.5 live births for every 1,000 population in 2003,
      which is a 1.5 per cent decrease from 2002. The birth rate has de-
      creased 25.4 per cent in the past decade.
 –   The U.S. Department of Agriculture opens the border to nearly
      all Canadian beef products.
20   Isabelle Roy, an aide to former public works minister Alfonso
      Gagliano, offers testimony before the Public Accounts Commit-
      tee that contradicts Gagliano's, saying the minister was regularly
      involved in the sponsorship program.
 –   Fadi Fadel, an aid worker with the International Rescue Commit-
      tee, returns to Canada after being held hostage in Iraq for eight
      days earlier in the month.
21   Statistics Canada reports that the number of people who were un-
      employed for over a year peaked in 1994 when about 17 per cent
      of those looking for work could not find any. This number has
      fallen to 10 per cent in 2003. The study compiled employment
      statistics from 1976 to 2003.
 –   The House of Commons approves a private member's bill that
      acknowledges the 1915 genocide of Armenians by the former Ot-
      toman Empire.
22   Chuck Guité, who oversaw the federal sponsorship program from
      1996 to 1999, testifies before the Public Accounts Committee.
      Guité denies any wrongdoing and says he filed all the necessary
      paperwork.
25   The Dalai Lama speaks to thousands at the SkyDome in Toronto.
 –   Over 43,000 health-care workers go on strike in British Colum-
      bia.
26   About half of all college and university graduates from the class
      of 2000 left school owing money for their education. Most of this
      debt is in the form of government student loans.
27   Anne McLellan, deputy prime minister of Canada, announces a
      new $690-million national and foreign security initiative.

29   Prime Minister Paul Martin makes first official visit to Washington, D.C., to meet with President George W. Bush.

MAY

3   A last-minute deal averts a province-wide general strike by British Columbia's public-sector employees.
4   70,155 couples filed for divorce in 2002. This number is down 1.3 per cent from 2001 and 1.4 per cent from 2000.
–   Naji al-Kuwaiti, an importer-exporter, is released after being held by Iraqi abductors for a week. He is the third Canadian to be taken hostage in Iraq.
7   Statistics Canada reports that employment increased by an estimated 50,000 full-time jobs in April. The unemployment rate fell to 7.3 per cent, which is the lowest rate since September 2001.
10   Chuck Guité and Jean Brault, the two men at the centre of the sponsorship scandal, plead not guilty to six fraud-related charges and are released on bail.
11   The Public Accounts Committee votes to end hearings on the sponsorship scandal and to begin working on an interim report.
12   The federal and the Nova Scotia governments announce a 10-year, $400-million plan to clean up the Sydney tar ponds.
17   Ken Dryden, former goalie for the Montreal Canadiens, announces he will run for the Liberals in the riding of York Centre.
–   Statistics Canada reports that, during the 1980s and 1990s, the earnings of new immigrants fell as the result of a series of factors such as the value of foreign job experience, language abilities, and nation of origin.
18   Greg Sorbara, Ontario's finance minister, tables the Liberal government's first budget. A new health premium is introduced that will range from $300 to $900 depending on annual personal income.
–   A report is released by the three federal opposition parties claiming that the Public Accounts Committee hearing into the federal sponsorship program exposes a 'gross abuse of power.'
20   Statistics Canada reports that after-tax family income demonstrated no significant change from 2001 to 2002 – this after five years of growth. In 2002 families of two or more, after inflation, made an estimated $60,500, up only marginally from $60,300 in 2001.
21   In a case brought by a Saskatchewan farmer, the Supreme Court of Canada rules in favour of U.S. biotechnology corporation

Monsanto, saying that because Monsanto holds a patent on a gene in its canola seed, it can control the use of the plant.

23 Governor General Adrienne Clarkson dissolves the House of Commons; a general election will be held after a thirty-six-day campaign.

27 Citing the prairie drought and the mad cow crisis, a Statistics Canada report reveals that 2003 farm incomes fell to their lowest level in twenty-five years.

– Alfonso Gagliano launches a $4.5-million lawsuit against the federal government and Paul Martin for wrongful dismissal, loss of wages, and personal damages.

31 Statistics Canada reports that real GDP advanced 0.6 per cent in the first quarter of 2004.

JUNE

1 Smoking in all bars and restaurants is banned in Toronto and surrounding municipalities.

– 928 hate-crime incidents occurred during 2001 and 2002, according to a survey of twelve major Canadian police forces.

4 Statistics Canada reports that 56,000 new jobs were gained in May, with a subsequent 0.1 percentage drop in the unemployment rate to 7.2 per cent.

5 Former U.S. president Ronald Reagan dies at age ninety-three.

10 The federal government goes to the Ontario Court of Appeal seeking to reverse a December 2000 decision by Ontario's Superior Court of Justice that grants retroactive pension payments to same-sex partners back to 17 April 1985.

11 With exports growing at over six times the pace of imports, in April Canada records its second-highest trade balance ever.

15 1.2 million Canadians were unable to find a regular medical doctor in 2003, according to results from the Canadian Community Health survey.

– Statistics Canada reports that 1.7 per cent of Canadians aged eighteen to fifty-nine consider themselves to be gay or bisexual.

18 Between 1988 and 2003, municipal governments increasingly relied on local taxpayers to pay for community services and infrastructure projects.

24 Statistics Canada reports that national net worth grew to $4.1 trillion through the end of the first quarter of 2004.

28 The Liberal Party of Canada wins a minority government. Seat

distribution is: Liberals 135, Conservatives 99, NDP 19, Bloc 54, and 1 independent.

29 According to preliminary results from Elections Canada, voter turnout continued to drop, with only 60.5 per cent of eligible voters casting ballots.

30 Wait times represent the number-one barrier to accessing specialized health-care services in Canada, according to the 2003 Health Services Access Survey.

JULY

1 Canada celebrates its 137th birthday.

6 U.S. Air Force Major Harry Schmidt is found guilty of dereliction of duty for his actions in the 2002 friendly-fire incident that resulted in the deaths of four Canadian soldiers in Afghanistan.

– Statistics Canada reports that police and court records from 1997–8 to 2001–2 reveal that family members convicted of most forms of violent crimes against their spouses, children, and parents were less likely to go to prison than other violent offenders.

8 Statistics Canada reports that 64 per cent of Canadian households had a least one person regularly use the Internet in 2003. This was a 5 per cent increase from 2002.

9 Statistics Canada reports that an estimated 25,000 jobs were added in June. The unemployment rate rose 0.1 per cent as more people were searching for work.

12 Ralph Klein announces that Alberta is debt-free.

14 The Yukon becomes fourth jurisdiction in Canada to legalize same-sex marriage.

– The Canadian ambassador to Iran is recalled after Canadian observers are denied access to the trial of the man charged with killing photojournalist Zahra Kazemi.

17 The Canadian ambassador to Iran remains and is one of the foreign observers given access to the trail of the man charged with killing photojournalist Zahra Kazemi.

18 Canada again recalls its ambassador to Iran after abrupt ending to the trial of the man charged with killing photojournalist Zahra Kazemi.

19 Nicolas Gill is chosen to be Canada's flag bearer for the opening ceremonies of the Olympic Games in Athens.

20 Prime Minister Paul Martin announces his new cabinet. New faces in cabinet include Ken Dryden, Scott Brison, and Ujjal Dosanjh.

21　Statistics Canada reports that an estimated three million people admitted to using cannabis at least once in 2002.

23　The federal government announces a plan to purchase twenty-eight twin-engine Sikorsky S-92 helicopters at a cost of $3.2 billion to replace the fleet of Sea King helicopters.

24　The accused killer of Iranian-Canadian journalist Zahra Kazemi is acquitted of charges of 'semi-intentional murder.'

28　Counterfeiting, property crimes, and minor offences account for a 6 per cent increase in Canada's national crime rate in 2003.

30　According to an independent audit, André Ouellet, suspended president of Canada Post, spent $2 million on travel and hospitality over an eight-year period.

–　University enrolment rose 4.3 per cent in 2001–2 with a record number (886,800) of students enrolling in schools across Canada.

AUGUST

2　Local 503 of the United Food and Commercial Workers Union receives accreditation from the Quebec Labour Relations Board. The union will represent 180 workers at the Wal-Mart store in Jonquière, Quebec – the first unionized Wal-Mart in North America.

6　Statistics Canada reports that only 9,000 jobs were gained in June as the unemployment rate fell 0.1 per cent to 7.2 per cent.

–　Svend Robinson pleads guilty in a Vancouver court to a charge of theft over $5,000. He is given a conditional discharge and thus will not have a criminal record.

12　André Ouellet resigns as head of Canada Post.

13　The Summer Olympics officially begin in Athens, Greece.

–　Parks Canada employees walk off the job across the country.

19　Revenue for post-secondary institutions in Canada grew sharply in 2002–3 largely because of increasing tuition fees and federal government grants. Student fees now account for over 20 per cent of total revenue.

–　U.S. officials announce the creation of a new command centre along the Canada-U.S. border south of Vancouver. A new plane with sensor equipment, marine units, and a Black Hawk helicopter are to be deployed. Similar centres in New York, Montana, North Dakota, and Michigan will also be built.

23　Canada's police chiefs want wiretap laws updated so as to gain better access to Internet and cell phone communications.

– Citizenship and Immigration Canada instructs the Canadian Bible Society to stop handing out bibles at citizenship ceremonies.

24 Justices Louise Charron and Rosalie Abella are nominated to the Supreme Court of Canada.

29 Closing ceremonies for the Summer Olympics take place in Athens, Greece. Canada won twelve medals, which is the lowest medal count since the 1988 Summer Olympics in Seoul, South Korea.

31 Statistics Canada reports that real GDP rose 1.1 per cent in the second quarter of 2004.

SEPTEMBER

3 Over 300 people are killed and 600 injured after commandos storm a school in Beslan, Russia, in an attempt to end a three-day stand-off.

7 Testimony begins in the public inquiry, headed by Justice John Gomery, into the sponsorship scandal.

8 Employees at the Canada Revenue Agency begin a strike against the federal government.

– The number of American soldiers killed in the war in Iraq surpasses 1,000.

– The Bank of Canada raises interest rates to 2.25 per cent from 2 per cent.

10 Statistics Canada reports little change in employment numbers for August. Job gains are up 0.7 per cent from 2003 for the first eight months of 2004.

13 The prime minister and the premiers meet in Ottawa for a two-day conference on the state of health care in Canada.

– Canada's first same-sex divorce is filed in Ontario.

15 Canada's first ministers reach a deal that will inject an extra $18 billion into health care over the next six years.

16 Same-sex marriage is legalized in Manitoba.

– Statistics Canada reports that national net worth totalled $4.2 trillion through the end of the second quarter of 2004.

– NHL owners lock out players over a salary-cap dispute, putting the upcoming hockey season in jeopardy.

18 John Tory is elected as leader of Ontario's Progressive Conservative Party.

22 The federal government announces that it is forgiving the debts of Senegal, Ghana, and Ethiopia.

- Fairuz Yamulky returns to Canada after having been held captive in Iraq for sixteen days.
24 Same-sex marriage is legalized in Nova Scotia.
25 Ontario government hurriedly passes legislation that bans Life Line Screening, a private health-care firm from Cleveland, from running a one-day diagnostics clinic in the Hamilton-Niagara area.
- Results of an RCMP internal investigation of the Maher Arar affair are released to the public. Although heavily censored, the document reports several instances of impropriety by the RCMP.
27 Statistics Canada reports that life expectancy for people born in 2002 increased only for men. According to the report, men can be expected to live to 77.2 years, which is up 0.2 years from 2001, while women can be expected to live 82.1 years, which remains unchanged since 2001.
- Newfoundland and Labrador Health Minister Elizabeth Marshall leaves the provincial cabinet, saying she disagrees with the management style of Premier Danny Williams.
- After thirteen years of deployment, Canadian peacekeepers leave Bosnia-Herzegovina.
29 Statistics Canada reports that the national homicide rate fell 7 per cent in 2003. The rate of 1.73 victims per 100,000 people is the lowest in over three decades.
- Forty-four North Korean asylum seekers scale the walls of the Canadian embassy in China.
- The Montreal Expos play their last home game ever. The team will be moving to Washington, D.C., for the 2005 season.
30 Air Canada emerges from bankruptcy protection.

OCTOBER

1 Governor General Adrienne Clarkson's term is extended one year.
- Anti-smoking laws take effect in New Brunswick and Manitoba.
5 Speech from the Throne delivered to first minority Parliament in twenty-five years.
6 Combat systems engineer Lieutenant Chris Saunders succumbs to injuries after a fire aboard HMCS *Chicoutimi* – a refurbished submarine recently purchased from the United Kingdom.
8 Statistics Canada reports that an estimated 43,000 jobs were

gained in September, with the unemployment rate decreasing 0.1 per cent to 7.1 per cent.

9 Hamid Karzai wins Afghanistan's first presidential election since the U.S.-led invasion in 2001.

11 Striking Parks Canada employees reach a tentative deal with the federal government.

12 More than 10,000 members of the Public Service Alliance of Canada reach a deal with the federal government after a one-day strike.

13 Federal Finance Minster Ralph Goodale announces that the federal government posted a $9.1-billion surplus for the 2003–4 fiscal year.

14 Striking Revenue Canada employees reach a deal with the federal government that will give them a 10 per cent pay increase over four years.

15 Ontario announces a plan to ban pit bulls. Current owners will be allowed to keep their dogs so long as the dogs are leashed, muzzled, and spayed or neutered.

16 The World Health Organization says that, since March, at least 70,000 people in Sudan's western Darfur province have died because of poor conditions in camps for internally displaced people.

17 The Top Ten for CBC's *Greatest Canadian* contest are announced. The list includes Don Cherry, David Suzuki, Alexander Graham Bell, Tommy Douglas, Wayne Gretzky, Pierre Trudeau, Lester B. Pearson, Frederick Banting, and John A. Macdonald.

20 The government of Ontario announces a plan to ensure the availability of healthy foods in all of the province's schools.

– The Canadian dollar closes at US$0.8029, its first time above $0.80 since 1993.

25 Alberta's provincial legislature is dissolved and an election is called for 22 November.

26 Premier Danny Williams walks out of a First Ministers Conference in protest against the federal government's offer on the Atlantic Accord.

28 Supreme Court of Canada rules that Newfoundland and Labrador was justified in deferring a $24-million pay-equity payment for women in 1991.

– The Boston Red Sox win the World Series of Baseball for the first time in eighty-six years.

29 Statistics Canada reports that beer remains the alcoholic beverage of choice for Canadians.

NOVEMBER

2 George W. Bush wins a second term as president of the United States.

– Statistics Canada reports that foreign-controlled firms in Canada possessed 21.7 per cent of assets in 2003, which represents little change from 2002.

– Ken Dryden, social development minister, announces $1 billion for a new national childcare program. The announcement comes after the release of an OCED study which found Canada's system to be chronically underfunded.

5 Same-sex marriage is legalized in Saskatchewan.

– Statistics Canada reports that 34,000 jobs were added in October, while the unemployment rate remained unchanged at 7.1 per cent as more people entered the labour market in search of employment.

11 Yasser Arafat, leader of the Palestinians, dies in hospital outside Paris.

10 Up to 700 Canadians are forced to flee the Ivory Coast as violence erupts in response to a French bombing raid on the Ivory Coast's air force – the French raid was in response to a bombing by the Ivory Coast's air force that killed nine French peacekeepers.

15 The Securities and Exchange Commission files a fraud suit against Conrad Black and Hollinger Inc. in Illinois.

12 The Saskatoon Police Department fires constables Bradley Senger and Lawrence Hartwig after they are implicated in the freezing death of native teen Neil Stonechild fourteen years ago.

18 Supreme Court of Canada rules that governments must consult with Aboriginals before allowing such activities as logging or mining on disputed crown land.

– Carolyn Parrish, MP for Mississauga-Erindale, is expelled from the Liberal Party caucus.

21 The Toronto Argonauts win the Grey Cup for the first time since 1997.

22 Ralph Klein and his Conservative Party win another majority government in Alberta.

24 Jamal Akkal, from Windsor, Ont., pleads guilty in an Israeli military court to conspiracy and illegal military training for planning attacks on Jews in Canada and the United States. He is sentenced to four years in prison.

25 Governor General Adrienne Clarkson's $19-million budget is cut by $417,000.

–   The Canadian dollar briefly cracks US$0.85 and closes the day at US$0.8492.

26 Ontario's Court of Appeal rules that same-sex couples in the province are entitled to survivor's benefits under the Canada Pension Plan dating back to 1985.

–   Two mechanical failures result in the spillage of close to 1,000 barrels of oil into the Atlantic Ocean from the Terra Nova off-shore-oil production platform.

29 Tommy Douglas is voted the Greatest Canadian by viewers of the CBC television series.

30 U.S. President George W. Bush thanks Canada for its role in restoring order to Afghanistan during his first official visit to Canada.

–   Statistics Canada reports that real GDP increased 0.8 per cent in the third quarter of 2004.

–   Stan and Frank Koebel, the two brothers at the centre of Walkerton's tainted water tragedy, plead guilty to common nuisance in Ontario.

DECEMBER

2   The twentieth anniversary of the world's worst industrial accident is marked in Bhopal, India. At least 10,000 people died and 555,000 were made sick when 40 tonnes of poisonous gas leaked from a pesticide plant owned by Union Carbide. The site has never been cleaned up.

3   Statistics Canada reports that employment rates remained relatively unchanged for November. However, with more people in search of work, the unemployment rate increased 0.2 per cent to 7.3 per cent.

7   An immigration hearing begins that will decide whether Jeremy Hinzman can remain in Canada. Hinzman, considered a deserter by the U.S. military, fled to Canada as a conscientious objector to the war in Iraq.

8   Canada's special operations military unit, Joint Task Force 2, receives a U.S. Presidential Unit Citation for heroism in battle for operations in Afghanistan. JTF2 is only the second Canadian unit to receive such a commendation.

9   The Supreme Court of Canada says the federal government can

change the definition of marriage, giving gays and lesbians the legal right to marry.

10 Captain Miles Selby dies after a mid-air collision of two Canadian Forces Snowbirds over Saskatchewan.

19 Prime Minster Paul Martin visits Libya, the first Canadian prime minister to do so.

21 Same-sex marriage is legalized in Newfoundland and Labrador.

26 A 9.15-magnitude earthquake, the second largest ever recorded, sends giant waves crashing into coastal areas of Southeast Asia. The resulting death toll is more than 225,000 people.

27 The federal government announces a commitment of up to $40 million for the Indian Ocean earthquake relief effort.

CANADIAN ANNUAL REVIEW OF POLITICS
AND PUBLIC AFFAIRS 2004

EDITOR'S INTRODUCTION –
THE YEAR IN REVIEW

Whereas the past several years had been dominated by international questions, in 2004 Canadian politics was decidedly inwardly focused. It is not that issues of foreign policy and defence were not important, particularly with the evident deterioration of the war in Iraq and Canada's ongoing involvement in Afghanistan, but rather that the year was defined by a federal general election. The Liberal Party had governed with a seemingly unassailable majority for a decade, and it had begun the year energized by a leadership convention that was marked by unparalleled unity. By the year's end, while still in government, the Liberals were reduced to a minority in the House of Commons and had been forced to accept amendments to their Throne Speech to avoid a second election in the year. At the same time, outside Parliament, Justice John Gomery was overseeing a commission of inquiry into the so-called sponsorship scandal, an issue that had plagued the Liberals for years and was seen as partly responsible for the collapse in their support in June's election.

There was little to foreshadow the significant shift in the political geography of the country as 2004 dawned. Paul Martin was newly elected leader of the Liberals and finally held the prime minister's office he had so obviously long coveted. The convention itself was little more than a big celebration of the (apparent) final act of the Chrétien-Martin battle, since there was no meaningful leadership contest. All but one of the potential candidates opposing Martin had withdrawn, and the one, Sheila Copps, managed just 6 per cent of the leadership vote. The Liberals had a strong majority in Parliament, a popular leader who had been a very well-respected finance minister, and an opposition that was struggling to overcomes years of bitter division.

On the opposition benches, the year began with a scramble to forge the new Conservative Party that had been born from the merger of the Progressive Conservatives (PCs) and the Alliance, a merger that was concluded only by a court ruling in December 2003. The Conservative

Party did not have time to hold a full policy convention, but it did need a leader. The early weeks of 2004 saw a small field of candidates emerge, as a series of well-known Canadian conservatives announced that they would not seek the leadership, including, the outgoing PC leader, Peter MacKay, as well as Jim Prentice, Chuck Strahl, Bernard Lord, Ralph Klein, and Mike Harris. The Alliance leader, Stephen Harper, did stand and was challenged by former Ontario cabinet minister Tony Clement and a young political outsider, Belinda Stronach. The election of Stephen Harper on 20 March, and on the first ballot, did not appear to mark the end of the fissures within the Canadian right. A number of members of Parliament crossed the floor or sat as independents following the final merger of the two former right-wing parties. Most notably, the former Progressive Conservative prime minister, Joe Clark, ended his days in Parliament as an independent and announced before leaving that he would henceforth support the Liberals.

It was in this context that Prime Minister Martin visited the governor general on 23 May, calling an election for 28 June. The election campaign, however, did not go as the prime minister would have planned. The Liberals faced a concerted attack from the three major opposition parties on their record, and particularly on the issue of the sponsorship scandal. There was a strong whiff of corruption about the sponsorship program, and to the opposition it smelled like blood. Particularly in Quebec, the scandal drove voters away from the Liberals, and with the Conservatives seeming to make inroads in Ontario, there were few places the Liberals would be able to replace lost Quebec seats. For their part, the Conservatives under Harper strove to appear safe and moderate: fiscally conservative but in the Canadian mainstream socially. The election team recognized that the danger was in allowing the Liberals to paint them as dangerous social radicals, intent on importing U.S.-style views on issues such as abortion and gay marriage that were out of step with the increasingly urban country. For much of the campaign, this strategy appeared to work, and polls suggested the election might even produce a Conservative government, but, fortunately for the Liberals, Harper's control over his members was not complete, and a number of off-message statements on key hot-button issues swung voters away from the Conservatives in the final days of the campaign.

The result of the June vote, therefore, was that Canada had its first minority government in a quarter-century. The Liberals lost their majority as both the Conservatives and the Bloc Québécois (BQ) picked up over twenty seats each and the New Democratic Party (NDP) gained five: the Liberals finished with 135, down from 168 at dissolution; the

Conservatives rose from 72 to 99 and the Bloc from 33 to 54; and the NDP returned with 19 members. It was also an election that saw voter turnout fall to its lowest level since Confederation, 60.9 per cent, down from 61.2 per cent four years earlier. There was a sense, however, that the election was unfinished, and that a second election could soon follow to provide a more decisive evaluation of the political state of play in Canada. Indeed, through the second half of 2004, the country was reminded of how precarious minority governments can be, even though the situation in Parliament did not (quite) result in a second election.

Following the summer recess, the new Parliament heard the now minority Martin government's second Speech from the Throne in October. The first had been read in February to guide a session that ended up lasting only three months. A Throne Speech to a minority Parliament was a rather different experience from the previous one, and so many that it had followed. The speech triggers a motion of confidence designed to demonstrate to the House that the government's program, as outlined in the speech, has the support of the Commons, and what became quickly clear was that this speech did not have such support. A defeat would trigger a second election that none of the parties really wanted – this time the Grits, and the other parties as well, really were chicken! However, the government was not willing to rely on election-aversion, and so it accepted a number of amendments to the speech, only the third time a Canadian government had amended its Throne Speech.

The political pressure on the government was not limited to the House of Commons. The sponsorship scandal had played a significant role in the election, and the result did nothing to put the scandal to rest. The prime minister had attempted to distance himself from the sponsorship program, cancelling it as almost his first act after the December 2003 leadership convention. However, in February the auditor general, Sheila Fraser, released a scathing report on the program, saying she was 'shocked' by the abuses. Again Martin attempted to mollify the public and escape the political fallout of the affair. He immediately fired Alfonso Gagliano, who had been at the heart of the program but sent to be ambassador to Denmark by the former prime minister. The Public Accounts Committee of Parliament, at this point still controlled by the majority Liberals, launched an inquiry. Of perhaps greatest political significance, however, Martin appointed Justice John Gomery to head a public inquiry into the affair. The inquiry began in September, but the main event seemed to be postponed to the new year, with both Martin and former prime minister Chrétien due to appear – although only Martin agreed publicly to do so.

Amid the political theatre that dominated the year, there was some movement on important areas of public policy, although any advances were rendered uncertain once the government lost its majority. In his first Throne Speech, Martin had outlined his ambitious 'New Deal for Cities,' including a full Goods and Services Tax (GST) rebate and enhanced infrastructure spending. The first element would provide much needed funding directly to cities, which were trying to cope with consistent, massive expansion; the second would be an important move to redress what nearly all observers agreed was the crumbling, virtually obsolete infrastructure across the country. However, the election results dealt a blow to the cities agenda. The point-person on the file, former Winnipeg mayor Glen Murray, was defeated in the June vote, and facing an uncertain Parliament, Martin watered down his agenda, substituting a 'new deal for communities.' The change in language was significant, since it brought in the interests of the small towns and rural communities across the country, which were quite different from those of the large urban areas the deal was originally designed to serve. There was some good news for cities, at least in Ontario, where the provincial government announced that it would transfer significant new powers to its large cities, starting with a new piece of legislation, the City of Toronto Act.

The provinces and the federal government were also able to reach an agreement on perhaps the most vexing of Canadian public issues when, in September, a First Ministers Conference on health care produced a health-care accord. The agreement saw the federal government commit over $40 billion to the provinces over ten years, in exchange for which the provinces agreed to a number of federal proposals designed to increase accountability and coherence in the fragmented Canadian health-care system. However, the deal fell short of instituting true national standards, and indeed it was touted by Jean Charest as a victory for Quebec and by Stephen Harper as more like a deal he would have signed than one to be expected from the federal Liberals.

One of the most significant results of the terrorist attacks on the United States in 2001 had been the breakdown of the distinction between internal security and the defence of the realm. In 2003 this had produced the reorganization of the security apparatus of the Canadian state with the development of the Department of Public Safety and Emergency Preparedness. In early 2004 the government put forward its integrated vision of security in this new environment with the release of *Securing an Open Society: Canada's National Security Policy*. It was the first time the government had enunciated an integrated national-security policy, and it was organized around three priorities: the protection of Canadians at home and abroad, ensuring Canada was not used as a base from which to threaten others, and the contribution of Canada to international security. The first reflected the elision of internal and external security in an era in which transnational terrorism was seen to pose the predominant threat. The second was largely an attempt to offset the stubbornly held belief south of the border that Canada's open society could provide fertile ground for terrorists bent on attacking the United States – exemplified in the persistent view that some of the 9/11 attackers had entered the United States through Canada, despite this being demonstrated to be false. The third priority was an attempt to connect Canada's traditional global engagements, and the more recent contributions to Afghanistan, to the new security environment.

The title of the national-security policy document, *Securing an Open Society*, was intended to draw attention to the vulnerabilities that can be created by liberty. It was not intended to be ironic, but one could forgive people from reading it in just that way – particularly, one could forgive it of Maher Arar. Arar was the Canadian who suffered 'extraordinary rendition' at the hands of the United States in 2002. He had been sent by U.S. officials to Syria, the country he had left as a teenager to move to Canada, and there was imprisoned and tortured on information that appeared to have been provided by Canada in some form. The Chrétien government had refused calls for an inquiry into Arar's ordeal and the role of the Canadian security services, but Paul Martin's government announced in January that Justice Dennis O'Connor would lead a public inquiry into the affair. The inquiry convened in June, but through much of the second half of the year it was taken up in struggling with the government to release the information needed for the inquiry to do its job, since the documents that were grudgingly provided were heavily censored. An open society indeed!

The case of another Canadian held abroad was also prominent this year. In 2003 Zahra Kazemi, a Canadian photojournalist who also held Iranian citizenship, died in Iranian custody. The summer of 2004 saw Reza Aghdam Ahmadi tried by the Iranians for her killing. The trial precipitated a diplomatic rift between Canada and Iran, with the Canadians withdrawing their ambassador in July after the Iranians first shut down two opposition newspapers as the trial was set to begin, and then denied the Canadian ambassador access to the court, despite an agreement to permit him to attend. He was then recalled a second time after the trial, since Canada did not accept that it had been a fair process – a view also held by international human-rights watchers. Kazemi's son called on the government to take stronger action against Iran in protest, but he was ultimately unsatisfied with Canada's response, which included appointing a new ambassador in November and tabling a resolution at the UN General Assembly on 'Iran and Human Rights.'

Canada's contributions to international security focused on the ongoing operations in Afghanistan. In 2004 Canada took its turn leading the International Security Assistance Force (ISAF), the North Atlantic Treaty Organization (NATO) mission to which Canada was contributing. General Rick Hillier assumed command of ISAF in February. General Hillier had significant command experience, including having served as the commander of NATO forces in Bosnia-Herzegovina. The year 2004 marked the end of the latter commitment, as the NATO mission in Bosnia was replaced by the European Union (EU) and the Canadian Forces (CF) withdrew from a theatre where it had been stationed since 1993. While the mission was a success, its end was welcome to the CF, which was increasingly overstretched by its lengthy overseas commitments. Indeed, in Afghanistan, the Canadian contingent was reduced in 2004 from 2,000 to 700. Extra forces were useful, for at the end of February Canada sent troops to Haiti to help maintain order in the aftermath of the ouster of President Jean-Bertrand Aristide.

Not only were the Canadian forces operationally stretched, but they continued to face equipment issues, several of which emerged prominently in 2004. On 1 October, Canada formally took command of the last of the four submarines it had purchased from the United Kingdom when HMS *Upholder* became HMCS *Chicoutimi*. However, the *Chicoutimi*'s initial Canadian voyage was extremely brief, as an electrical fire left the boat powerless and several members of its crew injured – including one who died as he was being evacuated to hospital in Ireland. The submarine then had to be 'towed' across the Atlantic, and its three sister submarines were also taken out of service for preventative maintenance. In July the government finally announced the replacement for the Sea King helicopters, a procurement process that had bedevilled the Liberal government since it cancelled the contract to purchase EH-101s soon after taking office in 1993. Even at that time, the Sea Kings were on their last legs, and now a decade later a new contract was reached for the purchase of twenty-eight S-92 Cyclones, the first of which, however, were not due to be delivered until 2008.

The Canadian relationship with the United States continued to be of central importance to our foreign policy, with three key items on the agenda: cross-border trade, in particular beef and wood; the return of missile defence, and the visit of the U.S. president to Canada. Beef producers in Canada struggled throughout 2004 with the ban on Canadian beef that had been instituted the year before in response to the discovery of a case of BSE (more popularly known as mad cow disease). While the ban was partially lifted in April, it was not until December that the United States announced that live cattle would be permitted back into the country, and even then not until March 2005. Softwood lumber remained an irritant, as Canada continued to win support in rulings from both the World Trade Organization and North American Free Trade Agreement (NAFTA) panels, but the United States retained its penalties on Canadian wood.

The Martin government equivocated on the question of joining the U.S. missile defence program throughout 2004. In the early months of the year it seemed the government was leaning toward accepting the U.S. invitation to participate, part of its attempt to improve relations with the Americans following the Chrétien years. In January the two countries exchanged letters on missile defence, building on the decision the previous year to hold talks on the issue. More significantly, in August the North American Air Defence (NORAD) agreement was amended to allow data collected by NORAD to be used by the U.S. military for the purposes of missile defence. Martin even expelled one of his own MPs from caucus for her outspoken attacks on the U.S. administration and its policies, including missile defence. In his end-of-year interviews, however, Martin questioned the feasibility of the system and so it was unclear whether he would lead Canada into formal participation in 2005.

Soon after his re-election in November, U.S. President George W. Bush paid his first visit to Canada. Part of his agenda was to push for Canada's participation in missile defence. However, he added Halifax to the usual visit to Ottawa in order to pay tribute to the contribution Nova Scotians had made in hosting Americans stranded when U.S. airspace was closed after 9/11. Despite his re-election, the U.S. president and his policies were not popular in Canada, and he faced a series of protests, including one of 5,000 in Ottawa.

With the November 2004 election over, the United States would have the same administration for the next four years. The same could not be said of his hosts. As 2004 drew to a close, the Liberal government faced a boisterous Parliament with a majority sitting on the opposition benches. It had been forced to amend its own Speech from the Throne, and the corruption scandal that had contributed mightily to its diminished status was under the spotlight of a public judicial inquiry. There were certainly no guarantees that 2005 would not see another federal general election, and were that to happen, no certainty over its outcome.

The present edition of the *Canadian Annual Review of Politics and Public Affairs* marks another step in the changes to the volume I first announced in 1999. It is a real pleasure to be able to include, starting this year, a section on Canada's First Nations. The lack of a separate treatment of First Nations in the *Review* has been perhaps its single greatest omission. The federal and provincial governments are created by the Canadian Constitution Act (1867) as the loci of governance in Canada, and they have served as the organizational foundation of the *Review*. However, First Nations governance is not simply an issue of the public policy of the other levels of government. In a number of cases the First Nations are treaty partners with the federal or provincial governments, and, in an attempt to right historical wrongs, they are increasingly being accorded governing autonomy. Yet, as the inaugural section on our First Nations will show, there was in 2004 still a very long way to go in redressing the situation in which Canada's engagement with its Native peoples has left them.

The lack of basic necessities – housing and safe drinking water – continue to plague our First Nations communities, despite an apparent focus on First Nations affairs in the first Martin Throne Speech of the year. The violence of the state in its relations with First Nations people came under public scrutiny this year, however, with public inquiries into 'Starlight Cruises' (the practice of police driving Native men out of town and stranding them) in Saskatchewan and into the killing of Dudley George at a protest in Ipperwash, Ontario. There was also continued attention to the legacy of another manifestation of state violence, the residential schools program, though no resolution was forthcoming in 2004.

The addition of a First Nations section to that on municipal affairs means that the *Review* now more properly reflects the range of Canadian political institutions that help shape our politics and public affairs, and we hope that it thereby provides a more useful and insightful account of the year.

ROBERT EVERETT

Parliament and politics

In November 2003 Paul Martin scored a massive victory in the contest to elect a successor to Jean Chrétien as leader of the Liberal Party and prime minister of Canada. When he took the oath of office the following month, the highly regarded former finance minister presided over a highly popular government buoyed by the change at the top. The Official Opposition, the Conservative Party, leaderless and bereft of a platform following its November 2003 birth out of a merger of the Reform Alliance and Progressive Conservatives, lagged badly. Yet, just weeks before the conclusion of the country's thirty-eighth general election on 28 June, Martin's main rival, new Conservative leader Stephen Harper, was openly musing about a move into the official residence at 24 Sussex Drive. This sharp and stunning change of fortunes seemed destined to result in the ouster of the Liberals from government after nearly eleven years when the balloting ended. However, a late surge gave the Liberals enough seats in traditional strongholds to hang on to the reins of government, albeit with a precarious minority in the House of Commons. Despite a dramatic reprieve, the chastened Liberals were weakened to the point where they had to accept, for only the third time in history, amendments to the Speech from the Throne that conceded a degree of control over the agenda to the opposition parties.

In any election year, there is a risk that the ebb and flow of partisanship will overwhelm substantive issues and impede the pursuit of policy. Coming as it did at the mid-point of the year, the election of 2004 created two prolonged periods during which the legislative calendar was thin. Many of the substantive issues that did command attention surfaced thanks to legal proceedings (such as the spate of lower court rulings tending towards upholding same-sex marriages), the ineluctable dynamics of federalism (especially evident in yet another accord with the provinces about health care), dicey decisions inherited from the government of Jean Chrétien (for example, the implications of assigning a more aggressive mission in Afghanistan to Canadian troops), and unresolved dilemmas (including those concerning an action plan in support of commitments made under the Kyoto pact on climate change). Seizing an opportunity created by Liberal vulnerabilities, the opposition parties used the Throne Speech amendments to elevate vexed issues such as electoral reform, tax cuts for lower-income earners, and the so-called 'fiscal imbalance' between the federal and provincial governments. The American government, hoping for a friendlier approach with Martin at the helm, made no secret of its hope and expectation that Canada would cooperate with its Ballistic Missile Defence (BMD) plan. Control of the agenda was difficult to regain once the majority vanished. The Liberals had to ponder issues with extra care, and defer action when it was possible. Sometimes this was due to the muscularity of the opposition, and sometimes it was attributable to divisions within the party itself.

Contributing to the Liberals' woes in 2004 was the lingering taint of scandal. In February, Martin bowed to partisan pressure (and sought political capital) by agreeing to establish an official inquiry into the mismanagement of a sponsorship program aimed at enhancing the image of the federal government and federalism in Quebec through advertisements and other promotional activities. Revelations about slipshod administration and a worrisome web of cozy relations between senior officials and a select number of private firms – possibly rising to illegal conduct – had tarnished the government of Jean Chrétien. The ongoing saga had also eroded support for the Liberal Party in Quebec, and provided other parties with inexhaustible opportunities for vilification. In addition, a public inquiry was launched into the case of a Canadian-Syrian citizen, Maher Arar, who was apprehended in New York in 2002, spirited off to Syria under the cover of suspect American anti-terrorist statutes, and abused during interrogations while incarcerated. Charged with illuminating the role of Canadian services in this episode, the commission was hindered by bureaucratic invocations of national security, heavy censorship of documentation, and the indifference of both Syria and the United States.

Liberals took some comfort from a relatively strong economy and healthy fiscal situation symbolized by another budget surplus and further drops in the government's debt. Yet even good news generated political headaches. Positive financial circumstances of the kind heralded by Finance Minister Ralph Goodale inspired the opposition parties, provinces, interest groups, increasingly activist pro-urban and anti-poverty alliances, think tanks, and sundry others to call upon Ottawa either to spread the wealth around or to curb its appetite for revenue. The cabinet assembled by Martin also tested several innovations in governance that it hoped would redeem a pledge to overcome the 'democratic deficit' that the prime minister extolled as a leitmotif of his tenure. They received a mixed response. New realities meant that the Liberals' greatest success during the year was simply surviving.

The thirty-eighth general election

The country went to the polls on 28 June after a thirty-six day campaign that began when Prime Minister Martin asked the governor general to dissolve Parliament on 23 May. Speculation about the timing of an election began as soon as Paul Martin was installed as the new leader of the Liberal Party and successor to Jean Chrétien as prime minister in November 2003. The instantaneous prognostication was perfectly understandable. On the positive side, the Liberals were surely tempted to capitalize on Martin's unprecedented momentum after he had deterred and defeated a host of rivals, prospective and real, on the road to an epic landslide. The party's membership coming out of the leadership convention of 2003 was unified, and its organization appeared robust and ready. An election was due sometime in 2004, but the political calculus was especially tricky. April passed and May was nearly over before Martin acted.

Of course, long before the 'issuing of the writs' – the arcane term to describe the actions of the chief electoral officer that set a campaign in motion – parties and candidates were preparing for the election. It was a particularly busy winter for the Conservative Party of Canada. Although there was no time for a formal policy convention before the election, the party had no choice but to find its first-ever leader.

Conservative Party leadership

In late 2003, over the vociferous and litigious protestations of a rump of its members, Progressive Conservative members joined their counterparts in the Canadian Reform Conservative Alliance to reconstitute under a single banner. The merger of the two right-wing parties was formalized on 8 December 2003 when Elections Canada registered the Conservative Party of Canada. Despite a handful of high-profile defections, primarily from the 'Red Tory' wing of the old Progressive Conservative Party – its more secular and ostensibly centrist faction – the Conservatives set about the task of establishing itself on the political terrain.

The first order of business in 2004 was to elect a party leader. Veteran Alberta MP Grant Hill was chosen to serve as interim head of the party for the duration of the parliamentary session (10 Jan.), succeeding Senator John Lynch-Staunton in the post. Several plausible candidates declined to enter the fray. Notably absent was the last leader of the Progressive Conservatives, Peter MacKay, who announced that he would not pursue the leadership on 13 January. Although clearly interested, MacKay admitted to funding shortfalls. Coupled with this was a surplus of baggage owing to a controversy surrounding a pledge not to enter into merger talks with the Canadian Alliance in return for the support of his chief rival, David Orchard, at the final PC leadership convention in 2003. Another past Progressive Conservative leadership hopeful, Jim Prentice, also cited money woes in announcing his decision to sit out the race (12 Jan.). British Columbia MP Chuck Strahl backed away as well despite some encouragement. Incumbent provincial premiers Bernard Lord of New Brunswick and Ralph Klein of Alberta demurred, as did former Ontario premier Mike Harris, a darling of the right.

This left the field to the last leader of the Canadian Reform Conservative Alliance, Stephen Harper, who signalled his entry on 12 January, and a pair of relative newcomers to the federal scene from Ontario, Tony Clement and Belinda Stronach. Clement, who had served as health minister in the hard-right Ontario cabinet of Mike Harris in the 1990s, formally declared his intentions on 15 January. Stronach, a complex figure with no electoral experience, launched her bid on 20 January. Although a novice candidate, Stronach was possessed of a formidable résumé. She had been entrusted by her father to run the industrial branch of Magna, a leading parts supplier to the North American automotive industry, while still in her thirties. Talks between the Reform Conservative Alliance and the Progressive Conservatives were facilitated by her patronage. Although Frank Stronach had been a Liberal candidate with suspicions about free trade, his daughter was adamant that Liberal hegemony was ruinous. A plethora of greying eminences gravitated to her camp, either as paid mentors or volunteers. For all this she was viewed in some quarters as an interloper, and the tabloid and serious press alike made much of her fortune and comfort with celebrity.

Clement gamely appealed for support in roughly the same geographical and ideological terrain occupied by Stronach. As a former cabinet minister with a keen partisan edge, he proved attractive to those who felt that the more cerebral Harper might be too tame for merciless Liberals. It was nevertheless difficult for him to develop traction. He was able to raise only a third of the money secured by Stronach, the frontrunner in donations. Stronach was entrenched in the Atlantic provinces and Quebec while Harper sealed up the western provinces. As is often the case in leadership campaigns and general elections, votes in populous Ontario proved decisive.

The voting method adopted by the Conservatives was unique. Each riding was assigned 100 points which were then allocated to candidates based on their share of the vote. The goal, which was part of the merger bargain, was to mitigate the disproportionate strength of the old Reform Party and placate those in smaller ridings. A preferential system was also adopted. If the count of first-choice votes was indeterminate, the trailing candidate's second-choice votes would be redistributed. This proved unnecessary. Harper won an outright victory with 56.2 per cent of the vote on the initial tally. Stronach finished a respectable second with 34.5 per cent. Strong in the eastern zones of the country, her momentum halted at the Quebec-Ontario border. The sheer weight of veteran Reform partisans was sufficient to tip the scales for Harper. Following Harper's triumph, he named MacKay as the deputy leader (22 March) and the Conservatives began in earnest to prepare for the election to come.

Preliminaries

Turbulence followed on the merger. Liberals defected to the Conservatives. Conservatives bolted in the opposite direction. The entire system reoriented in a landscape without a 'progressive' Conservative party in sight and with a relatively conservative leader at the helm of the Liberals. Keith Martin, who had once sought to lead the Reform Alliance, left the Conservative caucus on 14 January and declared his hope of wining the Liberal nomination in the British Columbia riding of Esquimalt-Juan de Fuca. John Herron also fled the Conservatives to sit among a blooming roster of independents in the House (6 Feb.). He planned to seek a Liberal nomination for the next round of voting. Hamilton-area Liberal MP John Bryden moved in the opposite direction (17 Feb.). Elsie Wayne, who was one of a pair of lonely Progressive Conservatives in the House at her party's nadir in the early 1990s, readied herself for retirement. Joe Clark, a Tory prime minister resolutely opposed to the unite-the-right cause, ended his days in the House as an independent on 2 February and subsequently declared that he would be supporting the Liberals (25 April). On 20 January, André Banchand resigned from the Conservative caucus to sit as an independent. Like Clark, he would not run again.

A number of former Liberal cabinet ministers vacated the national scene in the run-up to the election. Quebec's Martin Cauchon (tabbed as a possible prime minister), one-time agriculture minister Lyle Vanclief, and the Ontario trio of Bob Nault, Jane Stewart, and Art Eggleton decided to leave for various reasons, but all were significant players of the past who had been overlooked by Martin when his cabinet was assembled. There were other comings and goings that had less to do with ideology than idiosyncrasy. Among the departed was long-serving Svend Robinson, one of the NDP's strongest personalities, who resigned over a career-damaging shoplifting offence. The NDP lured former leader Ed Broadbent back to run in Ottawa Centre and nominated Monia Mazigh, partner of Mahar Arar, in the neighbouring riding of Ottawa South. A handful of notable independents ran in the election, including former Saskatchewan premier Grant Devine and Larry Spencer, a former Conservative MP who had been expelled from caucus in late 2003 for uttering anti-gay remarks.

Adjustments in the number of ridings necessitated by population growth revealed in the 2001 census resulted in an increase in the size of the House of Commons to 308 seats from 301 in the previous election. Ontario was allotted an additional three seats (to a new total of 106). Alberta and British Columbia grew by two seats each to 28 and 36 respectively. In two ridings the subsequent boundary changes created overlapping constituencies that necessitated nomination contests between intransigent sitting MPs of the same (Liberal) party. In Mississagua-Erindale, Carolyn Parrish prevailed over former cabinet minister Steve Mahoney (7 March) in a straightforward affair. In Hamilton East the fray was far more intriguing. It was there that Sheila Copps, who had dared challenge Martin to the very end of 2003 leadership race, faced Tony Valeri, an early convert to the Martin cause. Valeri won the day (6 March). Following the verdict, Copps complained bitterly about machinations that had blocked her way. She flirted with the possibility of running as an independent or as an NDP candidate. After a cooling-off period, Copps abandoned that idea and set about penning her memoirs.

The Liberals, Conservatives, and New Democrats were the main contenders. The Bloc Québécois fielded candidates only in Quebec. Also in the running were the Green Party (with candidates in 308 ridings), the Marxist-Leninist Party (76), the Marijuana Party (71), the Christian Heritage Party (62), the Canadian Action Party (45), the Communist Party (35), the Progressive Canadian Party (16), and the Libertarian Party (8). The Greens excepted, these parties were largely excised from media coverage. The Green Party also failed, once again, to persuade the Canadian Radio-television and Telecommunications Commission (CRTC) and a consortium of national broadcasters that its leader should be allowed to participate in the television debates.

On the hustings: health care or something else?

Reprising a refrain from recent Liberal campaigns, Prime Minister Martin declared that the election would be about fundamental values. Although the Conservative Party had bleached the contentious positions of the old Reform Party, it remained resolutely of the right. This was especially true in terms of social mores. The Liberals and other parties wanted voters to believe that the rebranding of the Conservative Party was a cosmetic solution to a partisan quandary rather than the abandonment of an agenda that would turn Canadian politics on its head.

One of the clearest dividing lines was health, and party platforms reflected contrasting visions. The opening salvos located health care at the heart of the matter. This was not just a matter of substantive differentiation. The Liberals tried to position the Conservatives as hostile to universality and receptive to further privatization of services, strategies that would be a tough sell. In this they were aided by the Conservative government of prosperous Alberta. It planned to make a major announcement in June about significant changes in its health system – a so-called third way – that was expected to embrace greater privatization as a panacea. This was manna to the Liberals and Alberta's cabinet knew it. The announcement was deferred until the election was over but not before a link was forged in the public imagination between Alberta's plans and those of the federal Conservative Party.

The leaders of the four parliamentary parties squared off on consecutive nights for debates in French and English. Other parties were excluded from these events (having challenged, without success, the rules of participation). While most commentators agreed that the events were not pivotal, they nevertheless added piquancy. The French debate was held on 14 June. With his superior command of the language and home-field advantage, Bloc leader Gilles Duceppe was able to steer many of the exchanges. Duceppe suppressed talk of sovereignty, his party's raison d'être, so as to focus attention on the Liberals' record. Martin had to weather persistent attacks from the others on stage about his ethics – his party's and his own. Many of the ripostes turned on the question of whether or not a vote for the Liberals or Conservatives would end up enriching the Bloc and by extrapolation the sovereignty cause.

In the English-language debate on 15 June, Martin tried in vain to switch off the sponsorship scandal with repeated warnings about the Conservatives. He contended that a Harper government would consider using the 'notwithstanding clause' of the Charter of Rights and Freedoms to override court rulings favourable to same-sex marriage, limit reproductive choice, move away from the principles of Medicare, cozy up to the Americans, and run down the nation's finances. James Travers of the *Toronto Star* judged the debates 'more tense and combative than revealing or enlightening' and invoked 'the spectacle of three birds of prey methodically picking at a once fierce predator now wounded and fallen on hard times' (16 June). He and many other pundits felt that Harper had fared well (a conclusion borne out by opinion polls) by adopting a cleverly understated tone of exasperation.

As always, the campaign served up a healthy dose of mudslinging, missteps, and misstatements. No party was immune from the intense scrutiny as journalists scouted out and exploited gaffes and controversies. A distracting dust-up followed on NDP leader Jack Layton's accusation that Martin could be blamed for the deaths of homeless individuals (27 May). Layton also raised eyebrows when he revealed that he would repeal the Clarity Act, aimed at a clearer construction of any future referendum question about Quebec sovereignty, and would not support an exit from the North Atlantic Treaty Organization (28 and 29 May). Overly aggressive Liberal candidates caused furores when they stepped over the bounds of decorum.

The Conservatives suffered most. Polls intimated a minority government, or better. Harper worked tirelessly, and often successfully, to make blandness a virtue and conservatism a painless if not pleasing prospect. Yet the party had difficulty reigning in its more opinionated candidates and allowed its more unvarnished positions to seep out. Scott Reid, running in rural Ontario, lambasted near-sacrosanct official bilingualism and in doing so recalled the kind of redneck sensibilities that doomed Reform in much of Canada. The party website promulgated, but then quickly retracted, salvos at the Liberals and the New Democrats for coddling child pornographers. Rob Merrifield suggested that women should be subjected to mandatory family counselling before obtaining an abortion while Cheryl Gallant equated abortion with terrorism. British Columbia candidate Randy White, upset that courts across the land had ruled in favour of same-sex marriage, argued that pernicious jurists could be thwarted by invoking the notwithstanding clause of the Charter. The social conservatism espoused by individual candidates was too far out of the mainstream, and it left voters who had flirted with the idea

Party preferences, select Ipsos-Reid polls, January to June 2004

	Liberals	Conservatives	New Democrats	Bloc Québécois	Green	Other
24 January	48	19	16	10	4	3
30 April	40	23	18	11	5	–
22 May	35	26	18	12	5	4
5 June	32	31	17	11	6	3
19 June	29	32	16	12	7	–
22 June	34	28	16	13	6	3
25 June	32	31	17	12	6	2

of voting Conservative confused about the true nature of the party. At the mid-point of the campaign, the Conservatives moved ahead of the Liberals. Second thoughts turned the tide against them.

The results

By convention, the party with the most seats is given the opportunity to face Parliament unless another grouping can demonstrate to the governor general that it can command the House. The Liberals were thus able to escape the full wrath of the electorate, but they barely clung to power after losing more than thirty seats. There was no real possibility of the Liberals forming a coalition or arriving at a looser compact with another party, as Martin quickly confirmed (29 June). An accommodation with the Official Opposition Conservatives or the separatist Bloc was out of the question. The New Democrats could not have helped even if they were so inclined, having fallen fractionally short of the twenty seats that could have been added to the Liberal total to equal reasonably firm control of the House. This would be a go-it-alone, finesse-or-fall, risk-laden sort of minority. Minority governments are not unusual in Canada. This was the tenth time that a governing party had secured a plurality rather than a majority of seats. The most recent experience was in 1979 and the short-lived government of Progressive Conservative Joe Clark. Some commentators recalled with fondness the accomplishments of the 1972–4 Liberal minority when Pierre Trudeau's government took an activist turn with the prodding of the NDP, or more generally extolled the moderating benefits of forced coalition building. Others were less sanguine about the prospects of productivity and longevity given the complex ideological divisions within the House and the ramped-up aspirations of other parties.

For the Conservatives, ending the estrangement of the right wing did not produce the bountiful electoral harvest predicted by merger advocates. Indeed, the recombined right's share of votes was actually lower than the total obtained by right-wing parties in 2000. Yet the consolidation of candidacies helped lift the Conservatives by upwards of twenty seats. The left fared better. New Democrats nearly doubled their share of their popular vote even though their putative rivals, the Greens, saw gains in the hundreds of thousands. The separatist Bloc Québécois, also of a progressive bent, soared. Deciphering the meaning of the national trend was no easy task, however, since ideological trajectories were hard to follow. Conveniently, if not necessarily fortuitously, the persistent provincial and regional imprints on Canada's political make-up made it easier to tell the tale of the Liberals' victory. The Liberals took twenty-two seats in the four Atlantic provinces compared to the Conservative total of seven and the New Democrats' haul of three. All four governments in Atlantic Canada were held by the Conservative Party, and all four premiers endorsed their federal kin. The voters showed a more independent streak.

Quebec tilted heavily towards the Bloc Québécois. The Bloc captured fifty-four of seventy-five seats and 48.9 per cent of the vote. Only the Liberals, with twenty-one seats (most of them picked up in urban, largely anglophone or allophone enclaves), dimmed the Bloc's otherwise dazzling performance. After two elections in which it dropped seats, the Bloc gained sixteen, a turnaround that Duceppe attributed to the renewed confidence in his party felt by the voters of Quebec. Just as plausibly, it was a verdict meant to punish the Liberals.

Ontario, as always, was the principal battleground of the election. The Conservatives made considerable gains in the province and ended up with 24 of 106 seats and just under 32 per cent of the popular vote. The NDP picked up seven precious seats despite setbacks for star candidates, including Layton's partner, Toronto city councillor Olivia Chow. The Liberals, though, retained their supremacy with seventy-five seats and 44.7 per cent of votes. Although positive, it was simply not enough to offset the forfeiture of Quebec.

Conservative fortunes improved in Manitoba. Seven seats went to the right, while the Liberals could win in only three ridings, fewer than the NDP's total of four. Saskatchewan proved to be surprisingly barren electoral ground for the NDP even though it was in power at the provincial level. The party was shut out entirely as the Conservatives translated 39.1 per cent of the vote into thirteen of fourteen seats, with

Number of seats, by party, in 2000 election, at dissolution, and following the 2004 election

Party	Seats Following 2000 Election (301 Seats)	Seats at Dissolution (301 Seats)	Seats Following Election (308 Seats)
Liberal Party	172	168	135
Conservative Party of Canada		72	99
Reform Conservative Alliance	(66)		
Progressive Conservatives	(12)		
Bloc Québécois	38	33	54
New Democratic Party	13	14	19
Green Party	–	–	–
Independent	–	10	1
Vacant	–	4	–

Share of popular vote and change from 2000 to 2004, by political party

Party	Share of Vote, 2000	Share of Vote, 2004	Change in Share of Vote
Liberal Party	40.8	36.7	–4.1
Conservative Party		29.6	–8.1 (hypothesized)
Reform Conservative	(25.5)		
Alliance	(12.2)		
Progressive Conservative			
Bloc Québécois	10.7	12.4	+1.7
	(Quebec 39.9)	(Quebec 48.9)	(Quebec +9.0)
New Democratic Party	8.5	15.7	+7.2
Green Party	0.8	4.3	+3.5
Other Parties / Independent	2.2	1.2	–1.0

the Liberals holding on to a single riding thanks to Finance Minister Ralph Goodale. Bedrock Alberta returned twenty-six Conservatives, with fully 61.7 per cent of voters in that province supporting the right-wing party. The Liberals clung to two seats in the working-class precincts of Edmonton.

The evening's tally with British Columbia voters sent twenty-two Conservatives to the Commons. The Liberals took eight seats. Despite the imbalance, this was astonishingly welcome news for nervous Grits. Aspiring to a near sweep on the west coast, the Conservatives actually shed six ridings while the Liberals gained two. The New Democrats went from two to five ridings, and the loyal voters of North Surrey stubbornly chose independent Chuck Cadman, an erstwhile Conservative, as their representative. All three seats in the country's northern territories went to the Liberals.

Smaller parties receded in this election. This was not true for the Greens. Calling it a 'coming of age' for his party, Green leader Jim Harris pointed proudly to a surge to 570,000 votes. With 4.3 per cent of the national vote, the Greens qualified for annual public funding of more than $1 million (parties exceeding a threshold of 2 per cent qualified for $1.75 for each vote cast). Although unable to win a single electoral seat, it was clear that the Greens had become a force.

At 60.9 per cent, the voter turnout was down from 61.2 per cent in 2000. It was the worst figure since Confederation in 1867. Parliament and Elections Canada had worked out a number of reforms designed to ease and widen voter participation, regulate campaign spending, and expand public financing for eligible minor parties. These technical tinkerings, however commendable, could not vitiate an obviously profound alienation.

Parsing the outcome

How did the Liberals cling to power? A *Toronto Star* editorial headlined 'Canadians Chose a Stronger Nation' argued that voters ultimately settled for a 'socially progressive alternative' to the far-right vision offered by the Conservatives even as they registered their justifiable anger over Liberal 'corruption, waste and arrogance' (29 June). The *Globe and Mail*'s editorialists were convinced that the results 'owed more to doubts about Stephen Harper's Conservative alternative' and the inability of Harper to 'persuade Canadians that he is what he says he is: a politician of the Canadian mainstream' (29 June). So much depended on Ontario. Ian Urquhart of the *Toronto Star* opined that Ontario voters were '"scared off" by the idea of a Conservative government propped up by the Bloc Québécois' – a decentralizing combination – and opted for the preferable course of 'a Liberal minority government with the NDP holding the balance of power' (29 June). For the better part of six weeks, Paul Martin and the Liberals were the issue. At the end of the day, it was Stephen Harper and the platform of the Conservatives that seemed crucial. A consensus formed around the view that this was merely the first round of the debate. The next election, whenever it came and however it was caused, would end with a more definitive sense of the mood of the electorate.

The ceiling for women candidates

The number of women successfully competing for nominations and winning seats in federal elections continued to be meagre. Parties had a dismal record when it came to nurturing women despite their public professions and intensifying pressure from advocacy groups. Only 23 per cent of candidates in the 2004 election were women. At just 245, the number of women running was actually down from a high of 436 in 1993. Overall, the proportion of women in the new House was virtually unchanged from 2000 at 21.1 per cent, with sixty-five women elected. New Democrats fielded the most candidates, and Liberal women enjoyed the highest rate of success at the polls. Groups that had sprung up to promote women candidates included Equal Voice. Its chair, journalist Rosemary Speirs, attributed the pattern to systemic discrimination against women at the local level and the reluctance of parties (with the possible exception of the NDP) to actively recruit and support females (*Toronto Star*, 29 June). Prime Minister Martin drew criticism when his new cabinet contained two fewer women than the pre-election ministry. All of the newcomers were men. Speirs called this 'disgraceful' and argued that the reduction in numbers was especially offensive given Martin's professed emphasis on merit as the criterion for inclusion in his campaign (*Toronto Star*, 22 July). The disappointment in his selections was not tempered by the naming of eight women as parliamentary secretaries.

National institutions

The new cabinet

Prime Minister Martin announced his post-election cabinet line-up on 21 July. He tapped thirty-nine Liberals to serve in the government. Thirty-three were named to senior positions and six were designated for roles at the junior minister of state level. A minority situation meant that experience was at a premium. Thus, it was not surprising that Martin chose to retain twenty-eight ministers from the outgoing cabinet in his new ministry. In addition, room was made for six seasoned backbench MPs, including former Conservative leadership candidate Scott Brison. Five rookie MPs also made the team, among them star candidates such as former British Columbia NDP premier Ujjal Dosanjh, B.C. forestry executive David Emerson, hockey legend Ken Dryden, and Jean Lapierre, a defector from the separatist ranks of Quebec. Each of them landed relatively important tasks. Martin also resurrected the career of Stéphane Dion, a key player during the latter Chrétien era at intergovernmental affairs. Dion returned from exile to tackle the environment file.

Six cabinet ministers went down to defeat in the general election (Stan Keyes, Gar Knutson, Rey Pagtakhan, David Pratt, Helene Scherrer, and Robert Speller). Pratt, the minister of national defence, had the highest profile. The others were of junior or middling rank. No one else in the upper echelons lost their seats, and, Martin included, thirteen senior ministers held onto their previous jobs. Those returning to familiar offices were:

- Anne McLellan, deputy prime minister and minister of public safety and emergency preparedness;
- Ralph Goodale, minister of finance;
- Irwin Cotler, minister of justice and attorney general;
- Reg Alcock, president of the Treasury Board;
- Joe Volpe, minister of human resources and skills development;
- Jim Peterson, minister of international trade;
- Jim Efford, minister of natural resources;
- Jacob Austin, government leader in the Senate;
- Joe McGuire, minister responsible for the Atlantic Canada Opportunities Agency;
- Judy Sgro, minister of citizenship and immigration;
- Geoff Regan, minister of fisheries and oceans; and
- Aileen Carroll, minister for international cooperation.

In addition, Joe Comuzzi continued as minister of state for the Federal Economic Development Initiative for Northern Ontario and Carolyn Bennett stayed on as minister of state for public health.

Eleven senior ministers were transferred to new posts, one full cabinet member was moved to a ministry of state, and a junior minister changed assignments. The most eye-catching swap involved the transfer of Bill Graham from Foreign Affairs to National Defence. Writing in the *Toronto Star*, James Travers argued that the odd decision to name a dovish intellect to head up Canada's armed forces might actually help to re-create a sorely needed coherence between the country's foreign and military affairs (22 July). Pierre Pettigrew was rewarded for a dutiful stint in the difficult Health portfolio with the plum assignment of Canada's foreign minister. The other shuffled ministers were:

- Jacques Saada, minister of the Economic Development Agency for the Regions of Quebec and minister responsible for la francophonie (from government leader in the House);
- Lucienne Robillard, president of the Queen's Privy Council for Canada and minister of intergovernmental affairs (from Industry);
- Andy Scott, minister of Indian affairs and northern development and interlocutor for Métis and non-status Indians (from the Ministry of State for Infrastructure);
- John McCallum, minister of national revenue (from Veterans Affairs);
- Albina Guarnieri, minister of veterans affairs (from associate minister of national defence and minister of state for civil preparedness);
- Andy Mitchell, minister of agriculture and agri-food (from Indian Affairs and Northern Development);
- Tony Valeri, leader of the government in the House of Commons (from Transport); and
- Liza Frulla, minister of Canadian heritage and minister responsible for the status of women (from Public Works and Government Services).

Claudette Bradshaw, who had held the full-cabinet Labour portfolio, was demoted to minister of state for human resources development. Ethel Blondin-Andrew, who had to survive a recount in her riding, emerged as the minister of state for northern development after a previous stint as the minister of state for children and youth.

There were eleven new faces on the scene. In the mix of former backbenchers and novices were:

- Stéphane Dion, minster of the environment;
- Ujjal Dosanjh, minister of health;
- Ken Dryden, minister of social development;
- David Emerson, minister of industry;
- Joe Fontana, minister of labour and housing;
- Jean Lapierre, minister of transport;
- Scott Brison, minister of public works and government services;
- Mauril Bélanger, deputy leader of the government in the House of Commons, minister responsible for official languages, minister responsible for democratic reform, and associate minister of national defence;
- Raymond Chan, minister of state for multiculturalism;

- John Godfrey, minister of state for infrastructure and communities; and
- Tony Ianno, minister of state for families and caregivers.

Three new positions resulted from the reorganization: a minister of state for infrastructure and communities; a minister of state for families and caregivers; and a combined labour and housing portfolio under a full minister who would also have responsibility for the Canada Mortgage and Housing Corporation. Four ministers were dropped from the Martin cabinet: Jean Augustine (the previous minister of state for multiculturalism and status of women), David Emerson (formerly at Environment), Denis Coderre (president of the Privy Council), and Denis Paradis (minister of state for financial institutions). The regional cast of the new ministry was not markedly different, but it did not escape notice that only nine ministers were women. Martin also picked twenty-eight parliamentary secretaries, some assigned to policy fields and others attached to specific departments. All were sworn in as privy councillors, a designation allowing them to participate in cabinet discussions.

Speeches from the Throne

Governor General Adrienne Clarkson read speeches from the throne on two occasions. The first gave rise to a lively but typically harmless debate in the House when a pro forma endorsement of the government's agenda was adopted by a vote along party lines. The second speech resulted in a riveting test of wills between the opposition parties and a weakened minority government. Failure to secure agreement on the wording of a motion would have forced a second general election within six months.

The House resumed in February after the Liberal leadership race and the amalgamation of the Canadian Reform Conservative Alliance and Progressive Conservatives. The Throne Speech kicking off a new session was interpreted as a preview of the Liberals' campaign platform. It promised concrete initiatives to help cities cope with their challenges, to enhance a wide spectrum of educational programs, to reduce waiting lists for treatments of various kinds, and to clean up toxic hot spots at military bases, abandoned mines, harbours, nuclear facilities, and other sites around the country. Big city mayors had been pressing the government through intense lobbying and advertising campaigns, and they professed themselves delighted with the government's overdue recognition of the so-called urban agenda. Municipalities were promised a

full rebate of the 7 per cent Goods and Services Tax and sped-up timelines for disbursals under a national infrastructure program. The speech
stressed that this was just a down payment. Other commitments included a review of Canadian foreign policy, assorted democratic reforms,
and legislation to remove barriers to affordable treatment of HIV-AIDS
in Africa. Carefully chosen phrases implied an awakened sense of activism informed by the view that 'government has an enabling role.' This
was understood in some quarters as Martin's way of countering charges
that he was 'tilting the federal government to the political right,' and, although listeners across the political spectrum heard the message, 'more
than a few ... expressed doubts about Martin's sincerity' (*Toronto Star*,
3 Feb.). Others felt that the agenda reflected the cautious and conservative persona of the prime minister.

Following the election in June, the thirty-eighth Parliament of Canada was inaugurated with a Throne Speech that tried to dampen expectations while calling on listeners to work together to ensure the success of
the new minority government (5 Oct.). Still not out of the woods over
the sponsorship scandal, the government said it would foster greater
transparency and accountability. Without giving specifics, the speech
nodded towards the NDP's demands for greater vigour in the pursuit
of electoral reform. A theme of fiscal prudence was sounded. Deficits
would not be countenanced, and the government reiterated its goal
of reducing its debt-to-gross domestic product (GDP) ratio to 25 per
cent in ten years. Programmatic priorities included a renewed drive to
improving the lives of Aboriginal peoples aided by benchmark indicators. Health care would remain a priority, but the recently completed
$41-billion accord with the provinces was the foundation of further en-
deavours. The new government also restated intentions to establish a
national system of childcare. This time they came wrapped around the
principles of 'quality, universality, accessibility and development.' The
urban agenda faded to some degree, but an unspecified share of the levy
on gasoline purchases would be targeted for direct use by cities. An
expanded, enriched military would be matched by a Canadian corps of
foreign-aid workers. A *Globe and Mail* editorial depicted the speech as
bland and diffuse, repetitive and shopworn, upbeat in tone but lacking
in definition (6 Oct.).

The speech over, the opposition pounced in search of still more
concessions. Conservative leader Stephen Harper was adamant that
the government must accept amendments to the speech since it had
not consulted other parties, but he stopped shy of declaring a bottom
line. Gilles Duceppe and the Bloc Qubécois, offended by ongoing and

planned intrusions on provincial jurisdiction, were rather less timid about bringing the government down. The NDP, baited by the promise of initiatives dear to its heart, was expected to grant the government time but could not, on its own, muster enough votes to prop up the Liberals. It was the beginning of a 'dangerous political game,' with the 'Conservatives and Bloc Québécois seeking to humiliate the Liberal government by demonstrating their power to control the political agenda' and the 'Liberals warning that they won't be pushed around' (*Globe and Mail*, 6 Oct.).

No party wanted an election. This provided the incentive and space to cobble together a face-saving escape. The matter was resolved over the course of several weeks. First a subamendment moved by the Bloc was defeated by the other parties on 7 October after an eleventh-hour agreement. The climax came on 18 October when the House approved an amended motion after protracted negotiation involving all parties. As a result, the government was required to

- consider tax cuts for low- and middle-income families as the state of the economy permitted;
- allow a vote on Canadian involvement in the U.S. missile-defence system rather than act by cabinet fiat;
- study reforms to the federal electoral system (such as proportional representation);
- examine the possibility of an independent budget office for Parliament; and
- ensure that surpluses in the employment-insurance program were used to help workers.

New department

The Martin government moved towards the creation of a new Department of Public Safety and Emergency Preparedness when it restructured the cabinet in December 2003. The department's creation was formalized with passage of Bill C-6 (31 March). This new entity consolidated responsibilities formerly lodged with the solicitor general, including the Royal Canadian Mounted Police (RCMP), the Canadian Security Intelligence Service (CSIS), the Canada Border Services Agency, the Canadian Firearms Centre, the Correctional Service of Canada, and the National Parole Board. The auditor general's February report nevertheless cast a harsh light on the coordination of security and intelligence.

Speaker

When Parliament resumed in October, the question of who would emerge as the presiding officer in the Commons took on greater urgency than is customary. There was some speculation that the Liberals would help engineer the election of a member of the opposition to the post of Speaker in order to cushion their thin margin in the House. Alternatively, the opposition parties could have attempted to seat a member of their choosing. This was all speculation. Satisfied with his performance since January 2001, MPs unanimously returned Liberal Peter Milliken to the office.

Ethics Commissioner

In 2002 the Liberals promised to create an independent ethics commissioner to replace the ethics counsellor of the past. On 31 March enabling legislation finally passed. Bill C-4 established this new post together with a separate Senate ethics office. It was the commissioner's responsibility to enforce codes of conduct for cabinet ministers and establish a new code for backbenchers and opposition members. Significantly, and in contrast to the ethics counsellor, the commissioner would report directly to Parliament rather than to the prime minister. However, the prime minister would continue to have the final say on reprimands for those found to be in conflicts of interest. The government nominated Bernard Shapiro, a former president of McGill University, to be the first incumbent of the new office. The Standing Committee on Procedure and House Affairs unanimously approved the appointment on 27 April.

Senate

Having reached the mandatory retirement age of seventy-five, eight senators were requited to end their terms. In addition, Richard Kroft of Manitoba resigned his place in the red chamber (24 Sept.) and in doing so surrendered the chair of two committees. Those who retired were the following:

• Gérald-A. Beaudoin of Quebec, a long-serving member and prominent member of the increasingly thin Conservative ranks in the Senate (15 April);
• Alasdair Graham, a Nova Scotia Liberal who had served as leader of the government in the Senate for two years (21 May);

- Brenda Robertson, a one-time provincial cabinet minister and Conservative from New Brunswick (23 May);
- Eileen Rossiter, a Conservative who came to the job after a business career in Prince Edward Island (14 July);
- Edward Lawson of British Columbia, a former labour leader who served as an independent senator from 1970 until he was welcomed into the Liberal caucus in 2003, in the final months of his tenure (21 Sept.);
- Jean-Robert Gauthier, a former Liberal MP from Ontario who had the unusual distinction of having been named to the Senate on two occasions by the same prime minister, the second time following an unsuccessful run for a House seat (22 Oct.);
- Laurier Lapierre, a former broadcaster and Ontario Liberal (21 Nov.); and
- Herbert Sparrow, a Saskatchewan Liberal who, having been appointed in 1968, was the last remaining senator to have been elevated by Lester Pearson (28 Nov.).

Martin, in no need of replacements to fortify the government's hold on the upper chamber and in no hurry to risk criticism in the heated political milieu, deferred the selection of new senators to 2005. The Liberals lost one vote when maverick Senator Anne Cools left to join the Conservatives in the middle of the election campaign (8 June).

Changes at the Supreme Court

Two of the court's nine puisne or associate justices formally ended their terms on 30 June. Frank Iaccobucci, who announced his resignation on 22 March, left after thirteen years of service to take up the post of interim president of the University of Toronto. Justice Iaccobucci was no stranger to the academy, having served as both a university vice-president and a law school dean at the University of Toronto prior to joining the court. The other vacancy was created when Louise Arbour, a distinguished international law expert, left to take up the post of human rights commissioner for the United Nations. Arbour had headed the prosecution on behalf of the United Nations at the International Criminal Tribunals adjudicating crimes in the former Yugoslavia and Rwanda before her Supreme Court appointment.

In the past, a government would have simply announced replacements after quietly canvassing the upper echelons of the legal community. When the two nominees were announced on 24 August, the government also set out a new process designed to create more transparency. The nominations were reviewed by a special committee composed of three Liberal MPs, two Conservatives, and one from each of the NDP and the Bloc Québécois. This membership was augmented by Julian Porter, from the Law Society of Upper Canada, and John Richard, chief justice of the Federal Court of Appeal, representing the Canadian Judicial Council. The nominees themselves did not testify. In a single-day hearing, Minister of Justice Irwin Cotler opened by commenting on the nominees' suitability for the job. Participants grappled with their role, especially without the candidates present, as the questioning unfolded. The committee quickly drew up a report for the prime minister, who accepted its advice to appoint the nominees. To be sure, the new process added a modicum of openness to the method by which justices are named, but it was generally considered to be an unsatisfactory compromise or an awkward first step.

The new justices were a pair of colleagues from the Ontario Court of Appeal, Madame Justice Louise Charron and Madam Justice Rosalie Abella. It was well known that Abella had been in line for a job on the highest court and was passed over in 1998 when Jean Chrétien opted for Ian Binnie.

Auditor general's reports

Auditor General Sheila Fraser released two major reports during the year. The first was issued on 10 February. Headlines were dominated by her investigation of the handling of the government's sponsorship program. The auditor general was 'shocked' by the nature and scope of the abuses. Rules were routinely bypassed by senior officials through 'fictitious contracts, artificial invoices and elaborate accounting devices' designed to move tens of millions of dollars from the Communications Coordination Services Branch of the Department of Public Works to firms friendly with the Liberal government (*Ottawa Citizen*, 11 Feb.). The government had misled Parliament about the program, and senior officials in bureaucracy and crown corporations had mischaracterized their roles in the scheme. Former minister Alfonso Gagliano was singled out for criticism. He was instantly fired from his post as ambassador to Denmark by the Martin government. According to Susan Riley of the *Ottawa Citizen*, the litany of abuses detailed in the thirty-four-page report amounted to a 'how-to manual for fraud artists' but also an exposé of 'an approach to politics ... practiced by other politicians of all stripes" (11 Feb.). Fraser passed on her findings to the RCMP.

Although the abuses had occurred during the tenure of Jean Chrétien, and the program had been cancelled, the Martin government inherited the fallout. In response, Martin established a public inquiry. Treasury Board President Reg Alcock and Public Works Minister Stephen Owen were assigned to clean up the mess internally and they announced plans to appoint a special counsel to retrieve unearned or ill-gotten money, whistleblower legislation to protect informants within the public service, and a review by a Commons committee. Opposition parties tried mightily to tie Martin to the scandal in the days following the report. There was no evidence of his personal involvement, but questioners in the House wondered how someone so intimately acquainted with Quebec politics could have avoided knowing about the problems. He may not have signed any cheques, but, as finance minister, Martin also had a fiduciary duty. Still, Martin insisted that he had no idea what was transpiring around him.

The sponsorship angle dominated media coverage of the report, but the audit also turned up poor coordination and administration of national security and intelligence prior to the establishment of Public Safety and Emergency Preparedness Canada in December 2003. In addition, Fraser was critical of the regulation of medical devices and plant biotechnology products. Health Canada was found wanting in its inspection of products in use, exposing the public to heightened risk and the department to liability. Further, Ottawa had not always or fully complied with agreements reached with First Nations and Inuit; a review of outlays for public-opinion surveys found instances when the government violated its own guidelines; and the March 2002 purchase of Challenger jets – on the last day of the fiscal year – was rushed, untendered, and insensitive to the articulated needs of government departments.

The second report was published on 23 November. As she (and predecessors) had done before, the auditor general rebuked the government for piling up surpluses in the employment-insurance fund that were diverted to other purposes. She was certain that Parliament had never intended that the plan would generate a pool vastly exceeding actuarial needs. Additionally, despite spending $1 billion each year on Aboriginal education programs, graduation gaps between Aboriginal and non-Aboriginal students were actually widening, and the Department of Indian Affairs was faulted for its oversight of the $273 million invested in post-secondary initiatives. Fraser found, too, that Ottawa had overspent on prescription drugs by overlooking generic brands and bulk-quantity purchases, and that it had delayed a time-sensitive program to upgrade fighter aircraft for the military.

National economy

Economic indicators

Conventional indices of economic activity and trends showed an improvement in overall performance in 2004. The GDP grew by 2.8 per cent compared to a 2.0 per cent increase in 2003. This relative robustness was attributed to a surge in consumer spending and exports, a phenomenon that was particularly noticeable in the second half of the year. Growth translated into labour-market vitality, with some 226,000 net new jobs taken up by employees. By December, unemployment had fallen to 7.0 per cent, a mark that was superior to the annualized average of 7.2 per cent and lower still than the level of 7.6 per cent achieved in 2003. Despite these gains, inflation was largely contained, falling to 1.9 per cent after a 2.8 per cent burst during the previous twelve months. Growing confidence in the economy by domestic and international investors was expressed in a sharp increase in the value of the dollar against the benchmark American currency. The dollar rose steadily to 77.0 cents in American currency, up from 71.6 cents in the previous year. The prime lending rate stood at 4.0 per cent compared to 4.7 per cent in 2003.

For all of the apparent good news, there were some worrisome trends. Canada's growth rate was a little more than half of the global average (albeit a figure that was heavily conditioned by unmatchable increments in China and a minor boom south of the border). Worse was the unevenness of results. Alberta zoomed ahead with growth of 4.3 per cent (and unemployment below 5.0 per cent), thanks to steep hikes in oil prices benefiting producers in that province, while employment struggles continued in the Atlantic region, especially Newfoundland and Labrador. The surplus in the trade of goods was $67.0 billion, but the overall current account balance was half as high, $33.8 billion. These data helped crystallize the truth that Canada's economy was increasingly dependent on unprocessed resources. Energy alone accounted for 16.1 per cent of exports. Meanwhile, the industrial sector shed investment and jobs. Trade was still not diversifying. Fully 85 per cent of all exports headed to the United States, creating a dependency on southbound shipments that was only partly diminished by rising sales to China. This was especially portentous if the soaring dollar discouraged manufacturing or undermined the service sector or if the American economy faltered. Income disparities also continued to track upward as the affluent received disproportionate benefits from the country's economic health.

Budget 2004–5

Tasked with delivering the first budget speech of the Martin regime, Finance Minister Ralph Goodale offered up an ensemble of middle-ground measures reminiscent of the approach taken by his predecessor and boss (23 March). Pre-election budgets often emphasize tax cuts or costly new programs. Eschewing this in favour of modesty represented a restoration of the managerialism favoured by Martin and was in striking contrast to the more free-spending approach of the 2003 budget of John Manley in the final days of the Jean Chrétien era.

Even so, the government was acutely aware of the need to address concerns of attentive voters. Indeed, the first part of Goodale's speech had less to do with money than with accountability and transparency: it asked for renewed trust in the Liberals' ability to administer the public purse. Goodale opened by accepting blame for past laxities and giving assurances that they would not be repeated. The rededication to probity included pledges to re-establish the Office of the Comptroller General to oversee spending and the creation of a national securities agency to monitor the investment sector. A special waste-trimming cabinet committee was charged with finding savings of $3 billion within four years. Given the Liberals' perilous standing in the polls, there was, according to John Ibbitson of the *Globe and Mail*, a 'certain pleading quality' to the budget (24 March). Conservative leader Stephen Harper dismissed the gambit as a lame effort to paper over the government's failings. To him, it was hollow rhetoric rather than authentic rectitude.

The speech came following a year in which economic growth had tapered off to 1.7 per cent. Although growth was reckoned to be stronger in 2004 and 2005, this was a sobering context. In terms of programs, the budget recycled promises to transfer $2 billion to the provinces for health care. A new Canada Public Health Agency was given $400 million from Health Canada to develop emergency-preparedness plans for crises such as the SARS outbreak of 2003. This was accompanied by $165 in funding for disease monitoring and treatments. Post-secondary accessibility for students from low-income families was the goal behind a blend of increased grants and loans under the Canada Student Loans program and a new Canada Learning Bond. Although Goodale trumpeted this commitment, critics argued that the impact would be blunted by limiting dollar amounts and restricting eligibility to those born after 2003. Extra money was also earmarked for the councils funding university research (an extra $90 million), for Genome Canada, and for early-childhood education. Responding to the so-called urban agenda, the government restated its intention to funnel $7 billion to cities over ten years by manipulating the GST. Payouts of $1 billion to municipalities under an infrastructure fund were accelerated to five years from ten. An additional $250 million was set aside for the Afghanistan mission, along with another $50 million for peacekeeping in troubled Haiti. Personnel in harm's way would be relieved of income tax during their tour of duty, an exemption estimated at $30 million annually. Advocates for the military were disappointed by the lack of money for the armed forces. Provision was made to decontaminate toxic sites, including the notorious tar ponds around the site of a former coal mine in Sydney, Nova Scotia ($400 million), and to help the beef industry ($1 billion).

There were no major tax changes in the budget. The exception was a minor adjustment to the cost allowances for computing and data systems for businesses. Many business organizations complained that the country's competitiveness was at risk because of the country's tax burdens but some found consolation in the greater prudence demonstrated by the government in this budget. This was exemplified by the return of the $3-billion contingency fund used for debt reduction if not required by unforeseen circumstances. Another $1 billion was held in reserve for the same purpose. The government had succeeded in reducing the debt-to-GDP ratio over the years, and Goodale forecast that it would fall to 25 per cent from 42 per cent over a ten-year period.

This was the seventh consecutive budget to project a surplus. Looking ahead, the government expected at least to balance the books for many years to come. Once again the conservative prognosticating by the Liberals drew flack from the opposition. Gilles Duceppe of the Bloc Québécois argued that Goodale was 'hiding surpluses like Paul Martin did' even as the provinces struggled, and the NDP's Jack Layton concluded that this sleight of hand meant future dividends of up to $200 billion would be diverted to paying down the debt rather than investing in the environment, health care, and social programs (Gloria Galloway and Jane Taber, *Globe and Mail*, 24 March). Finally, the government decided that it would sell off the last of its shares in the once government-owned Petro-Canada. Analysts noted that the budget had uniquely valued the asset sale prior to the transaction taking place.

Writing in the *Globe and Mail*, Jeffrey Simpson argued that the Conservatives would almost certainly try and exploit the budget scenarios in their election campaign given their ideological predilection for a smaller state: they would pitch tax cuts and spending reductions (24 March). In a similar vein, an editorial in the *Hamilton Spectator* commended Martin for 'promoting prudent management and protection of core social programs over expected Conservative promises of tax cuts at the expense of them. It's a gamble. But at least Martin has shown his cards' (24 March).

Autumn economic and fiscal update

In the ritual autumn appearance made by finance ministers before the House Finance Committee, Ralph Goodale told a familiar tale of budget surpluses vastly exceeding expectations. At $8.9 billion, the net surplus for the fiscal year was more than double the original estimate. Even after $3 billion had been set aside for the so-called contingency fund to pay down the national debt, the government had $6 billion at its disposal. The finance minister rejected accusations that he had deliberately concealed this size of this windfall, a charge levelled by impatient members of all opposition parties. Why would he, like his predecessor Paul Martin, withhold such good news? Critics charged that it was done in order to dole out unexpected gifts, or to downplay expectations that funds would be available for planned investments (especially favoured by the NDP), enriched transfers to the provinces and a restoration of equilibrium in the employment-insurance plan that had been turned into a deficit-busting cash cow (pet projects of the Bloc Québécois), and tax cuts (the Conservative demand). Downhearted business groups agreed that that the government should have taken measures to enhance Canada's competitiveness by easing corporate burdens and instituting durable, broad-based tax cuts. Goodale and his champions continued to extol the virtues of a more balanced approach entailing a combination of tax relief, spending, and debt reduction, but, in this instance, they pointed to commitments made to the provinces for health care and adjustments to the equalization formula when fending off calls for another round of tax breaks.

Goodale broke with the recent past when he confirmed for his listeners that the government was likely to have at least a balanced ledger well into the future. Even so, he cautioned that surpluses would not match the arresting totals of the recent past. In another concession, the finance minister also agreed to an independent review of how estimates were determined and appointed the Bank of Montreal's chief economist, Tim O'Neill, to take on the task (*Globe and Mail*, 17 Nov.).

Major policy areas

Finished and unfinished business

Despite the distractions of scandals and election campaigns, the House managed to pass some major pieces of legislation. Among those receiving royal assent prior to Parliament rising were amendments to the Patent Act and the Food and Drugs Act – entitled the Jean Chrétien Pledge to Africa – aimed at facilitating drug treatments for HIV-AIDS (C-9). The amendments made it possible for non-patent holders to provide low-cost versions of medicines for export to countries with insufficient capacity. The House and Senate also agreed to amend the Criminal Code to create a national registry of sex offenders (Bill C-16).

Other bills stalled. The Senate continued to dither over legislation to curtail cruelty to animals (Bill C-22). Bill C-2, which would permit wider distribution of foreign programming to counter the spread of unauthorized satellite transmissions in the so-called grey market, made it only as far as the committee stage. A similar fate awaited legislation to decriminalize possession of small amounts of cannabis (C-10), beef up drug-related impaired-driving penalties (C-32), amend child-pornography laws (C-12), enshrine property-taxation powers for First Nations (C-23), and establish procedures for the disclosure of wrongdoings in the public sector (C-25). Many of these were controversial but were likely to be revived in some form when the Liberals plotted out their 2005 agenda.

Federal-provincial health-care accord

Two months after the election, Prime Minister Martin convened a much anticipated First Ministers Conference on health care. The conference lasted slightly longer than planned but resulted in an agreement that injected more federal dollars into provincial health plans. Most of the work was done behind closed doors and in a tense atmosphere. When they emerged on 16 September, Martin and the premiers announced a deal providing for an infusion by Ottawa of $41.3 billion into provincially run systems over a span of ten years. Most of the money would be doled out directly and in guaranteed increments. In the first two years the provinces and territories would receive $3.5 billion in additional transfers, with $2.1 billion up front. The deal also featured an 'escalator clause' (operable to 2015) which would see transfers rise by

6 per cent annually. The total emolument over six years amounted to $18 billion.

On top of this basic funding, the parties worked out a series of complicated arrangements for targeted priorities. Special attention was given to cancer, heart disease, cataracts surgery, lower-joint replacement, and improvements in diagnostics. As summarized by the *Toronto Star* (17 Sept.), the provinces and territories accepted the following conditions in return for Ottawa's largesse:

- annual indicators reports based on terms to be decided by 31 December 2005;
- common benchmarks for waiting times;
- targets for the training, recruitment, and retention of health-care providers;
- enhanced home and mental health care;
- deductible-free palliative-care programs; and
- a national pharmaceuticals strategy including a comprehensive drug formulary (a list of drugs covered by a particular benefit plan).

The provinces also promised to respect the principles of the Canada Health Act.

Few panned the breakthrough, but many remarked on its shortcomings. Each signatory still had to confront rising costs stemming from merciless demographic trends and ever rising costs. Dismay was inspired by the relatively soft accountability provisions or by the apparent willingness of Ottawa to achieve consensus at any cost; and there were centripetal aspects to the accord. Calling it a tremendous victory for his province, Quebec Premier Jean Charest secured a side deal allowing his government to implement its own strategies. This was justified by Martin on the grounds of Quebec's distinctiveness, but he stressed that other provinces would be able to negotiate unique arrangements as well. For better or worse, it was evident that 'asymmetrical federalism' had taken root in federal-provincial relations. It was not lost on Conservative Party leader Stephen Harper that the pact was more to his liking in this regard, and he observed that 'the great irony with this deal [is that] it looks a lot more like a deal I would have signed than a deal Paul Martin would have signed if you'd listened to the platforms and the rhetoric during the election campaign' (*Toronto Star*, 17 Sept.). Roy Romanow, the author of a major study on Canada's health-care dilemma, was worried that the deal fell short of enacting truly national standards (*Toronto Star*, 17 Sept.). Indifferent or hostile to the outcome, Alberta Premier Ralph Klein marched away from the conference after a single day. In Canada, only wishful thinkers dare hope for entirely happy endings.

Afghanistan and the military

In late 2003 the government confirmed that soldiers would continue to form part of the multinational force in Afghanistan in 2004, and a larger deployment was readying to rotate into the Afghani theatre. Made up in the main by members of Quebec's Royal 22nd Regiment (nicknamed the Van Doos, based on the French *vingt deux*), the contingent arrived in Kabul on 20 January for a six-month stay. Their job was to help stabilize the central precincts of the capital city as part of a multinational force formed out of troops from NATO signatory countries. Shortly thereafter, one Canadian was killed and three others injured by a suicide bomb outside the main base of Camp Julien (27 Jan.). Command of the International Security Assistance Force in Afghanistan was passed to a Canadian, General Rick Hillier, on 9 February. He held that position until replaced in August.

Canadian forces had been engaged in Afghanistan since the American-led occupation began in 2002. Troop levels and missions had changed in that time, and decision makers in Ottawa had to face the future. On 4 February Prime Minister Martin announced that Canada would scale back its commitment to approximately five hundred soldiers when the Van Doos completed their tour in August. This was later refined to a deployment of a six-hundred-strong battle group and a two-hundred-member air force support group. The government also agreed to extend the mission until the summer of 2005 (15 April).

The Van Doos handed off to a Norwegian contingent in August, having suffered no causalities. In addition to regular patrols, the regiment provided logistical assistance with a variety of infrastructure projects. Fighting continued elsewhere in Afghanistan as the displaced Taliban regrouped and regained footholds in the provinces. Occupation forces had been unable to stem the opium trade, wrestle local control from 'warlords' in far-off locales, or effectively extend Kabul's authority outward from the capital. Although the international community rallied around the American effort to unseat the Taliban after the events of 11 September 2001, doubts about the long-term strategic viability of the occupation had not subsided and were indeed growing.

Missile defence

Dusting off an old and (many said) discredited concept, the Bush administration embarked on a costly anti-intercontinental ballistic-missile program after withdrawing from the 1972 Anti-Ballistic Missile Treaty. If it worked, the capacities developed under the Ballistic Missile Defence umbrella, so reminiscent of the Ronald Reagan-era Strategic Defence Initiative (or 'Star Wars') of the 1980s, would make it possible to locate and destroy nuclear warheads launched by the baneful rogue states so despised by American neo-conservatives. The threat may have been exaggerated, and the science behind honing in on a target whizzing through space might be the stuff of fantasy, but the Republican White House was unswerving. Owing to staggering costs and technical requirements such as widely dispersed radar installations, the Americans set about building an alliance of allied countries amenable to participating in the program. Ever-eager Australia promptly enlisted. But no state had more at stake than Canada. Already closely tied to the United States through the NORAD treaty, Canada was under great pressure to sign on to the missile-shield scheme.

It was clear where two parties stood. Both the New Democratic Party and the Bloc Québécois voiced their opposition to the concept. The Conservatives were somewhat coy, and dodged the question pending a substantive proposal to consider. The Liberals were clearly torn. Relations with the United States had been strained during the Chrétien years, in part because of Canada's decision to stay clear of the invasion of Iraq despite American blandishments. In ways that recalled the agonizing debate over Iraq, Liberals sent mixed signals about missile defence. Backbenchers were far from united on the issue. The prime minister categorically opposed the weaponization of space (23 June) but also maintained all along that Canada had to be in on the conversation about BMD. Yet Defence Minister Bill Graham insisted that Canadian contributions to a missile-defence system should not be equated with sending forces to Iraq since the aim was to defend North America. As a partner in NORAD, Canada was already committed to the principle of mutual aid against weapons of mass destruction (29 Sept.).

NORAD became the government's beacon for navigating through treacherous waters. On 6 August, Ottawa signed an addendum to the treaty permitting an exchange of information that could be used in operational situations by BMD installations (the first of which had been established in Alaska over the summer). Graham denied that this was a provocative first step towards formal membership in the BMD club,

but opponents could not help but notice that the amendment was ratified without parliamentary approval and they worried that the process
of entanglement would be driven inexorably forward. Later in the year,
the government hit on the notion of tying discussions about BMD to
talks over the renewal the NORAD treaty, due to expire in 2006. This
bought the government time, even though an impatient President Bush
discarded a carefully arranged diplomatic understanding to raise the
matter on the occasion of his state visit to Ottawa (30 Nov.).

There was no resolution as the year came to a close. Even so, the
all-party amendment to the Speech from the Throne explicitly provided
for a debate in the House of Commons before the government acted,
a concession that would likely result in either a weak affirmation or
a resolution opposing Canadian involvement given the disposition of
MPs if the matter came to the floor before another election.

Same-sex marriage

In the face of provincial court rulings sanctioning same-sex marriages,
the Liberal government of Jean Chrétien prepared a draft bill to legalize
such unions in 2003. The legislation was then referred to the Supreme
Court of Canada together with three specific questions turning on the
authority of Parliament to regulate in this domain, the consonance of
such legislation with provisions of the Charter of Rights and Freedoms,
and whether or not the Charter permitted religious bodies to exercise
their own right not to conduct same-sex marriage services. The prospect of same-sex marriage sharply divided the House. The NDP and
Bloc were prepared to support legislation while the Conservatives were
steadfastly against. However, members of each party had reservations
and some were likely to go against the party line on a vote. The fate
of the proposition lay with the Liberals. A majority appeared to be in
favour, but a significant and vocal minority would undoubtedly part
ways with the rest of the caucus. Two ministers, John Efford and Joe
Comuzzi, wavered over the matter. Backbencher Pat O'Brien indicated
that four others in the cabinet had doubts and would side with opponents if the vote was a matter of conscience rather than subject to party
discipline.

The Supreme Court decision was rendered on 9 December. In its ruling the court confirmed that Ottawa had the authority to change the
definition of marriage. Unlike many lower courts, it was silent when it
came to the question about whether or not the Charter obliged a more
expansive definition of marriage. The court did agree, as expected, that

religions and religious leaders could not be compelled to perform same-sex marriages. Meanwhile, judges in Manitoba (16 Sept.), Nova Scotia (24 Sept.), and Newfoundland and Labrador (21 Dec.) ruled in favour of same-sex marriages in their provinces. On 26 November the Ontario Court of Appeal upheld a lower court decision that survivors in same-sex relationships were entitled to benefits from the Canada Pension Plan, a position contested by the federal government.

Decriminalization of marijuana possession

On 22 July Prime Minister Martin confirmed that the government would reintroduce legislation to de-penalize possession of small amounts of marijuana. A similar bill (C-38) had lapsed with the end of Parliament in May. Under the old proposal, ticketed fines would replace harsher penalties for those caught in possession of fifteen grams or less of cannabis and one gram or less of hashish. Possession would be illegal, but transgressions involving small quantities would not result in criminal convictions that would stigmatize users, curtail travel abroad, and stymie employment searches. Opponents of the initiative argued that this would complicate policing and encourage use. The American government was among those against the bill, and it threatened to tighten borders.

Bill C-17 was presented to the House on 1 November and, as summarized in the *Toronto Star* (2 Nov.), it had the following elements:

- decriminalization of possession under fifteen grams of cannabis, with fines ranging from $100 for youth to $150 for adults;
- decriminalization of possession of one gram or less of hashish, with fines of $200 for youth and $300 for adults;
- higher fines if the offender was operating a motor vehicle, was in the vicinity of a school, or was in the commission of another offence;
- decriminalization of the production of three marijuana plants or fewer, with fines of $250 (youth) and $500 (adults); and
- a doubling of the maximum penalty for large-scale growers – fifty or more plants – up to fourteen years.

In a separate bill, the government proposed amendments to the Criminal Code permitting tests for suspected drug use paralleling procedures for alcohol intoxication (Bill C-2, 1 Nov.). Jurisprudence on the matter of sanctions for cannabis possession was often inconsistent, but during the year the Supreme Court ruled that existing statutes did not violate the Charter of Rights and Freedoms (9 Feb.).

Controversies

The sponsorship scandal

Freshly installed as prime minister, Paul Martin cancelled the controversial sponsorship program that had plagued the final years of Jean Chrétien's tenure (13 Dec. 2003). It was one of his first acts on the job, and his decision was clearly intended to differentiate him from his predecessor. He did not, however, bow to demands for a full public inquiry. This would all change early in 2004.

In the long saga of the sponsorship scandal, the date of 10 February 2004 was especially momentous. That day auditor general Sheila Fraser issued her detailed report on the government's mismanagement of the program from its inception in 1995. In addition to forensic examination of the books, her staff interviewed four cabinet ministers, five senior civil servants, and the president and a vice-president at VIA Rail. Never one to mince words, Fraser declared: 'I think this is such a blatant misuse of public funds that it is shocking. I am actually appalled by what we've found' (*Globe and Mail*, 11 Feb.). Her office determined that senior officials within the government and five crown corporations had disregarded procedures and misappropriated millions of dollars. This included the RCMP, Via Rail, Canada Post, the Business Development Bank of Canada, and the Old Port of Montreal. Private communications agencies in Quebec were given fees and commissions amounting to more than $100 million, but often this income was unearned. Repeatedly, these firms acted as unnecessary conduits by simply transferring money from government coffers to crown corporations. This scheme enriched the companies involved but provided no benefit whatsoever to the government or citizens. Illustrations of malfeasance abounded in the report. They included instances of fictitious and unfulfilled contracts, destroyed bank records, and verbal agreements. Outraged by these continuous violations of approved protocols, Fraser also condemned the government's failure to act on past warnings about the laxity of administration, later telling the Public Accounts Committee of the House that she had described these problems as long ago as the year 2000.

Braced for bad news, the Martin government responded immediately. Martin fired Alfonso Gagliano, a former cabinet minister central to the program, from the ambassadorial job to which he had been shunted by Chrétien. More important, he named Justice John Gomery of Quebec to head a one-person inquiry into the scandal. Meanwhile, the Public Accounts Committee, chaired by Conservative John Williams, embarked on its own review.

Largely spared from scrutiny as the scandal mushroomed around Chrétien, Martin was now fully caught up in the maelstrom. In short order he was asked if he recalled a 2002 letter addressed to him by a Liberal official complaining about the partisan nature of the sponsorship program (he did not), grilled about his personal knowledge of misconduct (he knew nothing, despite intimacy with many of the key players), and hounded about possible dereliction of duty when, as finance minister, he administered the public purse. The prime minister insisted that the scandal was rooted in the Public Works ministry (11 Feb.), said he would testify before the inquiry if requested, and warned that any cabinet minister involved in the scandal would be dismissed (12 Feb.). He opined that bureaucrats were acting under obvious political guidance, a veiled criticism of his predecessor. As Martin became a focal point, a taciturn Chrétien refused comment altogether (15 Feb.) or downplayed the scandal's significance in choreographed huddles with the press (30 March).

The pace of the scandal accelerated, and related events overwhelmed the political scene. Treasury Board President Reg Alcock assured the Public Accounts Committee that whistleblowers in the civil service would be protected while those guilty of crimes would be punished (17 Feb.). Martin suspended the presidents of Canada Post, VIA Rail, and the Business Development Bank (24 Feb.). An Olympic athlete employed by Via Rail complained that she had been fired by Via Rail after questioning transactions, prompting the corporation's chair, Jean Pelletier, to demean her (27 Feb.). Two days later, and despite apologizing, Pelletier was fired. VIA Rail's president, Marc LeFrancois, followed Pelletier out the door on 5 March when Martin sought to restore public confidence in the company's management. Both men subsequently filed wrongful-dismissal suits against the government, and rejected allegations of impropriety when they were summoned to the Public Accounts Committee in April.

The House committee heard from lesser civil servants that they had not questioned irregularities because superiors at the highest levels had signed off. One conspicuous informant, Allan Cutler, laid the blame on former program director Chuck Guité, and said that problems could be traced as far back as 1994 (11 March). Gagliano testified that he was innocent of any wrongdoing on the same day that Fraser depicted his office's shoddy administration (18 March). Although Gagliano characterized his meetings with Guité as infrequent and unrelated to sponsorship matters, a string of former staff members remembered the two getting together as often as once a week to discuss payments. Gagliano, too, sued for lost wages on the grounds of wrongful dismissal.

Executives with private companies denied misappropriating funds but they had great difficulty convincing listeners that they had not benefited from cordiality with high-ranking government and Liberal Party officials. When Guité made his long-awaited reappearance before the committee (transcribed testimony from a 2002 hearing was released on 1 April), he disavowed accusations that he had bent the rules. Exasperated, committee chair Williams complained of Guité's stonewalling. On 10 May, Guité and Jean Brault, the founder of the Groupaction agency, pled not guilty to charges of fraud laid by prosecutors acting on an investigation by the RCMP.

The committee hearings ended on 11 May. Opposition members were furious with the Liberal majority for voting to terminate the public phase and begin drafting an interim report. Conservative, New Democrat, and Bloc Québécois members of the committee released their own report on what they called the flagrant abuse of power orchestrated by individuals all the way up to the Prime Minister's Office (PMO). The election call on 23 May put paid to further testimony and reporting but did not quell the furore. On 15 June past employees of Lafleur Communications made it known that they had been pressured into making donations – for which they were reimbursed – to Liberal candidates in the 1997 election.

The Gomery Commission commenced on 7 September. Day by day a parade of witnesses fleshed out testimony elicited by the Public Accounts Committee and shed fresh light on the proportion of the scandal. According to new documents, a draft 1996 review of the program identified flaws in administration, problems that went missing from the final iteration. It was learned that Guité had been specially selected for the job of running the program. Guité was again a star attraction. After a dispute over whether or not the immunity granted by the Public Accounts Committee should be waived, he was summoned by Justice Gomery in November. Prior to his turn on the stand, there was disagreement about how much Prime Minister Chrétien and Finance Minister Martin would have known about the program's inner workings, but some witnesses insisted that nothing so elaborate and sensitive would have been allowed without at least a tacit nod from the upper echelons. Guité's own words on this score were confusing and contradictory. Yet he was able to outline some of the ties that bound his work to the PMO through assorted deals. As the commission wound down in November and December, there was more evidence that companies were granted lucrative contracts and even supplemental fees for little or no work.

In a year-end interview, Justice Gomery stirred a hornet's nest by adumbrating his conclusions about the affair (averring that he shared the findings of Auditor General Sheila Fraser) and characterizing Guité as a 'charming scamp' (*National Post*, 16 Dec.). Gomery planned to hear from Chrétien and Martin in the new year. The new prime minister pledged his full cooperation. The past prime minister was not so forthcoming, and in fact was something of a lonely nemesis of the commission. Chrétien and his supporters noted that the lead lawyer for the commission had close ties to former Conservative Prime Minister Brian Mulroney, and were otherwise critical of the justice's handling of the investigation. Although Gomery's inquest was far from over, it was evident that the sponsorship program represented a major breach of the public trust. Most commentators focused, like Gomery, on the worrisome ethical and legal dimensions. Outside Quebec few dared to question whether or not it was legitimate for a government to invest so heavily in an attempt to buy the affections of its citizens or if it was practicable to substitute symbols for substance – ultimately, this was the goal of the program – in the cause of national unity.

Maher Arar inquiry

On 26 September 2002 Maher Arar, a Canadian citizen travelling home following a visit to Tunisia, was detained by security personnel at New York's Kennedy International Airport. Arar, who also held citizenship from the country of his birth, Syria, was interrogated in the United States on suspicion of ties to terrorist organizations. Some two or three weeks later – the timelines were blurred by the secretive nature of his detention and treatment – the Americans 'deported' him to Syria under a controversial law authorizing extradition to Middle Eastern countries of dual citizens. On 22 October, the federal government confirmed that Arar, an engineer and father of two, was in custody and under investigation for alleged ties to the Muslim Brotherhood. His partner, Monia Mazigh, rallied to his aid, as did domestic and international human-rights organizations. Government ministers, including the prime minister, offered their sympathy about Arar's well-being, registered concern about the denial of legal assistance, and expressed muted criticism of the actions of the Americans and Syrians. It was not until 6 October 2003 that his travails ended. Upon release, he headed home to Montreal.

Despite clamouring from growing legions of supporters throughout this ordeal, the Chrétien government refused to establish a public inquiry into the role played by the Canadian security and foreign affairs apparatus in Arar's ordeal. Things changed when the first Martin cabinet was installed. In late 2003 the Security Intelligence Review Committee, a government-appointed oversight body, announced that it would look into how the Canadian Security Intelligence Service responded (22 Dec. 2003). On 28 January, Anne McLellan announced that Justice Dennis O'Connor would head a public inquiry into the affair. By this time, Arar had filed a suit against the American government (22 Jan.). One day earlier, the RCMP conducted a raid on the home of *Ottawa Citizen* reporter Juliet O'Neill while investigating the publication of leaked documents associated with the Arar case. On 9 March the Ottawa municipal police force confirmed that it had participated in a covert operation aimed at Arar, but it would not go beyond admitting that other security agencies had been involved. The story of Arar's tragic personal misfortunes was now spiralling into a vortex with potential consequences for many others.

O'Connor opened proceedings on 21 June with several days of testimony on the operations of various security services, including the information stored in databases that could be accessed by American authorities. He was advised early on that the Syrian government would not cooperate (5 July). The United States also formally declined to assist (21 Sept.). Testimony revealed that the RCMP had communicated with American agencies from the time of Arar's detention to his transfer to Syrian custody. These contacts were characterized as proper, but the RCMP acknowledged that some may have been 'unauthorized' (6 July).

From the outset, lawyers for Arar demanded that the inquiry order the release of any and all documents pertinent to the case without redaction. Until that point they had received altered versions. Government agencies were reluctant to comply, and on 14 July the inquiry was postponed to the autumn pending clarity on the matter of how evidence would be handled. On 29 July, O'Connor ruled that evidence would have to be vetted in camera and would be subject to customary national-security clearances. This decision resulted in additional delays.

Before the inquiry resumed, sections of the report on CSIS prepared by the Security Intelligence Committee were issued. The censored text concluded that CSIS had no prior knowledge of American plans to detain and deport Arar (14 Sept.). When an internal review by the RCMP was made public on 24 September, it suggested that the Mounties were not sufficiently experienced to handle an investigation on national-security grounds. Further revelations were blunted by the heavy censorship of documents released by the inquiry, including more than one thousand pages authorized for release by O'Connor on 26 November. Were the redactions warranted by national-security concerns, or did they hide unpleasant truths about the motivations and mistakes of the agencies involved? Arar's lawyers were confident that even a partial record would show culpability on the part of Canadian officials and claimed that his tortured interrogations in Syria were actively sought by Canadian officials. The batch of documents released on 26 November indicated that the RCMP resisted efforts to clear Arar's name even though they considered him peripheral, perhaps only a witness to the activities of others. In a ruling on 20 December, O'Connor expressed astonishment that the Department of Justice had sided with CSIS in blacking out a summary of closed-door testimony even though it was exculpatory. The year ended with a volley of lawsuits aimed at wining the release of additional material.

Paul Martin and Canada Steamship Lines

Paul Martin was among the wealthiest of parliamentarians. His fortune derived from ownership of Canada Steamship Lines (CSL) and offshoot companies. Although CSL's assets were placed in a blind trust in 1993, opposition parties made hay out of the fact that CSL was doing business in a federally regulated industry while Martin held the powerful Finance portfolio. Martin transferred the company to his offspring in 2003, but concerns lingered. Of particular interest was the extent to which Martin's businesses benefited from government contracts during his long stint in cabinet. Indeed, this was one of the principle topics on the minds of Conservatives when the House resumed in February.

In answer to previous probes by the opposition, a document was tabled in the House in 2003 pegging the value of CSL work for the government at $137,000 since 1993. As it turned out, this was wildly incorrect. According to a revised estimate tabled in January by the government leader in the House, Jacques Saada, the true amount was $161 million. The discrepancy was blamed on a clerical error. If true, it may have been the most prodigious mistake of its kind ever made. Conservatives charged that even the increased amount was erroneous. Martin insisted that he played no part in compiling the low amount since he was on the outs with the Chrétien government and distracted by his run for the Liberal leadership. To deflect constant questioning by Conservatives, the prime minister asked Auditor General Sheila Fraser to review the matter (3 Feb.).

Fraser reported back in November, saying that the upper figure seemed 'reasonably complete.' The qualifier was tacked on because she could not wrest full disclosure out of officials in some governmental quarters. Critics pointed out that the reckoning excluded dealings with federally mandated port authorities and other departments with which a shipping company might do business. Defending the arresting numbers, Martin argued that approximately half of the monetary value was attributable to contracts awarded while the Progressive Conservatives were in office in 1993. This did not satisfy critics still concerned about perceived conflicts of interest and material gains made by a high office-holder. Martin had always been sanguine about his ability to balance his political and business interests, but opponents, still seeking to tarnish the prime minister's integrity, felt that clearer, tougher guidelines should be instituted to cover such circumstances.

The dismissal of Carolyn Parrish

Veteran MP Carolyn Parrish, who had been returned to the House after defeating another sitting member in a spirited Liberal nomination contest, was possessed of an independent streak, a quality that might have made her an ideal parliamentarian at a time when backbench MPs were supposed to enjoy greater liberty and reborn influence. Instead, it led to an increasing ostracization that ended with her expulsion from caucus.

In the summer, amid the debate over Canada's possible involvement in the missile-shield defence system, Parrish likened those countries willing to partner with the United States in the initiative to a 'coalition of idiots.' No fan of the American president, she described George W. Bush as 'warlike' in the wake of his 'disappointing' re-election (*Toronto Star*, 19 Nov.) Outspokenness of this magnitude made her a media magnet. Naturally, television came calling. She agreed to participate in a skit during an appearance on the satirical program *This Hour Has 22 Minutes* during which she gleefully stomped on a Bush action figure.

Party brass were not amused, especially given the fragile nature of Canadian-U.S. relations and a pending state visit in Ottawa. Cautioned to show more restraint in future, Parrish responded by averring that she felt absolutely no sense of loyalty to Martin and his team. The prime minster acted. Saying that he 'could not tolerate behaviour that demeans and disrespects others' (*Globe and Mail*, 19 Nov.), Martin engineered an expulsion. Critics of the MP insisted that she had authored her own misfortunes, while defenders contended that the prime minister's churlish reaction was more a reflection of his inability to accept criticism of himself or the government. Parrish remained in the House as an independent.

Judy Sgro and 'Strippergate'

Minister of Immigration and Toronto MP Judy Sgro ruffled feathers when she suggested, in reference to a half-dozen individuals who had sought refuge in churches rather than submit to deportation orders, that Canadian churches abandon the time-honoured practice of providing sanctuary (25 July). Many religious and lay people considered this view deplorable even if it was expressed haphazardly.

Although the furore abated, Sgro was undone when a series of intersecting controversies proved too much for the prime minister. The first involved the accusation that non-partisan office staff had filed expense claims for trips to Toronto during the election campaign. Then came the more titillating word that an exotic dancer originally from Romania had been granted special temporary resident status, thereby permitting her to live in Canada for two years beyond the work permit's expiry and apply for citizenship. It was in the gift of the minister to make such dispensations, but the case did not appear to warrant such a high-level intervention. Critics seized the opportunity to grill Sgro. One, the NDP's Pat Martin, said that department officials had threatened to stymie the applications of constituents if he persisted in his questioning. There were also accusations of improprieties in campaign financing involving Sgro's riding association and applicants. The matter of the special permit was referred to the Ethics Commission on 22 November.

The trials of Svend Robinson

When he made his parliamentary debut in 1979, Svend Robinson was one of the youngest MPs ever elected. At the time he abandoned his re-election campaign in April 2004, he was one of the House's longest-serving members. Robinson's departure was precipitated by a stunning confession, made on 14 April, that he had taken an expensive ring from an auction showroom. He voluntarily returned the jewellery, and turned himself into police, before making the announcement. Attributing his actions to a lapse of judgment brought on by stress, the MP for the British Columbia riding of Burnaby quit the NDP caucus and paved the way for his assistant, Bill Siksay, to win the seat.

The sudden downfall ended, at least for the moment, the public career of one of Canada's most intriguing politicians. Despite repeated efforts to belittle and marginalize him, Robinson championed often unpopular causes with singular conviction. While serving in the House, he had served time in jail for his participation in protests against logging in the sensitive Clayquot Sound region of British Columbia. He vigorously championed Aboriginal causes, defended the right of Sue Rodriquez to end her life by means of assisted suicide, stood with protestors at the Summit of Quebec as they demonstrated against free trade, denounced policies of the Israeli and American governments, and sponsored an amendment calling for the inclusion of sexual orientation in the categories of hate crimes. In doing so, he attracted criticism from outsiders and occasionally from within his own party, as when his insistence that a reference to God in the Charter of Rights and Freedoms should be excised led to his demotion within the caucus in 1999.

As expected, Robinson entered a guilty plea to the charge of theft (6 Aug.). He was sentenced to one year's probation and one hundred hours of community service, but was spared a criminal record. Over the years he had received numerous awards in recognition of his advocacy of human rights. As he began a new phase of life, the more charitable partisan foes joined NDP stalwarts in acknowledging his contributions and courage.

Passages

On 16 December, Liberal MP Lawrence O'Brien succumbed to cancer at the age of fifty-three. The member for Labrador first entered the House after winning a by-election in 1996. Although not a well-known figure in the precincts of Parliament, he was remembered for his industry and compassion. He made headlines in October when he rushed to Ottawa from a hospital in Quebec in case he was needed to vote on the Throne Speech resolution.

CHRISTOPHER SPEARIN[1]

Foreign affairs and defence

When Paul Martin became prime minister at the close of 2003, one hope was that Canada would have a more assertive and recognized presence on the international stage. Certainly, the cabinet committee structure Prime Minister Martin put in place indicated this priority; whereas Prime Minister Jean Chrétien had no cabinet committees that dealt specifically with either foreign or military affairs, Paul Martin's structure had three (Global Affairs; Canada-U.S.; Security, Public Health, and Emergencies). To ensure renewed Canadian assertiveness abroad, Martin kept Bill Graham in his position as foreign affairs minister. This allowed the cabinet to continue to capitalize upon his experience garnered as an international law professor and as the former chair of the House of Commons Committee on Foreign Affairs and International Trade. The prime minister also named David Pratt to the position of minister of national defence. Pratt was a long-time supporter of the Canadian military, particularly while he was the chair of the House of Commons Committee on National Defence and Veterans Affairs.

However, in the wake of the 28 June 2004 federal election that saw the Liberals reduced to a minority position, Martin's international agenda was disrupted. David Pratt lost his seat for Nepean-Carleton to a first-time Conservative Party candidate. Because the Liberals lost a significant number of seats to the Bloc Québécois, Prime Minister Martin named Pierre Pettigrew to the prominent position of foreign affairs minister, a choice described as 'backfilling' (*Toronto Star*, 22 July). Bill Graham suffered a seeming demotion to become defence minister in order to make room for Pettigrew. Moreover, because the Liberals would have to rely on both the Bloc Québécois and the New Democratic Party in order to remain in power, this suggested that the

1 The author would like to thank Donald Spearin for his assistance in the preparation of this chapter.

Martin government would have to moderate its policies vis-à-vis foreign affairs and defence. It is in this 'weakened' context that many of the foreign- and defence-policy challenges and decisions in 2004 must be viewed.

Foreign affairs

President Bush's visit to Canada

At the end of November, President George W. Bush conducted, for two days, his first official visit to Canada. In terms specific to the United States, this was the president's first foreign trip after his re-election earlier in the month and was part of a larger outreach exercise to countries that had strained relations with Washington since the U.S invasion of Iraq in 2003. In terms specific to Canada-U.S. bilateralism, the trip was an opportunity to improve relations that had been tense, for a variety of reasons, since President Bush's inauguration in 2000. As part of this fence-mending gesture, the president visited both Ottawa and Halifax, the latter being important because of the role Atlantic Canadians played in hosting Americans stranded in the Maritimes when their planes were forced to land after the terrorist attacks of 11 September 2001. President Bush's words in Halifax were heartfelt: 'Canadians came to the aid of men and women and children who were worried and confused and had no place to sleep ... and you asked for nothing in return ... Thank you for your kindness to Americans in an hour of need ... Our two peoples are one family and always will be' (Canadian Broadcasting Corporation, 1 Dec.). President Bush also belatedly recognized the various ways Canada had contributed in the so-called war on terror: 'Afghanistan is a world away from the nightmare of its recent past, Mr. Prime Minister, and I want to thank you ...We share a history, a continent and a border ... Today, we're standing together against the forces of terrorism' (Canadian Broadcasting Corporation, 30 Nov.).

While the public-relations aspect of the trip was important, the prime minister and president pushed each other on a variety of challenges in the bilateral relationship. Prime Minister Martin raised cross-border trade disputes concerning softwood lumber and cattle (see below). President Bush, for his part, focused upon Canada's seeming hesitancy to endorse his country's plans for missile defence (also see below). To make his case clear, the president used the exact words of Prime Minister William Lyon Mackenzie King: 'We cannot defend our country and save our homes and families by waiting for our enemies to attack us. To remain on the defensive is the surest way to bring the war to Canada' (Canadian Broadcasting Corporation, 1 Dec.). Put differently, President Bush hoped that the two countries would 'move forward on ballistic missile defence co-operation to protect the next generation of Canadians and Americans from the threats we know will arise' (*Toronto Star*, 11 Dec.).

Additionally, while the trip may have been part of a larger charm offensive, President Bush made it plain that U.S. policies and priorities were not likely to change significantly in his second term. In reference to the U.S. election, President Bush commented that 'we just had a poll in our country that decided that the foreign policy in our country should stay in place for four more years' (Canadian Broadcasting Corporation, 30 Nov.). In this context, it was not surprising that many Canadians came out to protest the president's visit, not only in Ottawa and Halifax but also in twenty-three other locations across the country. The largest rally, 5,000 strong, occurred in Ottawa, on and around Parliament Hill, on 30 November.

Challenges in Canada-U.S. trade

Wheat

In the context of the ongoing battles between Canada and the United States concerning Canadian wheat production and export practices, Canada gained a degree of success in 2004. Earlier, on 31 March 2003, and in response to a U.S. request, the World Trade Organization (WTO) Dispute Settlement Body established a panel to review two issues: 1) the conformity of the Canadian Wheat Board (CWB) to WTO regulations; and 2) whether imported grain received less favourable treatment than Canadian grain. This request also coincided with the U.S. decision in 2003 to level anti-dumping and subsidization duties against Canadian wheat imports. Luckily for Canada, the WTO panel announced on 10 February 2004 that the CWB's practices fell within the acceptable parameters as laid out under Article XVII of the General Agreement on Tariffs and Trade (GATT) concerning state-trading enterprises.

As for the issue of national treatment, the WTO panel's findings were mixed for Canada. On the one hand, the panel found that Canada's program of allocating railcars to grain producers was permissible. On the other hand, it determined that Canada discriminated against imported U.S. grain by treating it differently. For the WTO panel, this difference in treatment existed in Canadian policies that required mandatory authorization for imported grain, prevented the mixing of eastern Canadian grain with imported grain, and provided the CWB with lower rail-transportation rates.

Given that the WTO panel upheld the legality of the CWB, a considerable victory for Canada, Agriculture and Agri-Food Minister Bob Speller was inclined to accent the positive rather than the negative: 'Considering the panel recognizes Canada's right to maintain our grain quality assurance system, the findings as they relate to the grain sector should have little impact on the Canadian industry' (Agriculture and Agri-Food Canada News Release No. 22, 10 Feb.). Although the United States appealed the WTO panel's finding regarding state-trading enterprises, the WTO Appellate Body upheld the panel's findings on 30 August. Because the appellate body was the last avenue of recourse under WTO rules, the United States had exhausted its efforts with the world body on this file.

For Canada, however, the fight was not over. This was because the WTO panel's findings dealt only with Canada's global trade policies and was not binding on Canada's bilateral trade relations with the United States per se. As such, the U.S. duties remained in place. In recognition that the fight would take place in several forums, the Canadian government requested on 9 April that the WTO examine U.S. claims that Canadian exports were harming U.S. grain producers. As well, the Canadian government and the CWB launched separate requests in the fall of 2003 for a panel to be struck under the North American Free Trade Agreement (NAFTA) to examine U.S. Department of Commerce (DOC) and U.S. International Trade Commission (ITC) policies vis-à-vis Canadian wheat exports to the United States. The NAFTA-panel examinations commenced later in 2004. Because the ITC had earlier voted to terminate tariffs on Canadian durum wheat and only a tied decision of 2-2 on the ITC maintained tariffs on Canadian spring wheat, thus revealing U.S. uncertainty, the CWB felt that it had a strong case. As argued by Louise Waldman, the board's spokesperson: 'It's not like they actually won their case originally. They had a tied decision, so what we're going after now is that decision piece by piece' (*Leader Post*, 30 Oct.). Success on these panels was important to Canada because, although the U.S. market accounted for only 10–15 per cent of Canadian grain exports, the value of Canadian spring wheat exports to the United States was still a handsome $250 million annually. Rulings from the NAFTA-panel examinations were not expected until 2005.

Beef

Similar to wheat exports, the situation regarding Canadian beef exports also improved, but in this case only after a long and often discouraging year. At the start of 2004, Canadian beef producers hoped that the U.S. border would fully reopen to the export of Canadian beef following its closure in the wake of a May 2003 finding that a sick cow slaughtered in Alberta in January 2003 suffered from bovine spongiform encephalopathy (BSE) or mad cow disease.[2] The United States partially lifted the ban in August 2003 to allow the export of boneless cuts and media reports indicated that it was to remove all restrictions in December 2003. These were encouraging signals for Canadian producers. However, on 23 December 2003, U.S. inspectors announced their finding of a BSE-infected cow in Washington State. Subsequent investigation determined that the cow was born on a farm near Leduc, Alberta, in 1997. Given that the Canadian beef industry had already lost $1.9 billion at the time of the Washington State finding, the comments of Dr Brian Evans of the Canadian Food Inspection Agency were understated: 'This is not a shocking discovery (but) it certainly does provide some disappointment to the industry' (Canadian Broadcasting Corporation, 7 Jan.). Despite the earlier hopes of Canadian beef producers, the restrictions on the cross-border movements of beef exports remained and the resulting depressed prices and backlog continued.

To compensate Canadian beef producers, the federal government released two pools of money that built upon financial-aid packages created earlier in 2003. On 22 March, Prime Minister Martin announced a farm-aid package that included $680 million for the Canadian beef industry: 'These are hard times. And as these farm families face these kinds of challenges we believe that the government must be there to help' (Canadian Broadcasting Corporation, 22 March). In light of these continuing hard times, the federal government offered on 10 September an additional recovery plan valued at $488 million. The goals of this plan were threefold: 1) to increase Canadian slaughterhouse capacity; 2) to expand foreign markets for Canadian beef (the United States imported 70 per cent of Canadian live cattle exports before the ban); and 3) to provide recuperation assistance to Canadian beef producers. For Minister Speller, a future goal was the reduction of Canada's reli-

---

2 Also on 20 May 2003, thirty-three other countries closed their borders to Canadian beef exports.

ance upon a continental production system that had developed in North America during the 1990s: 'We want to reposition the beef industry so that it can return to profitability with or without the border reopening' (Canadian Broadcasting Corporation, 10 Sept.).

Nevertheless, fully reopening the U.S. border to Canadian beef exports remained the primary focus in 2004. On 20 April, the U.S. Department of Agriculture (USDA) opened the border to beef products (ground, processed, and bone-in beef) from animals less than thirty months old, a move that immediately benefited the Canadian meatpacking industry. Nevertheless, it was only on 29 December that the USDA announced that Canada would be designated as a 'minimal-risk region' for BSE, with the resumption of imports of young Canadian cattle scheduled for 7 March 2005.

Although the new U.S. regulations still prohibited the import of older live cattle, 95 per cent of Canada's trade in beef and cattle to the United States could now resume. But, because the border's closure cost the Canadian beef industry and rural Canada approximately $5 billion, the repercussions, as expressed by Dennis Laycraft of the Canadian Cattleman's Association, were likely to be long term: 'I think it's going to, in some cases, probably take close to a decade for producers to recover from the type of impact that they've gone through' (*Calgary Herald*, 30 Dec.).

Swine

The case of Canada's export of live swine to the United States was also a mixed story in 2004. With 7.4 million hogs shipped across the border in 2003, valued at $554 million, the United States was the largest market for Canadian live swine exports. Since 1999, these exports had been relatively uncontroversial, thanks to U.S. government findings that Canada was a fair trader. However, on 5 March, the U.S. National Pork Producers requested that the DOC conduct countervailing and anti-dumping investigations regarding the U.S. import of live Canadian hogs. On 8 April, the DOC agreed to conduct these investigations.

On the one hand, Canada was able to achieve a degree of satisfaction because the DOC's preliminary countervailing decision, issued on 17 August, was in Canada's favour. On the other, the DOC determined on 16 October that Canada was indeed guilty of dumping hogs on the U.S. market. As a result, the DOC announced plans to impose duties ranging from 13.25 per cent to 15.01 per cent depending upon the type of pork. In light of all the problems Canada was encountering in its bilateral trade relations, Saskatchewan Agriculture Minister Mark Wartman argued that the DOC's decision was 'yet another example of an unwarranted U.S. challenge to legitimate trade in an integrated North American market' (*Leader Post*, 16 Oct.). The final ruling on the DOC's determinations was not to be made until March 2005.

Softwood lumber

Despite numerous findings supporting the Canadian position issued by both the WTO and NAFTA, Canada's trade dispute with the United States concerning softwood lumber, ongoing since 2001, continued throughout 2004. In terms of the WTO, on 22 March, a WTO panel found that the ITC's threat of injury determination was inconsistent with international trade regulations. Canada made the request for this investigation on 7 May 2003. For International Trade Minister Jim Peterson, the finding's message was unequivocal: 'The countervailing and anti-dumping duties imposed by the U.S. on Canadian softwood lumber exports are baseless' (DFAIT News Release No. 45, 22 March). The WTO further underscored the inconsistency of U.S. policy when another WTO panel determined on 13 April that the DOC's anti-dumping determination was also out of keeping with U.S. obligations towards the WTO. Later, on 11 August, the WTO Appellate Body announced that the U.S. employment of 'zeroing' was similarly not in keeping with WTO guidelines.[3]

In terms of NAFTA, the process investigating the ITC's threat of injury determination continued in 2004. Earlier, on 5 September 2003, the NAFTA panel found that the ITC's approach was inconsistent with U.S. law. Nevertheless, on 15 December 2003, the ITC issued a threat of injury-remand determination that contended that U.S. producers were indeed threatened. The back and forth continued in 2004 because, although on 29 April the NAFTA panel released a second report finding the ITC's threat of injury-remand determination to be similarly inconsistent, the ITC subsequently issued a second such threat on 10 June. The third NAFTA panel report's findings, released on 31 August, were that the second ITC's threat of injury-remand determination was also

---

3 As indicated in DFAIT News Release No. 90, 'zeroing is the practice of assigning a margin of zero to goods for which the export price exceeds the home market price. This difference is also referred to as a "negative dumping margin." Zeroing prevents the negative margin for one category of goods from offsetting a margin of dumping for another category of goods. This is an important issue because zeroing results in higher dumping rates.'

not in keeping with U.S. law. The wording of this third NAFTA panel report was particularly damning of the ITC: '[The commission has been] simply unwilling to accept this panel's review authority ... and has consistently ignored the authority of this panel in an effort to preserve its finding of threat of material injury' (Canadian Broadcasting Corporation, 31 Aug.). As a result, the ITC's third remand determination, released on 10 September, indicated that Canadian softwood exports were not a threat to U.S. producers. For representatives of the Canadian lumber industry such as Carl Grenier, the executive vice-president of the Free Trade Lumber Council, this was the ruling Canadian producers were hoping for: 'It cannot get any better than this ... It's total victory. They basically ran out of patience' (Canadian Broadcasting Corporation, 31 Aug.).

Nevertheless, it became evident that the victory was not to be total for the Canadian softwood-lumber industry. On 13 October, the United States indicated that it would file an Extraordinary Challenge Committee proceeding, as it was allowed to do under NAFTA guidelines, regarding the NAFTA panel's determination. Additionally, on 14 December, the DOC reduced only slightly its duty rates on Canadian softwood lumber. The new countervailing duty rate fell from 18.79 per cent to 17.18 per cent and the new anti-dumping duty rate stood at 4.03 per cent from the earlier rate of 8.43 per cent. As part of an obvious divide-and-conquer strategy, the United States also applied a particular duty-calculation strategy to British Columbian timber. Moreover, U.S. officials and U.S. lumber producers alike asserted that the earlier determinations against the U.S. position were not retrospective, and thus the monies collected would not be returned to Canadian producers. Since the imposition of U.S. duties in May 2002, U.S. Customs had collected approximately $4 billion in duties. Although collectively these moves were an attempt to force Canada back to the bargaining table, plans for a new round of bilateral negotiations were not forthcoming when 2004 ended.

Byrd Amendment

Canada, along with other interested states, continued the battle with the United States regarding the controversial Continued Dumping and Subsidy Offset Act of 2000, otherwise known as the Byrd Amendment. The act's terms permitted an extreme incentive measure such that U.S. companies supporting petitions for anti-dumping and countervailing-duty investigations were doubly rewarded. Not only did they benefit commercially from the imposition of duties, they were also entitled to receive direct payout of these duties held by the U.S. Treasury. Even although Canada and ten other co-complainants in September 2001 challenged the Byrd Amendment in the WTO and won, the United States, following an unsuccessful appeal, still did not repeal the amendment by the WTO deadline of 27 December 2003.[4]

In earlier years, the damage done to Canadian interests was small. Disbursements to U.S. producers, mostly in ball bearing, steel and other metals, and household-item sectors linked to Canadian exports, were US$5.2 million in 2001, US$2.5 million in 2002, and US$9.5 million in 2003. However, the Byrd Amendment was a particularly sensitive measure to Canada given the aforementioned softwood-lumber dispute. Although the U.S. government held the cash deposits for the countervailing and anti-dumping duties in trust, approximately US$1 billion annually could be distributed to U.S. lumber producers starting in 2007.

Because of these high stakes for Canada and U.S. intransigence, the latter not totally unexpected because 2004 was a U.S. election year, Canada and seven other co-complainants asked the WTO that they be granted retaliatory authorization.[5] In particular, they wished for a WTO-determined level of retaliation that would be linked to the dollar amount of U.S. disbursements. On 31 August, the WTO responded by permitting retaliation by the co-complainants of up to 72 per cent of the annual level of disbursement. This retaliation could take the form of tariffs on U.S. imports or the suspension of certain trade rules. On 23 November the Canadian government launched domestic consultations to determine what penalties Canada should impose. Finance Minister Ralph Goodale justified the government's approach: 'We want to hear from Canadian businesses themselves on the next steps that should be taken in challenging this U.S. measure ... The Government of Canada conducts public consultations every time retaliatory trade action is considered, and this dialogue will ensure that our upcoming response will be in Canada's best interests' (DFAIT News Release No. 134, 23 Nov.). The issue of retaliation was a sensitive one given the potentially nega-

---

4 The ten other co-complainants were the European Union, Australia, Brazil, Chile, India, Indonesia, Japan, Mexico, South Korea, and Thailand.
5 The seven other co-complainants were the European Union, Brazil, Chile, India, Japan, Mexico, and South Korea.

tive impact it could pose for bilateral relations specifically and the state of the world economy generally.[6] Therefore, while the public consultations ended on 20 December, it was not surprising that the government did not announce a decision before the end of the year.

Human and political rights

China/the Koreas

On 29 September, forty-four North Koreans scaled the walls surrounding Canada's embassy in Beijing, China.[7] This episode came on the heels of twenty-six North Koreans entering the Japanese embassy in Beijing earlier in September in search of sanctuary and eventual safe passage to South Korea. While the Chinese government had not done so in public cases, a treaty with North Korea nevertheless required China to classify all North Korean asylum seekers as economic migrants and return them to North Korea. Additionally, Beijing was in the midst of negotiating with Pyongyang to recommence the six-country talks regarding North Korea's nuclear-weapons program. The issue of asylum seekers threatened to upset the delicate bilateral talks. In light of this complexity, China asked that the Canadian embassy hand over the North Koreans.

Instead of giving the North Koreans to Chinese officials, Canadian diplomatic officials launched negotiations with the Chinese government that lasted for several months. Eventually, the negotiations achieved success; the Canadian embassy slowly transferred the North Koreans, out of the public spotlight, to South Korea. On 22 December, Minister Pierre Pettigrew announced that the last four North Koreans were now in South Korea and that both Canadian and Chinese officials were to be commended for handling a very sensitive matter: 'I would ... like to thank the Chinese government for working with us to resolve this issue in a way that is consistent with our international obligations and in keeping with our humanitarian concerns' (DFAIT News Release No. 156, 22 Dec.).

6 In the case of the European Union alone, approximately $4 billion in countermeasures was permissible.
7 The forty-four North Koreans came from five families. The group consisted of twelve men, twenty-six women, and six children. Chinese officials caught one man who was not able to scale the fence fast enough.

Zahra Kazemi

Even though Zahra Kazemi, a photojournalist with joint Canadian and Iranian citizenship, died while in Iranian custody back on 11 July 2003, the demands for justice by Canada and her family were not met in 2004. In the summer of 2004, controversy surrounded the trial of Mohammad Reza Aghdam Ahmadi, the Iranian agent charged with her 'semi-premeditated murder' (i.e., there was not the intent to kill). Iranian journalists reported that Saeed Mortazavi, Tehran's chief prosecutor, had pressured them to censor their coverage of the trial. Iranian officials also shut down two reformist newspapers at the trial's start. In addition, on 13 July, Canada announced the recall of its ambassador, Philip Mac-Kinnon, when he was denied access to the courtroom, despite Iranian agreement that he could attend. This recall was put on hold only when Iranian officials relented.

While the trial was under way, the Kazemi family's legal team, headed by Nobel Peace Prize winner Shirin Ebadi, wished to use the proceedings as a forum to investigate a number of points: 1) the accused was in fact a scapegoat for the actual killer, prison official Mohammad Bakhshi; 2) Saeed Mortazavi was responsible for covering up Kazemi's death and forging documents; 3) Kazemi was tortured before her death; and 4) her death was premeditated, not the result of a stroke as initially contended by Iranian officials. The judge, however, did not allow for the expanded focus and he brought the proceedings to a close on 18 July. In protest, the legal team did not sign the record of proceedings and Canada again recalled its ambassador.[8] On 24 July, the judge cleared the accused based on the 'lack of sufficient evidence.' For Minister Pettigrew, the trial did 'nothing to answer the real questions about how Zahra Kazemi died or to bring the perpetrators of her murder to justice' (DFAIT News Release No. 81, 25 July). United Nations human-rights experts also condemned the decision: 'Many reports indicate that the proceedings did not meet international standards of fair trial because key evidence that might have incriminated judiciary officials, the prosecutor's office as well as the intelligence ministry were ignored by the court' (Canadian Broadcasting Corporation, 27 July).

Throughout this process, Stephan Hachemi, Kazemi's son, continued to pressure the Canadian government to take more aggressive action

---

8 Another complicating factor was that Iranian officials again prevented the presence of other foreigners in the courtroom.

against Iran. He called for the government to bring the case to the International Court of Justice, to expel the Iranian ambassador to Canada, and to demand the return to Canada of his mother's remains. Although Hachemi did meet with Minister Pettigrew in Ottawa on 27 July, he was dissatisfied with the meeting's outcome: '[The minister] did not commit himself to any of the proposals I made to him ... The minister failed me and failed to have my mother's rights respected' (Canadian Broadcasting Corporation, 27 July).

On 23 November, the government announced that Gordon Venner would assume Canada's ambassadorship to Iran.[9] The rationale behind the move was threefold. First, Minister Pettigrew agued that this would allow Canada to argue forcefully the Kazemi case before Iranian officials: 'Justice denied is offensive to Canadians. This case will be pursued energetically' (DFAIT News Release No. 133, 23 Nov.). Second, the government wished to have representation in Iran to explain the Canadian decision to table a human-rights resolution regarding Iran in the UN General Assembly on 2 November. Finally, Canadian representation was key because Canada was then chairing the Board of Governors of the International Atomic Energy Agency (IAEA), a body examining in depth Iran's nuclear program. Canadian activism in the IAEA could be seen as an indirect punishment of Iran regarding its human-rights record and specifically its handling of the Kazemi case.

Maher Arar

Maher Arar's mission to learn exactly why Syrian officials detained him for a year as a terror suspect and what role Canadian officials played in his imprisonment continued throughout 2004.[10] On 22 January, Arar's legal team launched a lawsuit against the U.S. government in U.S. District Court for the Eastern District of New York in search of both an admission of wrongdoing and financial compensation. A few days later, on 28 January, Public Safety Minister Anne McLellan announced the creation of a public inquiry into the Arar case with the specific focus of assessing 'the actions of Canadian officials in dealing with the deporta-

9 Philip MacKinnon had moved on to become Canada's ambassador to Egypt.
10 On 26 September 2002, U.S. officials at New York City's Kennedy Airport detained Arar, a holder of dual Canadian-Syrian citizenship, as he returned to Canada via the United States from a vacation in Tunisia. They suspected him of having ties to al-Qaeda and deported him to Syria.

tion and detention of Maher Arar' (Canadian Broadcasting Corporation, 28 Jan.). Minister McLellan granted the head of the public inquiry, Justice Dennis O'Conner, the authority to examine classified documents and to consider review mechanisms.

During the course of the hearings, which started in Ottawa on 21 June, a somewhat murky picture was revealed regarding official Canadian involvement. On 30 June, RCMP deputy commissioner Garry Loeppky testified that material on police investigations, even related to innocent individuals, was kept on a national database that could be released to U.S. officials upon request. On 6 July, it became evident that the RCMP had interacted with U.S. officials shortly after Arar's arrest in New York. It also became evident that the release of sensitive information, some of which did not originate with the RCMP, may have been unauthorized. On 24 September, an internal RCMP report released to the inquiry showed that the RCMP lacked the experience to investigate the Arar case. On 14 September, the Security Intelligence Review Committee released a heavily censored report indicating that the Canadian Security Intelligence Service was unaware of U.S. plans to detain and deport Arar. A few days later, on 21 September, the U.S. State Department announced that it would not participate in the public inquiry. The clarity wished for by Arar was also denied on 26 November when Justice O'Connor released over 1,000 pages of RCMP documents in which over half of the content was blocked out owing to national-security concerns. The public inquiry continued into 2005.

The Khadrs

Because of a variety of developments, the Khadrs, Canada's so-called 'al-Qaeda family,' continued to be in the news in 2004. First, in the aftermath of the October 2003 gun battle with Pakistani forces that killed her husband, Ahmed Said Khadr, and paralysed one of her four sons, Karim Khadr, Maha Khadr indicated that, despite her earlier protestations, her husband was indeed a terrorist. As a result, thousands of Canadians signed a petition to demand the family's deportation. The petition proved to be unsuccessful.

Second, Abdullah Khadr, another son, who escaped the October 2003 gun battle, was on the run in Pakistan in 2004. Although he wished to return to Canada, Canadian diplomatic officials could not guarantee his safety nor prevent a potential arrest in Pakistan. It was additionally rumoured that Abdullah was the suicide bomber that killed Corporal Jamie Murphy in Afghanistan in January (see below). Although the Canadian military collected genetic material for testing from the bombing scene, a February interview with Abdullah conducted by the Canadian Broadcasting Corporation laid the rumour to rest: 'If I was the suicide bomber, I wouldn't be doing this interview with you right now' (Canadian Broadcasting Corporation, 26 Feb.).

Third, another Khadr son, Abdulrahman, conducted a battle with the Foreign Affairs Department in 2004. Abdulrahman returned to Canada in the autumn of 2003 following his capture by U.S. forces in Afghanistan in November 2001 and subsequent detention at the U.S. military prison in Guantánamo Bay, Cuba. In May 2004 Abdulrahman applied for a Canadian passport and was turned down by the Foreign Affairs Department without explanation. The lack of explanation was because no regulations were in place to withhold passports on security grounds; therefore, ministerial initiative was required to invoke crown prerogative to prevent the issuing of the passport. Although the government introduced new regulations to close this gap, the Federal Court of Canada ruled in December that Abdulrahman could proceed with a case against Ottawa regarding the denial. Abdulrahman's lawyer, Clayton Ruby, declared: 'Canadians should be pleased because this is the liberty of the ordinary Canadian ... Can government reach in, single you out and say, "Ah you, you don't get a passport"' (*National Post*, 11 Dec.).

Finally, Omar, the fourth Khadr son, remained imprisoned by the United States in Guantánamo Bay. U.S. forces had shot and captured Omar in Afghanistan in July 2002 after he detonated a grenade that killed a U.S. Army medic.[11] Since the start of his incarceration, U.S. officials had not charged Omar with a crime and were unsure as to whether to try him eventually before a military commission. But in October 2004, U.S. officials allowed Omar to speak to a lawyer for the first time. This was in response to a suit launched by other detainees in their demand for habeas corpus, the right to contest detention before a judge. Nevertheless, Omar's legal standing remained unresolved by the end of 2004.

Ukrainian elections

In the days leading up to the run-off vote for the Ukrainian presidency on 21 November, Minister Pettigrew underscored the importance of an appropriately run election in Ukraine: 'As the Ukrainian people pro-

11 At the time of his capture, Omar was fifteen years old.

ceed to the November runoff vote, Canadians are watching with a great deal of interest and are hopeful that this vote will be conducted in a free, fair and transparent manner' (DFAIT News Release No. 132, 19 Nov.). This was an important vote for Ukraine's budding democracy because irregularities and controversies had plagued the initial polls on 31 October.[12] As well, the vote was critical in determining the political direction Ukraine would take. The run-off pitted the Western-leaning opposition leader, Viktor Yushchenko, against Prime Minister Viktor Yanukovitch, the candidate strongly supported by outgoing President Leonid Kuchma and Russian President Vladimir Putin. The vote was also domestically important in Canada because, with a population of 1.2 million Canadians of Ukrainian descent, Canada was home to the second-largest Ukrainian diaspora after Russia. As a result of this domestic consideration, Canada contributed thirty-six individuals to a 600-member election-observer team organized by the Office for Democratic Institutions and Human Rights of the Organization for Security and Cooperation in Europe.

Unfortunately, the election monitors reported that the run-off vote suffered from severe irregularities ranging from ad hoc voting restrictions to rigged counting to manipulation of the media. Although monitored exit polls suggested a Yushchenko victory, the Ukrainian Elections Commission found that Yanukovitch won 49.42 per cent of the vote, whereas Yushchenko received only 46.70 per cent. Following this outcome, tens of thousands of opposition supporters filled Kyiv's Independence Square for seventeen days of continuous protest. Domestic and international pressure together led the Ukrainian parliament to bring down the prime minister's government on 1 December. Two days later, Ukraine's Supreme Court ordered a new run-off vote on 26 December.

In preparation for this second run-off, the largest number of Canadian election monitors in Canada's history travelled to Ukraine. The Ukrainian Canadian Congress sent a 500-strong delegation. In terms of an official Canadian response, the government selected 500 individuals from a pool of 4,000 applicants to form the Canadian Observer Mission. This mission, headed by former prime minister John Turner, was the first project of the Canada Corps of the Canadian International Development Agency (CIDA). Since many of the Canadian observers had no

---

12 One assertion, backed by medical evidence, was that Viktor Yushchenko became ill by dioxin poisoning. The poison may have been administered during a 6 September dinner with Ihor Smeshko, the head of Ukraine's successor organization to the KGB.

prior experience, they received two days of training in Canada and then a third day of training in Ukraine.

The results of the 26 December run-off vote made plain earlier problems; Yushchenko received 52 per cent of the vote versus the 44 per cent won by Yanukovitch. Although there were still some voting irregularities, Turner was confident of the election's validity: 'What I saw was quiet, well-organized and well-directed' (*Guardian*, 28 Dec.). The Ukrainian Canadian Congress was similarly impressed: '[The election] met essential democratic norms and the will of the people was expressed' (*Guardian*, 28 Dec.).

Sudan

By the end of 2004, violence had plagued Sudan's Darfur region for almost two years. The conflict pitted native Africans against pro-government Arab militias. During a period of twenty-one months, over 70,000 people, mostly native Africans, had been killed and an additional 1.5 million people were either displaced internally or forced to flee to neighbouring countries. Given that civilians endured the bulk of the suffering, the Arab militias stood accused of committing war crimes, crimes against humanity, and even genocide.

To try to counter the violence, the international community was involved in a number of ways. The United Nations Security Council issued Resolution 1556 on 30 July. This resolution called on the Sudanese government to disarm the militias, to respect human rights, and to bring to justice those who had violated human rights. Later, on 18 September, the council issued Resolution 1564, which featured the specific threat of sanctions with a particular emphasis on Sudan's oil industry. Meanwhile, the African Union (AU) facilitated negotiations among the different parties. To reinforce a somewhat shaky ceasefire, the AU sent 3,500 soldiers and 800 police to Sudan to bolster the 400 AU soldiers already present.

Canadian assistance came more in the form of money and materiel than in terms of military personnel. From the fall of 2003 to the end of 2004, Canada contributed over $37 million to help resolve the situation and to deal with the humanitarian challenges. In particular, Canada donated monies for the charter of helicopters to assist AU forces. However, although two Canadian military personnel were supporting the UN operation in the country and an additional two went to Sudan to determine and assess possible activities and locales for more Canadian personnel, greater numbers of troops were not forthcoming. For

Minister Graham, the assistance Canada provided was sufficient and the overstretched Canadian military needed time to recover: 'There's no question that our troops have been extraordinarily actively engaged for the past several years. We've made it clear – both to them and to the Canadian public – that we are taking time for their re-formation, for their training' (*Ottawa Citizen*, 2 Sept.).

This stance, however, did not sit well with many of the government's critics. For Stockwell Day, the Conservative foreign affairs critic, the government had to do more to show its resolve and to bolster that of the international community: 'We have to be actively involved in holding this regime accountable for what's happening in Darfur ... we have to support the African Union and report what's going on in that part of the world if we're going to avoid another Rwanda' (*National Post*, 13 Oct.). Rwanda was also on the mind of retired Lieutenant-General Roméo Dallaire, the commander of the ill-fated UN mission to the central African country in the mid-1990s. For him, the government's unwillingness to commit troops risked a repeat of the Rwandan genocide: 'It burns inside and the sentiments or the feelings that I had of abandonment in Rwanda are exactly the same that I feel today in regards to the Sudan ... I am just disgusted with the lame and obtuse responses coming from Canada and the western world' (*Ottawa Citizen*, 2 Sept.).

Prime Minister Martin, for his part, tried to bolster the image of Canadian resolve by visiting Sudan on 25 November. However, despite Martin's demand to Sudan's president, Omar al-Bashir, that he act to ensure the security of civilians in the Darfur region, his call fell on deaf ears: 'In the discussion with us, the president indicated with us that he was not able to control the janjaweed [the Arab militias]. That, in fact, they were operating on their own. The point we made to him is that we expect the janjaweed would be controlled. Period' (Regina *Leader Post*, 26 Nov.).

Asian Tsunami

As 2004 ended, the Canadian government faced the domestic and international repercussions of the Asian Tsunami of 26 December. An earthquake just off the Indonesian island of Sumatra, measuring 9.0 on the Richter scale, triggered the massive wave. With eleven countries severely affected by the disaster, estimates by year's end were that at least 100,000 people were dead and millions more were displaced. For UN Secretary General Kofi Annan, the Asian Tsunami was 'an unprecedented global catastrophe' (MSNBC, 31 Dec.).

Although the Canadian government initially pledged $1 million in assistance shortly after the disaster struck, it quickly raised the amount to $4 million on 27 December and to $40 million by 29 December. The government announced plans for debt relief for disaster-struck countries and an initiative whereby the government would match the private donations of Canadians dollar for dollar. As well, it added consular staff and resources to the region to track down and care for Canadians caught up in the disaster. As for military measures, the government arranged for two military flights to bring relief supplies to the region. It also sent an interdepartmental reconnaissance team of seventeen people first to Sri Lanka and then to Indonesia to assess how Canada might best contribute to relief efforts.[13]

Despite this activism, the government received a number of complaints about its handling of the international crisis. First, because the disaster struck during the December holidays, many key government officials such as the prime minister, Minister Pettigrew, and International Cooperation Minister Aileen Carroll were out of the country on vacation. As a result, only bureaucrats and Minister Graham served as the public face of the initial Canadian response. Then, as the level of the challenges in the region became more apparent, the cabinet members were criticized for only belatedly cutting their holidays short to return to Ottawa. Second, although the prime minister charged Minister Graham and Health Minister Ujjal Dosanjh to head up disaster relief in his absence, the opposition parties criticized Minister Pettigrew for not being adequately engaged with the crisis. For instance, Stockwell Day was surprised by the minister's silence: 'This is a foreign affairs issue. Certainly there is a tie in with Minister Graham related to security, but these are foreign friends and foreign governments that have been devastated and I am surprised that we haven't heard from Mr. Pettigrew on this' (*National Post*, 30 Dec.). Third, by the end of 2004, the government had still not announced whether it was sending Canada's Disaster Assistance Response Team (DART) to the region. Minister Graham suggested that DART was 'a wonderful tool, but it's for specific purposes, and we haven't seen where that's necessary at this particular point' (*Calgary Herald*, 29 Dec.). He also noted that Canada had not received any formal request from states in the devastated region. These

---

13 The group consisted of eleven personnel from the Disaster Assistance Response Team, three officials from Foreign Affairs, two officials from CIDA, and one person from the Canadian Public Health Agency.

comments came despite the fact that DART was designed for quick-response relief operations and that similar teams from other developed world countries were already on the ground in the region. Possible reasons for the government's resistance were threefold: 1) the cost of sending DART, estimated at $15–20 million, was too high; 2) Canada lacked the necessary airlift capacity to transport DART to the region in a timely manner; and 3) if Canadian airlift assets were used, they could easily break down, much to the government's embarrassment.

Defence policy

Federal election and defence issues

In the lead-up to an election call in the spring of 2004, the government announced a series of expenditures for the military, totalling approximately $7 billion. The government emphasized, in particular, the decision to move forward on the purchase of the Stryker Mobile Gun System, the Joint Support Ship program (see below), and the replacements for fixed-wing search-and-rescue aircraft and the Sea King helicopter (also see below). Critics, however, asserted that these announcements were mere ploys. Indeed, Prime Minister Chrétien's government had announced many of the expenditures or plans for the same projects. For instance, then Defence Minister John McCallum announced the decision on the Stryker in October 2003, a decision that was reiterated in the Martin government's first Throne Speech. Minister McCallum similarly announced the replacement for search-and-rescue planes in November 2003. The joint support ships were part of a strategic investment plan released in October 2003. As for the Sea King replacement, it was McCallum's predecessor, Defence Minister Art Eggleton, who announced in August 2000 that the government of the day was to launch the specification and procurement process. In December 2003 the Martin government, moreover, reiterated that it would continue this process.

During the election campaign, both the Conservative and Liberal parties focused on manpower issues. The Conservatives called for troop levels to increase by 27,600 in order to bring the forces' full-time strength to 80,000. The Liberals, in contrast, proposed a more modest manpower proposal, one that they hoped would differentiate themselves as the more 'dovish' party: an additional 3,000 reservists and 5,000 new full-time soldiers for a special peacekeeping brigade.

However, after the election, the Liberals' proposal received sharp criticism because no new monies were allotted towards raising the manpower. Already, the military had a $1-billion annual deficit for ongoing operations and the anticipated costs of the new brigade were substantial: $2.5 billion in start-up costs and $400–500 million annually for sustainment. Department of National Defence (DND) analysts concluded that, in order to make the increase feasible, the military leadership would have to contemplate mothballing the navy's three destroyers or reducing the air force's fleet of operating CF-18s by 25 per cent. The former would likely ensure that Canada would not play a leading role in multinational naval operations and the latter would likely upset Washington given the role the CF-18s played in continental defence. The government made no decision on any actual cuts in 2004.

Domestic and continental security

Canada's national-security policy

On 27 April, Minister McLellan tabled in the House of Commons the document 'Securing an Open Society: Canada's National Security Policy,' touted as Canada's first-ever integrated strategic framework to prepare for and respond to threats. As outlined by the minister, the government wanted a policy that would protect Canadians, both from threats and from unjustified government intrusion: 'A Government's most important duty is to ensure the safety and security of its citizens … The National Security Policy protects our collective security interests in a way that reflects core Canadian values of tolerance, openness and respect for fundamental rights and freedoms' (DND News Release, 27 April). The document's focal points were threefold: 1) the protection of Canada and Canadians both domestically and internationally; 2) the maintenance of diligence to ensure that Canada was not a base for threats to other states; and 3) the contribution of Canada to international security. The document outlined various measures in keeping with these general areas regarding intelligence, emergency planning and management, public health, transport security, border security, and international security.[14] To these ends, the government also allotted some $690 million in funding that went towards the following goals, plans, and new projects: an integrated threat-assessment centre, intel-

14 The document did not go into depth on international security measures. The government wished to expand on these measures in its foreign- and defence-policy statements to be released in 2005.

ligence enhancement, a government-operations centre, securing critical governmental information systems, a cyber-security task force, marine security, a passport-security strategy, and a real-time identification project for fingerprints.

However, criticism in a variety of forms did accompany the new policy. One criticism was that it was simply a knee-jerk reaction to a scathing report issued by the auditor general in March. That report outlined significant Canadian deficiencies dealing with intelligence communication, terrorist watch-lists, and passport controls. Another criticism was that the policy was not for a Canadian audience at all given the misgivings, justified or not, that many U.S. officials held about the Canadian security stance. Indeed, the timing of the policy's release seemed convenient because on 30 April the prime minister held meetings with President Bush and U.S. congressional leaders in Washington, during which he emphasized the security activism inherent in the new policy. Yet another criticism was that the policy was simply a pre-election manoeuvre taken by the Liberals. Certainly, the public seemed to want more vigorous security measures. A POLLARA public-opinion survey indicated that 55 per cent of Canadians wanted the government to increase spending on anti-terrorism measures. As well, 54 per cent wanted defence-spending increases. Lastly, near the end of the year, the Canadian Senate reported that despite the policy, the government had 'yet to demonstrate that it is prepared to match resources with its stated objectives' (noted in *Guardian*, 9 Dec.). In light of problems related to vulnerable seaports and airports, inadequate surveillance on the Great Lakes, and deficiencies in funding and manning for defence and intelligence, the Canadian Senate argued that the security of Canadians continued to be compromised: 'When it comes to national security and defence – issues that are not part of the everyday lives of most Canadians – the vast majority of citizens trust in luck … Unfortunately, luck is notoriously untrustworthy' (noted in *Guardian*, 9 Dec.).

The military and the north

In light of the global warming that raised the potential for regular maritime travel through the Northwest Passage, U.S. interest in developing northern oil reserves, the growing Canadian diamond industry in the territories, and assertions of Arctic sovereignty made by countries such as Denmark, the Canadian military turned its attention towards its northern capabilities in 2004. In the past, the military possessed considerable northern capabilities given the Arctic threat posed by the Soviet Union during the Cold War. However, with the end of the Cold War, subsequent budget cuts, and a shift in operations to places like Haiti, the Balkans, and Afghanistan, the military's northern presence had declined both qualitatively and quantitatively. In a 2000 report the Canadian Forces Northern Area (CFNA) contended that 'we have moved from a position where virtually every infantryman and a sizeable portion of the membership of the other combat arms had personal experience in such operations, to a posture where few junior personnel across the forces have ever experienced the Arctic in an operational context' (*Ottawa Citizen*, 7 Aug.). By 2004, the military's personnel levels in the north stood at only 150 regular force members and 1,500 Canadian Rangers.

In response to this recognized deficiency, the military conducted Exercise NARWHAL in the Cumberland peninsula area of Baffin Island, Nunavut, from 13 to 30 August. The $5.4-million exercise involved more than 600 personnel from the three services and was the military's largest joint exercise in the Arctic in over a quarter of a century. To underscore this point, with respect to the frigate HMCS *Montreal* employed in the exercise, this was the first time a Canadian naval ship had sailed north of the 60th parallel since 1974.[15] The exercise's objectives were to familiarize military personnel with Arctic terrain and conditions, to promote Canada's northern presence, and to discover the mock crash site of a foreign satellite. Concerning the second objective, for Lieutenant-Colonel Sandy Robertson, one of the exercise's planners, 'the bonus is that it demonstrates to the international community our determination to protect the sovereignty of our North' (*Ottawa Citizen*, 7 Aug.). As for the third objective, it was in keeping with the 1978 Operation MORNING LIGHT during which Canada tried to discover the remnants of the nuclear-powered Russian satellite Cosmos 954 that had crashed in the Arctic. To facilitate the contemporary scenario, the exercise included tests of a new satellite-surveillance system and an unmanned aerial vehicle (UAV) (see below).

The results of Exercise NARWHAL made plain the military's limitations both generally and in terms of its specific northern capabilities. First, during times in the exercise, poor weather grounded the fixed-wing and helicopter flights that supported ground personnel. Military officials, such as Lieutenant-Colonel Scott Archer, the CFNA chief of

15 Indeed, the vessel's design would not have been able to tolerate even the soft first-year ice.

staff, were worried about fuel limitations and the inability of aircraft to detour to remote locations: 'If you push the weather in the Arctic, more times than not you will be bitten by that ... There's not a war so we are taking peace-time safety very realistically here because we don't want to hurt anybody' (*National Post*, 20 Aug.). Yet commercial air flights in the region continued as usual. The operations manager for Kenn Borek Air, for instance, commented that he had 'no idea as to why the military is not flying' (*Ottawa Citizen*, 21 Aug.). Second, the weather-related grounding of air assets stranded two personnel overnight and outdoors on 23 August. Although the two soldiers were eventually saved, subsequent investigations revealed that they lacked the appropriate clothing, provisions, and training for such an incident that included snow, –18 degree Centigrade wind chills, and the possibility of polar bear attack. Third, an engine on the frigate's Sea King helicopter caught fire in the midst of transport flights of personnel and cargo. The helicopter remained grounded until a replacement fire-extinguisher bottle was shipped from the south. Owing to the increasing military, economic, and political salience of Canada's Arctic region and deficiencies such as those identified above, the military announced that it would conduct an even larger northern exercise in 2006.

Ballistic Missile Defence

The issue of whether Canada would 'participate' in the American Ballistic Missile Defence program remained unresolved in 2004.[16] From one angle, it appeared in 2004 that the government would eventually offer its support. Early in the year, on 15 January, Canada exchanged letters on missile defence with the United States. This built upon Canada's decision on 29 May 2003 to enter into discussions with the United States by laying out the areas to be explored in future meetings, including the potential role of the North American Aerospace Defence Command. The latter issue was addressed when, on 5 August, the government amended the NORAD agreement to permit the information collected from NORAD regarding missile warning to be available to the U.S. commands for BMD. This decision was meant to ensure the

16 Participation referred mainly to Canada offering its political sanction to the program and having a 'seat at the table' in terms of defining the BMD architecture and in responding to missile threats against North America. The United States was not looking for Canadian funding or the basing of interceptor missiles in Canada.

continued relevance of NORAD and it integrated Canada into one portion of the overall BMD architecture. To spur on public interest, DND officials revealed publicly that Canadian participation in BMD could lead to as much as $1.5 billion in related spin-off contracts for Canada. As well, although Minister Graham indicated that other bilateral defence issues were of greater prominence and that the threat posed by missiles was remote, he was nevertheless supportive of Canada offering its endorsement: 'Canada has long had a tradition of working with the United States on continental defence. I would like us to see if we could get an agreement that is satisfactory to us' (*Edmonton Journal*, 30 Dec.). The prime minister too, following President Bush's visit to Canada, indicated that Canadian participation was important: 'If there is going to be an American missile going off somewhere over Canadian airspace, I think Canada should be at the table making the decisions' (Canadian Broadcasting Corporation, 24 Feb. 2005).

Moreover, Prime Minister Martin seemed prepared to deal with Liberal caucus members who were publicly vehement in their opposition to Canadian participation, even in the context of a fragile minority government. On 18 November, the prime minister expelled maverick MP Carolyn Parrish from the Liberal caucus. Although the expulsion occurred shortly after Parrish stomped on a George Bush doll on the television program *This Hour Has 22 Minutes* and commented publicly that she had no loyalty to the government, her earlier opposition to BMD certainly contributed to Martin's eventual decision to dismiss her. On 25 August, Parrish, known for her anti-Americanism, asserted that Canada should avoid BMD participation: 'We are not joining a coalition of the idiots. We are joining a coalition of the wise' (Canadian Broadcasting Corporation, 25 Aug.).

From another angle, Canadian participation in BMD seemed unlikely by the close of 2004, regardless of the damage this would do to the prospects of improving Canada-U.S. relations generally and with the Bush administration specifically. Despite its statements and its seeming activism on the issue in 2004, the government had not elected to structure coherently and take charge of the domestic debate on BMD. In fact, in year-end interviews, and in contradiction to Minister Graham's comments and his own earlier statements, the prime minister questioned BMD's utility and feasibility. Indeed, a U.S. test of the system in mid-December, the first in two years, resulted in a malfunction. Additionally, in the minority situation, the government needed the support of opposition parties to remain in power and BMD was a potentially disruptive issue. The New Democratic Party and the Bloc Québécois stood opposed to Canadian participation, especially because of the potential BMD posed for the weaponization of space and its implications for arms control. Conservative Party leader Stephen Harper, although initially supportive, tempered his party's position to 'wait and see' in order to highlight the government's timidity regarding BMD: 'What we want to know is the nature of our proposed involvement, the costs of any obligations that we would incur, the nature and value of any benefits ... When does the Prime Minister intend to tell Parliament and tell Canadians about these things and about where the government's at in this program?' (*Toronto Star*, 11 Dec.). Certainly, considerable resistance within the Liberal Party itself also in part caused the prime minister's timidity. The Quebec Liberals and the women's Liberal caucus, in particular, opposed Canadian involvement. While the prime minister arguably had no choice in taking on Carolyn Parrish, these forces were much more difficult to deal with.

Bi-National Planning Group

In 2004, although a bilateral agreement regarding BMD did not come to fruition, Canada and the United States took further steps to enhance continental defence integration through the Bi-National Planning Group (BPG). Formed in December 2002 with a two-year mandate and located at Peterson Air Force Base in Colorado Springs, the BPG was designed to examine how the two countries collectively might respond to dangers such as terrorist incidents and natural disasters. Given the existence of NORAD, the BPG focused upon land and maritime threats. As well, it examined the sensitive issues of how military forces would interact with civilian authorities and first responders, how command and control would be exercised, and how troops from either country would move across land and sea borders. The government's Speech from the Throne on 5 October 2004 highlighted the continued importance of the BPG by stressing that Canada wished to intensify bilateral cooperation so as to deal with both man-made and natural emergencies. To this end, the government promptly renewed the BPG's mandate for an additional two years (to May 2006). For Minister Pettigrew, Canada's continued participation in the BPG was in keeping with the country's long-standing continental security obligations: 'Canada and the United States have, for decades, worked closely together to meet our shared security needs ... The Bi-national Planning Group is a key element of our cooperative response to new and emerging threats' (DND News Release 04.093, 29 Nov.).

Afghanistan

Suicide bombing

On 27 January a suicide bomber blew himself up beside a convoy of Canadian military Iltis vehicles conducting a patrol near Kabul. Unfortunately, Corporal Jamie Murphy died in the explosion and an additional three soldiers, Lieutenant Jason Feyko, Corporal Richard Newman, and Corporal Jeremy MacDonald, received injuries. All served with 3rd Battalion, Royal Canadian Regiment Battalion Group. The consequent board of inquiry found, on 24 August, that the incident was not preventable, that there was no known threat, and that the convoy itself was proper activity for the mission at hand. As well, the board determined that the Iltis vehicle, although lightly armoured, was appropriate for urban patrols in Kabul.

However, even before the release of these findings, DND announced steps to increase its procurement of the Mercedes-Benz G Wagon, the more comfortable and better-armoured replacement for the Iltis. In 2003 the government announced that it would purchase 802 vehicles and 150 Armour Protection Systems for $130 million. That contract included an additional option, which was exercised on 14 July 2004. The military was now to receive an additional 357 G Wagons and twenty Armour Protection Systems. General Raymond Henault, the chief of the defence staff (CDS), emphasized that this boost in equipment stocks would serve the military well both in Afghanistan and in other endeavours: 'The versatile G Wagon has been an important element in soldiers being able to conduct operations in Operation ATHENA and in helping our soldiers gain the trust and respect of the people of Afghanistan ... The G Wagon will contribute to the Land Force's requirement to conduct sustained, effective combat and support operations, and meet the peacetime training requirement' (DND News Release 04.051, 14 July).

ISAF command

On 9 February Lieutenant-General Rick Hillier, head of the Canadian army, assumed command of the International Security Assistance Force in Afghanistan, replacing Germany's Lieutenant-General Gotz Gliemeroth. Canada's leadership was fitting given that, at the time of the handover, Canada had contributed two six-month rotations to the force, which made it the leading troop contributor. For General Henault, who attended the handover ceremony in Kabul, Lieutenant-General Hillier's position was also a feather in the cap of the Canadian military: 'This appointment illustrates that our allies have confidence in the leadership and professionalism of the Canadian Forces' (DND News Release 04.008, 9 Feb.). After serving as ISAF's head for six months, Hillier transferred command to France's Lieutenant-General Jean-Louis Py on 9 August.

Overstretch

Shortly after the completion of a visit to Afghanistan, André Marin, the military ombudsman, released a November report critical of the workload of Canadian military personnel in the country.[17] In August, Canada had reduced its military presence in Kabul from 2,000 soldiers to only 700. Minister Graham had commented that the responsibilities of the remaining Canadians had correspondingly been reduced: 'What the Canadian public has to understand is that when we reduced our force in Afghanistan from 2,000 to 700, obviously we reduced the scope of the mission as well' (*Toronto Star*, 30 Nov.). However, Marin argued that many personnel were doing double duty by performing both their regular jobs and additional tasks to fill in the gaps. He identified resulting shortfalls in base maintenance, force protection, trades positions, and reconnaissance and surveillance capabilities. Simply put by Marin: 'The resounding message, from the lowest rank right on through the chain of command to the highest rank over there, is that they are overworked' (Canadian Broadcasting Corporation, 29 Nov.). As part of the remedy to the situation, Marin requested that the military look into providing the 700 soldiers, who were to return in February 2005, with a special 'decompression period' and to consider more closely the staffing requirements for future rotations of Canadian personnel to be sent to Afghanistan.

Friendly fire incident, 2002

The legal machinations triggered by the accidental U.S. aerial bombing of Canadian soldiers in Afghanistan on 18 April 2002 seemingly came

---

17 Also with respect to Afghanistan, the military ombudsman investigated issues pertaining to the air quality in Kabul and the treatment of Canadian snipers in Afghanistan in 2002 who, while having received the U.S. Bronze Star medals, were allegedly mistreated by fellow Canadian personnel both in Afghanistan and in Canada.

to a close in 2004. Earlier in 2003, one of the U.S. pilots, Major William Umbach, agreed to accept a reprimand and retired from service. However, the other pilot, Major Harry Schmidt, opted for the riskier option of a court martial, in the hopes of clearing his name fully. But on 25 June 2004 the U.S. Air Force announced that it would not court-martial Major Schmidt; instead, a non-judicial hearing was forthcoming. Though, as the result of that hearing, Schmidt could have received the maximum penalty of thirty days in jail, in the event he was forced to forfeit one month's pay (US$5,600) and received a written reprimand. For Marley Léger, the wife of one of the four dead Canadian soldiers, the reprimand was a relief: 'I feel somewhat at peace with the letter of reprimand and the acknowledgement by the American government that this was a blatant mistake and he disregarded an order' (Canadian Broadcasting Corporation, 6 July).

Other military operations

Bosnia-Herzegovina

The year 2004 marked the end of an era when, after thirteen years, the government announced the withdrawal of the Canadian military contingent from Bosnia-Herzegovina. Canadian military personnel first entered the region in April 1992, under Operations HARMONY and CAVALIER, as part of the United Nations Protection Force. Later, upon the signing of the Dayton Peace Accords in December 1995, Canada contributed to NATO's Implementation Force under Operation ALLIANCE and, as of December 1996, to NATO's Stabilization Force (SFOR) under Operation PALLADIUM. In a visit to Bosnia-Herzegovina in August 2004, Minister Graham outlined the various contributions that Canadian military personnel had made: 'CF members have conducted complex military operations, monitored de-mining efforts, assisted with elections and helped to reconstruct schools and water systems. In short, they have helped to bring peace, stability and hope to this part of the world' (DND News Release 04.066, 30 Aug.). These tasks were performed through some 40,000 tours of duty, which amounted to sending the entire army to Bosnia-Herzegovina twice.

The decision to end the Canadian presence was in keeping both with the military's wish to reduce its operational tempo and with an organizational handover in Europe. In December 2003 NATO announced that, because of the improving security environment in Bosnia-Herzegovina, its troop presence would drop from 12,000 to 7,000 by June. As a result,

Canada reduced its contribution to 650 personnel in April 2004. Then, during the NATO Summit meeting in Istanbul on 28 June, NATO indicated that its presence would end altogether; operations would become the responsibility of a European Union Force at the end of the year. Consequently, the Canadian military closed its camp outside Velika Kladusa in November. While Canada could congratulate itself for a job well done in Bosnia-Herzegovina, for General Henault, the departure was critical to reduce the military's overstretch: '[The] draw-down in Bosnia will help our forces to achieve the transformation that is underway in all NATO forces, giving them time to retrain and re-connect with their families' (DND News Release 04.066, 30 Aug.).

Haiti

A combination of disasters, some of them man-made, kept Haiti on the radar screens of Canadian politicians and the military alike in 2004.[18] Throughout February, violence came to a head between supporters and opponents of President Jean-Bertrand Aristide. Since his election in 2000, the president had been plagued by criticism from Haiti's business elite and by accusations of human-rights abuses and corruption. As the violence between the different camps grew in ferocity and spread across the country, French and U.S. officials pressured President Aristide to resign on 29 February. Although he eventually fled to South Africa, Aristide vowed that he was still Haiti's lawful leader and that he would return someday.

Canada was one of the countries that filled the vacuum upon the president's departure. Over the span between February and March, the Canadian military launched Joint Task Force PRINCIPAL, which featured 100 military personnel and four Hercules transport aircraft operating in the Caribbean. The mission included the deployment of JTF2 personnel to protect Canadian assets, officials, and foreigners in Haiti. During the course of the task force's operations, the Hercules conducted eleven flights to transport 340 individuals, including 200 Canadians, from the country. They also delivered humanitarian supplies. Later, on 5 March, DND announced Operation HALO. This was a ninety-day deployment of 450 personnel to the region, as well as six helicopters, to participate

---

18 To underscore the political and military significance of Haiti in Canada, the chief of defence staff, the minister of national defence, the foreign affairs minister, and the prime minister all visited the country in 2004.

in the United Nations Multinational Interim Force. The operation was extended, however, to allow for the successful transition to the United Nations Stabilization Mission in Haiti in June. As part of this new mission, Canada contributed 100 police officers.

Before Operation HALO personnel left the country in August, they dealt with the destruction wrought by severe flooding that had lasted for two weeks over the May/June span. The helicopters conducted rescues and humanitarian activities during the floods that claimed the lives of over 3,300 Haitians. Later, during September, the Canadian military was again involved in Haiti as the result of Hurricane Jeanne, which killed an additional 3,000 Haitians. Military flights, conducted by Hercules aircraft and the Polaris Airbus, delivered charitable donations on the behalf of Canada, the International Federation of the Red Cross, the government of Quebec, and Moisson Montreal.

Equipment and procurement

Submarines

In Faslane, Scotland, on 1 October, Canada formally accepted the last of the four used diesel electric submarines it had acquired from the United Kingdom. During a ceremony in which the submarine, HMS *Upholder*, was officially renamed HMCS *Chicoutimi*, Minister Graham suggested that the future of Canada's submarine fleet looked bright: 'HMCS *Chicoutimi*'s handover to the Canadian Forces illustrates the progress we are making in establishing a modern submarine fleet that will serve Canadians extremely well for the next 25 years' (DND News Release 04.04, 1 Oct.). On 4 October, the *Chicoutimi*, with fifty-seven crew, left Scotland en route to Halifax on the submarine's first transatlantic voyage under Canadian command.

The following day, disaster struck the *Chicoutimi* when an electrical fire broke out onboard the vessel. The fire left the submarine powerless in the ocean and with ten of its crew members suffering from smoke inhalation. Although the captain of the submarine, Commander Luc Pelletier, indicated that his crew required no further medical assistance, a Royal Navy doctor who was sent to the *Chicoutimi* felt that three sailors should be transferred to land for further treatment. The initial plans were for the three injured personnel, Lieutenant Chris Saunders, Petty Officer Denis Lafleur, and Master Seaman Archibald McMaster, to be airlifted to hospital in Londonderry, Northern Ireland. However, during the flight, Lieutenant Saunders's condition worsened and the helicopter was diverted to Sligo in the Republic of Ireland. Unfortunately, Saunders succumbed to his injuries while en route to Sligo.

On 12 October, Minister Graham ordered that Canada's three other submarines remain docked until investigators conducted their work (at year's end, they were still docked). As for the investigation itself, Vice-Admiral Bruce MacLean, chief of the Maritime Staff and commander of Canada's navy, launched a board of inquiry on 8 October. Of interest to the board were a number of issues: the chain of events that led to the fire, how the fire was fought, how the medical conditions of the crew members were treated, and what recommendations might be appropriate. Although the board was to submit its findings to Vice-Admiral MacLean by 30 November, it requested further time to explore the case given its complexity. After receiving substantial documentation and interviewing seventy-eight witnesses both in Canada and in Europe, the board submitted its report on 17 December. At the time, DND indicated that the report contained twenty-three recommendations, but the findings were not to be made public until February 2005.

On Parliament Hill, however, the *Chicoutimi* incident served as political fodder for opposition parties interested in investigating the Liberal government's defence policies, especially at a time when the Liberals were in a minority government situation. In October, because of their numerical dominance on the House of Commons Committee on National Defence and Veterans Affairs, the opposition members, such as the New Democratic Party's Bill Blaikie, were able to launch an investigation into the government's initial rationale behind the submarine project, which, even before the *Chicoutimi* disaster, had been plagued with setbacks and problems: 'It's certainly a refreshing change for me ... to have that motion pass without a Liberal goon squad coming in to kill it' (*National Post*, 19 Oct.). During this investigation, a Chrétien-era defence minister, David Collenette, suggested that the military had suffered because of budget cuts that, under the advice of then Finance Minister Paul Martin, the government implemented in the 1990s: 'My personal view is that, looking back over the 10 years, we have cut back too much on our military capability. I think that Canadians really have to face up to the fact that you can't have your cake and eat it too' (*Victoria Times Colonist*, 14 Dec.). The parliamentary investigation also revealed that the way the 1998 submarine deal was 'sold' to the Canadian public was misleading. Initially, DND indicated that the $750-million deal would, in fact, be free owing to the provision of training for British troops at Canadian bases. However, during the investigation, DND revealed that the 'bartering' training did not occur and that the price tag for Canadian taxpayers stood at $897 million.

As for the *Chicoutimi* itself, on 14 December, DND awarded EIDE Marine of Norway a $2.7-million contract to bring the submarine to Canada aboard a semi-submersible self-propelled transport vessel. Perhaps in trying to find the silver lining in the incident, Vice-Admiral MacLean indicated that the repair process, estimated to take several years and cost $100 million, would help to further the navy's development of its submarine fleet: 'By conducting the repairs in Canada, the Canadian Forces will be able to progress *Chicoutimi's* Canadianization work concurrently' (DND News Release 04.084, 4 Nov.). EIDE Marine was to transport the *Chicoutimi* to Halifax in January 2005.

Sea King helicopter replacement

On 23 July, Minister Graham announced the long-awaited replacement of Canada's original fleet of forty-one Sea King helicopters: twenty-eight twin-engine Sikorsky S-92 Cyclones. Two components made up the project's $5-billion cost: $1.8 billion was for the helicopters themselves and modifications to be done to Canada's twelve frigates that would carry them at sea and $3.2 billion was for a twenty-year service, training, and support contract. As part of the deal, $1 billion in subcontracts would go to Atlantic Canada and additional monies were to be generated for Aboriginal businesses. In short, for Minister Graham, the Cyclone was 'the right helicopter for the Canadian Forces at the best price for Canadians' (Canadian Broadcasting Corporation, 23 July).

This announcement was meant to put to rest a controversy that had dogged the federal Liberals since the election of Prime Minister Chrétien in 1993. In one of his first acts as prime minister, Chrétien cancelled the Mulroney-era contract for fifty EH-101 helicopters to replace both Canada's Sea Kings and search-and-rescue helicopters, citing them as too expensive with their $5.8-billion price tag. This decision cost the Canadian taxpayer $500 million in penalties. Later, the government split the contract for the Sea Kings and search-and-rescue helicopters in two, only to see a variant of the EH-101 win the latter contract in 1998. As this manoeuvring and stalling went on, Sea Kings continued to fly and embarrassing accidents and mishaps continued to occur.

After the announcement, controversy persisted on a number of fronts. First, although the military was pleased that the government had announced its commitment, many would have preferred the EH-101, the only other competitor, because this would have allowed for efficiencies and cross-training since similar helicopters were already in the Canadian fleet. Second, with only two engines, the Cyclone was seemingly less rugged than the three-engined EH-101. This led to accusations that DND, under political pressure, had 'dumbed down' some of the specification requirements in order to keep the Cyclone in the running and prevent the Liberals from being forced to choose the EH-101 again. Third, whereas the EH-101 was a proven military aircraft, the Cyclone had been previously manufactured only as a civilian aircraft. Canada, according to one media source, was taking a big risk: 'It's a paper aircraft ... Canada is going to be the guinea pig to see if this bird will fly' (*Toronto Star*, 24 July). Fourth, because the military variant was non-existent, let alone unproven, there was a fear was that Sikorsky would not be able to meet its commitments in a timely manner.[19] Already for some, the proposed timeline was considered too long because the first Cyclone was not to be delivered until 2008, with one additional helicopter being accepted monthly thereafter. This potentially left some Sea Kings in the air until 2012, an expensive and possibly dangerous proposition. Fifth, some commentators questioned Minister Graham's assertion that the Cyclone was a considerably cheaper aircraft, arguing that the Sikorsky bid was perhaps just 1 per cent less than that put forth by AgustaWestland, the maker of the EH-101. Lastly, others accused Minister Graham of suggesting that there was a competition in the first instance. Shortly after the announcement, DND revealed that the AgustaWestland bid had in fact been thrown out weeks before on technical grounds. Yet this was a virtual impossibility because DND had created a pre-qualification phase in 2002 that was meant to examine the desired capabilities so that the final decision would be made solely on price.

In the context of this considerable amount of criticism and controversy, AgustaWestland launched a lawsuit in Federal Court in September. Charging that the government's decision was 'biased, unfair and contrary to the rules of the procurement,' AgustaWestland demanded either that it receive the helicopter contract or that the selection process start anew (*Toronto Star*, 13 Sept.). Although the government finalized the contract with Sikorsky in November, the dispute remained unresolved by the end of 2004.

---

19 The contract did contain a penalty clause of $100,000 per day for every delivery delay, but this had a maximum of $36 million.

Joint Support Ships

On 16 April, the government released additional details about its earlier proposed Joint Support Ship program. At a cost of $2.1 billion, the navy was to receive three ships in order to replace its two thirty-three-year-old Auxiliary Oiler Replenishment vessels (AORs). These new ships, which would be the largest naval vessels ever entirely built in Canada, were to be multifunctional in three areas: at-sea replenishment, strategic sealift, and support of land-based forces. Initial specifications indicated that the crew complement was to be smaller than that of the AORs (247) and that the ships were to be able to navigate in first-year ice (up to 0.7 metres in thickness). The government sought to announce the winning bid in 2007 and for the navy to receive the first ship by 2011.

To facilitate this timetable, the government also revealed the three stages for the acquisition. Stage One was to be a pre-qualification phase during which interest was to be solicited from the defence industry and then evaluated. Stage Two was to involve project definition such that the field was to be narrowed to two competing consortia. Stage Three dealt with project implementation and was to feature two contracts: 1) design and construction; and 2) lifetime in-service support.

Unmanned aerial vehicles

In 2004 the Canadian military continued with an experimentation and test usage of UAVs that had started three years earlier. On the positive side, the military conducted successful experiments with the U.S.-made Silver Fox mini UAV system (weighing seven kilograms) and the much larger U.S.-built Altair UAV (the size of a fighter aircraft). Not only was UAV technology deployed in Exercise NARWHAL, it was used as well in two twenty-three-hour-long flights along Canada's east coast. These systems were under study for their utility in remedying challenges pertaining to command and control, surveillance, reconnaissance, and intelligence collection. Another focus was to examine the advantages of not having a human in an aerial vehicle. In this vein, Colonel Dave Burt, the director of air requirements, emphasized that 'you want UAVs to do the 3 Ds— everything that's dirty, dangerous and dull' (*Ottawa Citizen*, 13 Oct.).

On the negative side, the army's use of UAVs in Afghanistan faced considerable criticism in 2004. As a result of a series of crashes, collisions, and hard landings between the fall of 2003 and January 2004, all four of Canada's French-built Sperwer drones were out of service. Until the French firm Sagem replaced the drones, Canadian military personnel in Afghanistan were reliant upon the UAVs of German forces that were to have been withdrawn from the country but were kept on because of the Canadian losses. Moreover, the losses drew attention to the fact that these particular UAVs had been rushed into service. Because of potential problems that had been identified before their shipment to Afghanistan, the director of technical airworthiness had issued only a limited 'airworthiness clearance' rather than a certificate of airworthiness. Some military officials felt that the difficulties were not overly problematic given the severe topographical and meteorological conditions found in Afghanistan: 'The UAVs themselves are being operated in the harshest environment possible ... We are having to operate the UAV at the edge of its potential. As such, we've seen some accelerated wear of the equipment, but nothing that is really unexpected' (*National Post*, 20 Jan.). However, because of the rush, the Conservative Party's defence critic, Jay Hill, was less than sympathetic: 'It was obvious when the first one crashed in November, that the Sperwer isn't up to the job. Paul Martin repeatedly insists he'll provide our military with the best equipment possible. It's time for him to make good on that promise and stop sending troops into action with equipment that falls out of the sky' (*National Post*, 23 Jan.).

Policies and personnel

Recruitment, retention, and remuneration

On 14 April, as part of the build-up to the election campaign, the government announced that the employment income for all Canadian police and military personnel serving overseas in high- and moderate-risk operations would be exempt from income tax. In total, some 3,000 Canadians stationed abroad, regardless of rank or length of time deployed, were to receive this financial relief. For Defence Minister David Pratt, the tax break recognized the high operational tempo and the organizational, financial, and emotional strains inherent in manning Canada's overseas presence: 'Those who put their life on the line to protect Canadians deserve our support ... The tax break will improve the quality of life of our Canadian Forces members and their families' (DND News Release 04.028, 14 April).

Less than two weeks later, on 26 April, the government implemented pay improvements designed to boost the recruitment and retention of physicians and dentists in the military. At the time of the government's announcement, General Henault asserted that the increase was linked directly to Canada's overseas presence: 'In these times of high operational tempo, the Canadian Forces need doctors and dentists more than ever ... These pay improvements together with other non-monetary initiatives, will help us to attract and retain top medical and dental talent, which in turn will better enable us to meet our operational commitments' (DND News Release 04.030, 26 April). This increase was part of a long string of payment improvements for medical and dental personnel, starting first in April 1999 when the government launched the Medical and Dental Direct Entry Officer Recruitment Allowances program. Yet, despite the almost annual increases and bonuses since 1999, the military was still short, at the captain rank, of 42 per cent of the required medical personnel and 13 per cent of the required dental personnel.

Later, on 1 July, the compulsory retirement age for military members in both the regular force and the primary reserve increased from fifty-five years of age to sixty. Although the maximum calculation for pensionable service remained thirty-five years, the raising of the ceiling recognized many recruitment and retention problems the military had faced since the mid-1990s. Not only were senior members leaving early, thus creating a leadership and expertise vacuum, the military confronted a smaller youth population from which to draw new recruits. The shift also recognized that, because many personnel were joining the military later in life, it was often difficult to reach the thirty-five-year maximum with a retirement age set at fifty-five. Finally, this policy change put the military in line with comparable guidelines adopted by the Canadian Coast Guard and the Royal Canadian Mounted Police.

Chemical-warfare testing

A long-running battle between hundreds of Canadian veterans and the government came to a head in 2004. From the 1940s until the 1970s, but especially during the Second World War, the Canadian military conducted tests of chemical-warfare agents on largely unwitting Canadian soldiers who had volunteered in hopes of receiving extra pay and leave time. The tests on the approximately 3,700 soldiers took place at the Suffield Experimental Station in Alberta and at the Chemical Warfare Laboratories in Ottawa. It was only in 1989 that the governmental formally conceded that the tests had in fact occurred, and although veterans had been suffering the effects, extra compensation had not been forthcoming owing to secrecy, a lack of documentation, and incomplete medial records.

In early February, momentum concerning the veterans' plight increased when veterans launched a class-action lawsuit against DND, the National Research Council of Canada, the attorney general, and Veterans Affairs Canada. As well, Military Ombudsman André Marin publicly asserted in January that the foot dragging should end and that the government would have to make amends: 'It shouldn't go to court. This matter should be resolved out of a recognition that these people suffered long enough ... I see everyone nodding politely that we should do something, but no one is stepping up to the plate. It's been 50 years. That's long enough' (*National Post*, 13 Jan.).

In light of the lawsuit and a likely very critical report to be released by Marin, the government announced a compensation package later in February that gave each surviving veteran a one-time payment of $24,000.[20] As expressed by Minister for Veterans Affairs John McCallum, the government would work promptly to ensure that the veterans received their justly deserved compensation: 'They served our nation without the recognition extended to those who served elsewhere and without appreciation of the risks they faced ... We will respond quickly and compassionately in providing them with the services and benefits that they may be eligible to receive' (DND News Release 04.010, 19 Feb.). On 5 April, the program office for the Chemical Warfare Agent Testing Recognition Program, with a budget of $50 million, opened, and on 11 May retired corporal Roy Wheeler, the first approved applicant, received his $24,000 cheque. At the time of Wheeler's recognition, the program office had received 1,700 inquiries and 700 applications and had approved 100 applications.

Military ombudsman

Canadian military personnel lost a tireless advocate when André Marin announced in December that he was stepping down as Canada's military ombudsman. He was the only person ever to have served in this role, the government having created the position five years earlier. As for new opportunities, Marin was looking forward to becoming Ontario's ombudsman, responsible for independently investigating the complaints of Ontarians against provincial government departments: 'It's

---

20 In the cases of deceased veterans, there were provisions for beneficiaries.

got enormous potential. We're going to be putting the office on the map ... with investigations into issues that affect Ontarians' (*Toronto Star*, 16 Dec.). Marin was to begin his new duties on 1 April 2005.

Chief of the defence staff

After a secret vote on 17 November, NATO's twenty-six member countries elected General Henault to be NATO's chairman of the Military Committee. He won the position over the only other candidate, General Hans Jesper Helsoe, the chief of the Danish defence staff. Succeeding German General Harald Kujat, who assumed the position in 2002, General Henault was to begin a three-year term in June 2005. As the chairman of the Military Committee, a body consisting of senior NATO-member officers, Henault was to be the top uniformed adviser to NATO's secretary general, Jaap de Hoop Scheffer. This responsibility, both managerial and vision-oriented, brought into focus General Henault's desire to transform the military organization: 'I think I can bring to NATO and specifically to the NATO committee a continuation of change and that is really what I would want to do, to ensure that NATO is postured, especially from the military committee perspective, for the long term in this new security environment' (*Edmonton Journal*, 18 Nov.).

General Henault's selection was testimony not only to his own capabilities but also to Canada's position and contribution to NATO. Indeed, the selection was distinctive because Britons and Germans had usually served in the chairman's position; the only other Canadian to serve in the role was Admiral Robert Falls in the early 1980s.[21] For Prime Minister Martin, the decision of NATO members to choose Henault reflected well on Canada's stature in the organization: '[The decision was] an indication of the esteem in which Canada, and its military leadership, is held among member nations and signals Canada's commitment to the organization' (*Ottawa Citizen*, 18 Nov.). For others, Henault's selection was not to be viewed as an endorsement of Canada's defence policy, given the problems, particularly related to underfunding, which had plagued the country's military during the 1990s and into the new century.

General Henault's eventual departure to NATO headquarters in Brussels also sparked speculation as to what senior officer was to replace

---

21 In 1983 Admiral Falls left the chairmanship after he publicly criticized the U.S. decision to deploy Pershing missiles in Europe.

him as Canada's CDS. Reports suggested that the three top contenders were Lieutenant-General Hillier, Vice-Admiral Ron Buck, the vice-chief of defence staff, and Vice-Admiral Greg Maddison, the deputy chief of defence staff. While the position usually rotated among the three different services, in this case favouring either Buck or Maddison because the navy was 'up next,' Hillier was a strong candidate because he possessed considerable operational experience as a multinational commander in Bosnia and as the ISAF commander in Afghanistan. The government, however, did not announce Henault's successor in 2004.

EMMANUEL BRUNET-JAILLY AND WARREN
MAGNUSSON

Municipal affairs

The year 2004 began promisingly for Canadian municipalities. There was good reason to believe that Paul Martin, the new prime minister, would carry through on his promise of a 'new deal for cities.' In a number of important municipalities, including Toronto and Vancouver, there were freshly elected mayors who were pressing for changes that would allow them to take more aggressive action on a range of problems, from the infrastructure deficit to social distress. Most of the relevant interest groups and policy think tanks seemed to agree that cities needed more powers and more resources. Not only was there pressure on the provinces in this respect, but the federal government seemed alive to the 'urban agenda' in a way that it had not been for more than thirty years.

Nevertheless, the prospects for such an agenda were much bleaker by mid-summer. The Martin government, already enmeshed in the sponsorship scandal, lost its majority in the June elections, and Glen Murray, the Winnipeg mayor who was expected to be the standard-bearer for the federal new deal for cities, went down to defeat in his own constituency. In the subsequent months, vigorous and persistent municipal lobbying was required to prevent the federal government from backing off on its nascent commitments to cities. The fact that this campaign bore some fruit was encouraging, but there was an increasing contrast between the many signs of vitality at the municipal level and the apparent drift and confusion in Ottawa. Our focus here is on those signs of vitality, and on the apparent policy consensus associated with them.

Cities in the marketplace

If there is one theme that was most apparent during the year, it was the need for new levels of public investment in Canadian cities. At the Mayors' Summit on 23 January, Toronto Mayor David Miller argued that 'the absence of adequate investment in our cities – in everything from public transit, to affordable housing, to child care, to infrastructure – is reaching a crisis point' (*National Post*, 23 Jan.) Although the infrastructure deficit is what captured most attention across the political spectrum, there seemed to be growing recognition that other forms of investment were also required to sustain economic growth. At the same summit, the new federal parliamentary secretary for cities, John Godfrey, told the mayors that the next Throne Speech would include promises for more funding for municipalities. The prime minister dampened speculation about this almost immediately, but two things were evidently on the agenda: relief from GST payments for the municipalities and a municipal share in the federal gasoline tax. The latter was seen as one move towards broadening the revenue sources available to the municipalities and enabling them to begin the large infrastructure investments that they would need to make.

Why is it that the infrastructure deficit had become so severe? This is the question the Canada West Foundation (CWF) raised in a February 2004 report. As the CWF explained, most of the recent infrastructural investment in Canadian cities occurred after the Second World War and prior to the mid-1970s. Although urbanization continued at a rapid rate after that, investment slowed. In the 1980s and 1990s, governments focused on balancing budgets and reducing debt. Capital projects and infrastructure maintenance were cut. Even with good maintenance, public infrastructure eventually reaches the limit of its serviceable life. In 2004, 28 per cent of all public infrastructure was over eighty years old, while 31 per cent was from forty to eighty years old. Problems have been increased by the deferral of necessary maintenance. To the extent that there has been public support for increased government spending in recent years, it has tended to point in other directions. Thus, in 2004, 60 per cent of Canadians chose health care as their top priority for spending, and only 5 per cent chose municipal services and infrastructure. In the circumstances, overcoming the infrastructure deficit will not be easy.

As noted by the newly constituted National Forum on Economic Growth of Big Cities in Canada – also called Big City 22 (BC 22)[1] – Canada is a highly urbanized country. Pressure on the urban infrastructure is especially intense in the rapidly growing big cities, which have most of the jobs and attract newcomers from the rural areas as well as

---

1 The twenty-two members of the National Forum on the Economic Growth of Big Cities are Toronto, Vancouver, Montreal, Ottawa, Calgary, Edmonton, Quebec, Winnipeg, Hamilton, London, Ont., Kitchener, Ont., St Catharines, Ont., Halifax, Victoria, Windsor, Oshawa, Saskatoon, Regina, St John's, Nlfd., Sudbury, Ont., Saguenay, Que., and Sherbrooke, Que.

overseas. But the political demand to spread infrastructure more widely is intense – as became apparent when the federal government started to think twice about commitments that might be perceived as providing assistance to the already favoured cities at the expense of other areas.

The Conference Board of Canada, in its *Performance and Potential 2004–5 – Key Findings*, noted some slippage in Canada's relative performance with respect to the 110 indicators of the Organisation for Economic Cooperation and Development (OECD) on the economy, innovation, the environment, education and skills, health, and society. The Conference Board argued that 'Canada's competitive advantage increasingly will be based on our knowledge and our skills and will be centered in our major cities,' and it expressed concern in this context about the infrastructure deficit. It said that cities needed more sources of funding to offer services and enhance and maintain the quality of urban life. It considered various ways of addressing the deficit and emphasized that the problem could not be overcome without senior government involvement. The board also suggested that municipalities should control urban sprawl, employ user fees, and develop public-private partnerships. Urban sprawl increases the cost of services, and user fees allow for an itemization of the cost of services such as water, sewage, electricity, garbage, or highways. Public-private partnerships offer a way of financing infrastructure without relying entirely on public borrowing.

These views were echoed in a report by TD Bank Financial Group, which argued that a new approach to infrastructural investment is necessary. *Mind the Gap: Finding the Money to Upgrade Canada's Aging Infrastructure* made the case that 'neglect of the country's stock of public capital is one of the greatest risks facing the country's quality of life.' In location decisions, investors and mobile individuals look at infrastructure because it has an impact on productivity and quality of life. The TD valued the current infrastructure deficit at as much as $125 billion. The report suggested increasing user fees and bringing in the private sector, but, like the Conference Board, the TD spoke positively about the possibility of a municipal share in the federal gas tax. It also took favourable note of financial instruments now available to U.S. municipalities, but generally unavailable in Canada, such as tax increment financing (TIFs) and enterprise zones. The TD observed that, while infrastructure is primarily a local and provincial responsibility, the federal government is appropriately involved with respect to such matters as border infrastructure and immigration settlement. TD Bank also suggested the creation of an independent advisory body to provide advice to governments on infrastructure-investment priorities.

In a sign of changing attitudes, the Canadian Taxpayers Federation joined its voice to those calling for a transfer of a portion of federal gas-tax revenues to municipalities for roadway development. The federation defended the idea of treating the gas tax as a user fee and focusing expenditures on the construction and maintenance of roads and highways. This would mean reducing the overall gas tax to a level commensurate with road costs. According to the president of Canadian Federation of Independent Business, Catherine Swift, a recent survey of small business owners showed that three-quarters of its membership supported the idea of provincial governments giving municipalities more revenues for specific projects – but not increasing the overall capacity of the municipalities to tax. A question that kept coming back to civic leaders discussing the gas tax was whether cities were already overtaxing people and whether the cities' share of all taxes had increased more than that of other levels of government. The answer was 'no' in both cases, according to Canada West Foundation studies published in June and October 2004. In brief, these studies suggested that cities such as Vancouver, Edmonton, Calgary, Saskatoon, Regina, and Winnipeg do not overtax. The first study noted that most tax dollars in these cities go to protection, transportation, parks and recreation, and general expenditures: 'Virtually every dollar collected by the large western cities is spent to support programs, services, and infrastructure.' These cities have no or very few debts and overhead expenditures account for less than 10 per cent of total spending, which is very low. The foundation concluded that these cities' expenditures have increased but not sufficiently to compensate for inflation and population growth. In other words, there has been a reduction of per-capita spending across those cities. Furthermore, when comparing the overall tax increases from 1961 to 2000, it appeared that local taxes stood at 8.5 per cent of all taxes, while provincial and federal taxes accounted for 39.3 per cent and 52.2 per cent respectively. At the same time, local property taxes increased by just 7.6 per cent while personal income tax increased by 24 per cent (federal) and 14 per cent (provincial). In short, the complaint that municipalities' overall share of taxes is burdensome is misplaced.

The significant thing is that these studies emerged from groups that had often argued for tax relief and debt reduction in the past. By 2004, there seemed to be a general consensus that Canada's infrastructure had reached the end of a life cycle and that this posed a threat to the prosperity of the country's largest urban regions. The search was under way for appropriate fiscal solutions. Whether those solutions would involve new taxes, the transfer of federal revenues directly to the municipalities, or innovative fiscal instruments that involved the private sector were the matters at issue. All these things had to be considered in light of evident social changes.

The culture of cities

Immigration and migration are key engines of the cultural and social transformation of Canadian cities. By 2004, more detailed data from the 2001 Census were available. These data confirmed a pattern in which immigration from abroad tended to concentrate in a few centres – especially in and around Toronto and Vancouver – while Canadians themselves tended to spread out more widely. In 2004 Oshawa had expanded the fastest of all Canadian municipalities, thanks to its ability to draw people from within the greater Toronto area. Toronto ranked second and Calgary third. Whereas Toronto continued to draw heavily from abroad – 44 per cent of all new immigrants have settled in the Toronto region in recent years – Calgary attracted people mostly from other parts of Canada, adding many young, well-educated individuals lured by the booming local job market. Changes of the latter sort added to local diversity as well: Calgary was positioning itself to be a rival to Vancouver not only in its capacity to attract head offices but also in its character as a city committed to environmental sustainability and social diversity.

Many cities that have not been among the top destinations for immigrants are becoming aware of the social, cultural, and economic impact of immigration and working on making themselves more attractive to newcomers. For instance, Saskatoon, which attracted about 2.3 per cent of all new immigrants as recorded by Statistics Canada in 2001, noted that it had been much more successful in the 1980s, with numbers above 3 per cent. The city is now developing programs to welcome new settlers and these initiatives are echoed by the University of Saskatchewan, which is expanding its international student population, and by the local business community, which is recruiting more foreign workers. By 2025, immigration is forecast to account for 100 per cent of Canada's net population increase: it stood at 70 per cent in 2004. With about 225,000 new immigrants yearly, and about 18.4 per cent of the population foreign-born, immigration still shapes Canadian society. On average, immigrants bring about $30,000 into the country. They account for about 30 per cent of all new workers (compared to 10 per cent in the United States). Immigrants also tend to be more educated: in 2001, 15.4 per cent of Canadians had a university degree, but 80 per cent of skilled immigrants did, as did 20 per cent of those in the family class. Even

among refugees, 13 per cent had university degrees. The Conference
Board of Canada was among a number of organizations pointing to the
potential benefits of ongoing immigration.

High levels of immigration do involve challenges, however. There is
mounting evidence, for instance, that federal, provincial, and most local
governments struggle to support new immigrants and that recognition
of skills and credentials remains an obstacle to the full economic participation of new immigrants in Canada. The social and cultural transformation of Canadian society is also clearer in large urban centres than
anywhere else. This in turn leads to tensions between cities and rural
communities. Finally, according to Statistics Canada's *Social Trends*,
we are witnessing a sharp increase in the number of 'visible minority
neighbourhoods that are enclaves of about 30 per cent of people coming from one single ethnic group.' Indeed, whereas in 1981 there were
about six neighbourhoods in the country with 30 per cent of the residents from a single visible minority, in 2001 Statistics Canada counted
254. Nearly all those neighbourhoods are in the Toronto or Vancouver
areas. For some, this has raised fears about declining cultural and social
integration.

Regional governance

The year 2004 did not witness major municipal mergers (see our 2002
Review) or de-amalgamations (see Montreal, 2003 *Review*), but a mul-
titude of complex economic, social, and cultural issues arose across the
country. In Victoria, B.C., for instance, 2004 was yet another year of
growth. The city forecast 30,000 residents within two square kilometres
of the municipal hall by 2020. The picturesque downtown that has a
reputation across North America as a charming old-world city is attracting interest from developers. New condominiums are being built
and older heritage buildings are being refurbished and expanded. Also,
the city is planning growth in what had earlier been light-industrial and
commercial enclaves and on the Docksides lands, a large waterfront
area overlooking the inner harbour in need of remediation and development that totals about forty hectares. One issue is the development of
a dense or denser downtown, which means higher buildings and lower
development charges for developers. Clearly, building height is at the
core of this discussion, with the media reflecting the public's concern
with the need for balance between livability and historic conservation.
Preserving the Victoria's nineteenth-century charm and urban lifestyle
is what the community seems to want.

At the same time, panhandling has been an issue for a new coalition of businesses of the lower mainland and the greater Victoria region. The Safe Street Coalition and the Greater Victoria Chamber of Commerce were part of thirty such community groups that wanted B.C. Solicitor General Rich Coleman to change the Trespass Act along the lines of the very controversial law passed in Ontario in 1999 by Mike Harris's Conservative government. The 'anti-squeegee' law imposed fines up to $500 and six months in jail from the second offence. There is ongoing tension between demands to clean up the downtown to encourage middle-class uses, on the one hand, and concerns about homelessness and discrimination, on the other. In many ways, Victoria's downtown mirrors Vancouver's, where such issues were even more prominent.

Another subject of contention that divided Vancouver residents and led to serious contentions both with the 2010 Olympic Games organizing committee and with the province of British Columbia was the construction of the new Sea-to-Sky Highway from Vancouver to Whistler. The existing two-lane highway was deemed too narrow to allow for the effective movement of traffic during the Games. However, the new planned four-lane highway was to cut across the municipality of West Vancouver. Also, the project would require the expropriation of about forty-nine hectares of land owned by British Pacific Properties (one of the most exclusive developers in the region for a century). Environmental assessment suggested that it would have a disastrous impact on a major stand of arbutus trees and the creeks that flow down from the ridge. The province called for arbitration by the Environmental Assessment Agency, which laid out a complex picture: the West Vancouver idea to dig a tunnel would be more expensive, result in more accidents, and then serve the traffic capacity of the Vancouver/Whistler link for just twenty-five years, not the fifty forecast for the four-lane highway. That four-lane highway would cost only $130 million but cut a path sixty metres wide through an unspoiled natural area. This is symbolic of the sort of conflicts that arise in many urban areas.

In 2004 Calgary was in the news as one of the fastest growing urban centres in Canada, noted even by *USA Today*. Calgary is the main beneficiary of the current oil and gas boom, with over $40 billion in investments expected by 2025. Whereas Edmonton attracts oilfield service companies, including many construction workers and tradespeople, Calgary has been expanding in the financial, administrative, and engineering sectors. Both cities were nearing the one-million mark in population, with Calgary's economy growing by 4.6 per cent in 2004. But such expansion has its downsides. Transportation between Calgary and Edmonton remains an issue and the development of a high-speed rail link was again under discussion in 2004. Calgary also confronts challenges with respect to water supply, since it controls very little land in its watershed and faces competition from other stakeholders. According to Mayor Dave Bronconnier, there are acute infrastructure issues in the city: a number of currently discussed projects to build light rail, tunnels, and bridges cannot be addressed by property taxes. Homelessness is also a problem in Calgary and Edmonton, as it is in Vancouver and elsewhere.

Regina Mayor Pat Fiacco underscored that there was a huge gap in basic road repairs. Although the Martin government was suggesting that a municipal share in the gas tax could pay for better roads, transit, green space, and affordable housing, most mayors seemed to agree that the first item (roads) could easily engulf all available money for years. If so, the broader deficit in physical – let alone social – infrastructure would remain. Halifax Mayor Peter Kelly explained that the Halifax Regional Municipality had $123 million in infrastructural deficit and that the gas-tax annual portion of $30 million would help only with repairs, improvement, and replacement of roads and other basic facilities. Like other mayors, he wanted municipal relief from the GST, a share in the gas tax up to 5 per cent, and federal reinvestment in infrastructure. Such moves had been expected in Martin's new deal for cities.

The March 2004 federal budget speech was eagerly anticipated by the municipalities. In fact, it marked a significant but important change. The 'new deal for cities' was reborn as a 'new deal for communities.' Smaller communities did not want to be left behind and had lobbied Ottawa to prevent a focus on large and expensive urban transit systems. Montreal and other large city regions realized only in the summer that the new deal for communities also included small cities, towns, and villages. Including smaller communities in the 'new deal' meant that Canada's largest cities were about to be short-changed again – at least by their own lights. Faced with the altered federal strategy, the bigger cities first suggested that the 'new deal' should focus on public transit rather than roads. This was in response to a demand from smaller cities and communities that federal funding be redistributed on a per-capita basis, which would have made it difficult for the larger cities to address their public-transit needs. For instance, the Société des transport de Montréal records over 75 per cent of all of Quebec's transit ridership, in an area that has only 25 per cent of Quebec's population. A report for the Parti Québécois suggested increasing taxes on parking in Montreal, or a penny per litre in Quebec's gas tax, or again a $5-increase in car-registration fees, but none of these ideas were acted upon. Nationally, the bigger cities continued to lobby for a funding formula that would recognize their peculiar needs.

In Ontario, the provincial government unveiled its own infrastructure program, which committed $100 billion over thirty years to repairs and development of roads, transit systems, sewers, and hospitals and schools. On 17 September Premier Dalton McGuinty announced that Toronto and many other Ontario municipalities would be given new powers and funding to address a large number of local issues. McGuinty also declared that he would introduce a new modernized City of Toronto Act, explaining that 'it is a miracle it [Toronto] has delivered prosperity for so long and to so many – despite living in a legislative straitjacket' (*National Post*, 18 Sept.) This was a surprise move on the part of the Ontario government that addressed criticism by the Toronto and Ottawa mayors, David Miller and Bob Chiarelli, who had been advocating for more powers for their large municipalities. Both mayors had been upset by the province's agreement that summer to consult on funding, programs, and legislation with the Association of Municipalities of Ontario (AMO), because it failed to recognize the particular needs of the big cities. Toronto severed its ties with the AMO, arguing that it needed to have direct relations with the province, since it was the sixth-largest government in Canada, with a budget larger than those of most provinces. Alone, it was accommodating 40 per cent of all new immigrants to Canada. Chiarelli said that similar changes were expected for Ottawa and that the new act was 'a revolutionary step in the annals of Canadian municipal history' (ibid.).

Local democracy

The Quebec provincial government in 2004 was still struggling with the administrative implications of de-amalgamation. The situation was particularly complicated in Montreal. Jean-Marc Fournier, the minister in charge of the de-amalgamation, proposed to reduce the size of the city council from seventy-three to sixty-three. Even at the latter number, Montreal would still have an exceptionally large council: Toronto has forty-four councillors, Calgary fourteen, Ottawa twenty-one, and Vancouver ten. In Vancouver, there was a proposal to increase the size of the council to fourteen, and elect the members from wards rather than at-large. In an October 2004 plebiscite the proposal went down to defeat: with a voter turnout of only 23 per cent, 54 per cent voted against. The results were a disappointment to many of the supporters of the current mayor, Larry Campbell, who had promised during his 2002 election campaign to give Vancouverites a greater say in local politics. The ward system had long been on the agenda of reformers, who argued that poorer neighbourhoods and minority groups had less chance of representation on a council elected at-large.

In Nova Scotia, along with the regular civic elections, the big issue in 2004 was a province-wide plebiscite on Sunday shopping. Nova Scotians are the only Canadians who cannot shop on Sundays, and the main reason – reaffirmed again with the plebiscite – is that a majority of them do not want to: 98,729 people voted 'No' versus 81,110 who voted 'Yes.' The Halifax Chamber of Commerce voiced its disappointment, stating that Nova Scotia lagged behind the rest of Canada. The civic election that year was the second in the newly amalgamated Regional Municipality of Halifax. In the 'new' Halifax, the mayor is elected at-large but the councillors are elected in each of twenty-three districts. Peter Kelly was re-elected as mayor on 16 October. Kelly had won the 2000 election as mayor of Halifax after defeating Walter Fitzgerald. In 2004 his contenders suggested that he was ignoring downtown Halifax in favour of the region as a whole, and that he micromanaged the city rather than focusing on the big picture. Kelly's answer was that he attempted to balance all issues. The turnout in the mayoral election was 43.39 per cent, and Kelly won with 82.3 per cent of the vote or 102,865 votes.

Municipal elections were also held in all 104 municipalities of New Brunswick on 10 May. These elections marked the end of the three-year terms; elected officials now serve four years. In New Brunswick, as in most parts of Canada, these civic elections are non-partisan. Saint John's new mayor, Norm MacFarlane, won over incumbent Shirley McAlary. In Fredericton, Brad Woodside, who had stepped down in 1999, won again in the municipality. The incumbent was Les Hull. In Moncton, Deputy Mayor Lorne Mitton was elected over Councillor George Leblanc. Commentators noted that the electoral turnout was above 50 per cent across the province, which is high (the Canadian average for municipal elections is about 40 per cent), and that most incumbents were returned to their offices, suggesting that people were interested in local issues and the future of their communities but were also generally happy with their elected officials.

Cities in the confederation

In February, as part of his prospective new deal for cities, Prime Minister Martin had established an external Advisory Committee on Cities and Communities. The committee chair was past premier of British Columbia Mike Harcourt. Harcourt said: 'The government of Canada already has massive involvement in cities. It must ensure that its involvement is harmonized with provincial jurisdiction and with municipal priorities and needs, for the benefit of citizens in every community across Canada' (Office of the Prime Minister [2004] News Release, 'Prime Minister Names Members of External Advisory Committee on Cities and Communities,' 15 Feb.). John Godfrey, at that point still a parliamentary secretary, was supposed to work closely with the Advisory Committee to develop a long-term vision on the role that cities are to play in sustaining Canada's quality of life, provide advice on policies for cities and communities, bring regional- and community-related expertise to policy forums, and facilitate relevant discussions with the provincial, territorial, and Aboriginal governments. The ultimate goal, it was claimed, was to establish reliable, predictable, and long-term funding and to ensure a new relationship among orders of government that would allow cities to be at the federal-provincial policy table.

As noted above, however, the federal budget of 23 March marked a shift away from cities per se in favour of communities more generally conceived. As the minister of finance, Ralph Goodale, said, 'communities are the front lines for social issues and the engines for economic growth, attracting talent from around the world and forming the foundation for dynamic high tech clusters.' He introduced a budget that he said would put $7 billion 'into the hands of communities over the next ten years – starting with $589 million in 2004–05' thanks to a decision to give the municipalities a full rebate on the GST. He also promised to 'accelerate $1 billion committed last year to municipal and rural infrastructure so the money would flow over 5 years rather than 10.' Although these measures were supposed to be only a 'down-payment' on what the prime minister promised under the new deal for cities – and now 'communities' as well – the municipalities had reason to be nervous: much depended on the outcome of the anticipated federal election.

Having met in Toronto in January, as mentioned earlier, the mayors of Canada's twenty-two largest municipalities met again in Montreal on 11 June (less than three weeks before the election) to discuss their common position on the comprehensive partnership agreements they wanted with higher levels of governments. The public declaration 'invited' Canada's provinces and the federal government to 'recognize the important role of cities in the sustainable economic, social, cultural, and environmental development of the provinces and the country as a whole,' as well as 'the need to accelerate the development of Canada's city regions without increasing the tax burden of citizens so that city regions may improve their competitive position in comparison to other North American regions'; to 'specify the policies, the programs and the priority issues for each city region, particularly in terms of infrastructure affecting competitiveness and attractiveness, the sums of money to be invested by each partner, and the planning, coordinating, financing and monitoring mechanisms that will be set up to reach the objectives'; and to 'provide cities with a share of revenues that grow with the economy that reflect the wealth created by cities and enable them to reinvest in the competitiveness and attractiveness of their communities.' A key anticipated measure was a municipal share in the gas tax, previously promised but not yet implemented, owing in part to reservations from some of the provinces.

The Liberals lost their majority, as it turned out, and so faced Parliament in the fall in a much weaker position. The Speech from the Throne on 5 October spoke of the government's commitment to 'Canada's cities and communities. Communities are key to our social goals and our economic competitiveness. They are the front lines in building a better quality of life.' There was a promise to the municipalities of 'a portion of the federal gas tax, growing over the next five years,' and an indication that the government would 'expand the partnership approach used to develop the Vancouver and Winnipeg Agreements' which had provided funding to relieve inner-city distress. City leaders were unsettled by the Throne Speech, however, because they found the commitments, particularly with respect to the gas tax, too vague. On 6 October Toronto Mayor David Miller spoke publicly about a 'lack of understanding about what the new deal is about,' (*Toronto Star*, 6 Oct.). As far as he and other major city leaders were concerned, it was about addressing the specific problems of the larger cities, not spreading a relatively small amount of money around the country as a whole. Prime Minister Martin responded at a reception for municipal leaders later that day. He reaffirmed his commitment but noted that the Liberals could expect opposition from the Bloc Québécois and the Conservatives. The following two months were marked by intense negotiations, both between the federal government and the provinces and among the municipalities, which were seeking a formula for the gas-tax transfer that would satisfy both the big cities and the smaller communities. By the end of the year, the necessary compromises were beginning to take shape. Indeed, Gérald Tremblay, mayor of Montreal, had declared in June 2004 that this was a new partnership 'founded on the idea that city regions, as economic engines of the country, can create new collective wealth that will, in turn, generate the revenues needed to maintain and improve our communities' (Press release by Michel Lévesque, Communauté métropolitaine de Montréal, and Massimo Bergamini, Fédération canadienne des municipalités, 11 June). Ultimately, Tremblay and other municipal leaders believed that, despite difficulties, they had succeeded in advancing their agenda significantly.

KRISTIN BURNETT

First Nations

Federal developments

Speech from the Throne

The Speech from the Throne in February 2004 outlined a policy strategy designed to place greater focus on domestic rather than foreign and defence issues, and central to this new domestic policy were Aboriginal concerns. Prime Minister Paul Martin condemned the conditions under which First Nations people in Canada lived, and announced his intention to scrap the Aboriginal Governance Act (a name applied to a series of legislation created under the previous Liberal government). Former Prime Minister Jean Chrétien had introduced this act supposedly in an effort to make Aboriginal reserves more fiscally accountable.

The Assembly of First Nations (AFN) rejected the direction of the legislation because its design included very little Aboriginal consultation or input, and the legislation itself had the potential to undermine the nation-to-nation relationship. Martin promised that any future drafting of legislation affecting First Nations people would entail greater Aboriginal involvement (*National Post*, 11 Feb.). Such promises were reflective of Martin's efforts to distinguish his policies from Chrétien's. However, in spite of Martin's assurances, substantial improvement in the living conditions of First Nations people seemed unlikely as his government's new budget allocated no new money for housing or safe drinking water.

First Nations people face a severe housing shortage. A 2003 report noted that the greatest cause of debt for Aboriginal communities was housing, with an estimated 25,000 houses needed before the end of 2004/5 (*Windspeaker*, Jan.). Bill Montour, former Six Nations chief and former regional director general for the Department of Indian Affairs and Northern Development (DIAND), spent time working for the department on housing and raised concerns that the money allocated to Indian and Northern Affairs Canada (INAC) was not reaching the intended communities (ibid.).

In February the report of the National Assessment of Water and Wastewater Systems in First Nations Communities was released. It revealed that, out of 740 water systems inspected on 691 reserves, 218 or 29 per cent showed high-risk problems that had the potential to affect water quality negatively (*Windspeaker*, Feb.). Another 46 per cent of the water systems in the reserve communities examined needed some kind of repair, and only 185 of the inspected water systems had few or no problems (ibid.).

Indigenous participation

The federal government announced a positive step towards facilitating an Aboriginal voice in the creation of policy. Five federally recognized Aboriginal groups were to be called upon to send representatives to committee meetings whenever MPs considered legislation relating to First Nations people. These representatives were to have the same rights as MPs to ask questions but would not have a vote (*Globe and Mail*, 29 March).

Treaties and self-government

The Tlicho Agreement, ratified by the House in the fall, is perhaps the most significant treaty negotiated with First Nations people over the past century. This modern treaty is a comprehensive land-claim settlement and self-government agreement, and will affect 3,500 Aboriginal people in northern British Columbia. The treaty created a Tlicho government, transferred ownership of 39,000 square kilometres of land, and provided the Tlicho Nation with $150 million in operating funds (*National Post*, 9 Dec.).

Third-party management

The management of INAC received a scathing indictment in the auditor general's report released in February. Although the so-called sponsorship scandal received most of the public's attention, the report revealed serious problems with INAC's debt-intervention policy. When bands go into debt, the federal government immediately intervenes: first with advice; then, if the debt continues to grow, a co-manager is appointed; and finally, if the debt exceeds a certain limit, a third-party manager is selected. Placing bands into third-party management strips band councils of any authority or control over local matters. All band affairs are subject to the approval of an outside manager who rarely if ever visits the communities they supervise. Moreover, the selection of the third-party manager is not an open and transparent process and there are no agreed-upon qualifications for the position. Aboriginal communities have no choice in the selection of third-party managers. Nor does INAC monitor the performance of the managers in spite of the fact they are responsible for millions of dollars. The manager's salary of $195,000 to $312,000 a year is paid out of the band's operating funds. Fraser identified the third-party manager as the most harmful element of the debt-intervention process.

New funding

In September, following the First Ministers Health Care Summit, Paul Martin announced that the federal government was putting $700 million towards funding new health-care programs for status Indian, Inuit, and Métis people over the next five years (*Windspeaker*, Oct.). Of that money, $200 million was earmarked for sorting out jurisdictional battles between federal, provincial, and Aboriginal governments regarding the delivery of health-care services (ibid.). No comments were made about restoring non-insured health benefits (NIHB), such as medical transportation, drugs, dental and vision care, medical supplies and equipment, crisis intervention, and mental-health counselling. These services are particularly expensive in remote communities (ibid.). The NIHB branch of Health Canada's First Nation and Inuit Health division experiences a yearly shortfall ranging from $31 to $115 million (ibid.).

Some Aboriginal spokespersons were not impressed with the prime minister's announcement for new health-care funding. In particular, Cindy Blackstock, the executive director of the First Nation Child and Family Caring Society of Canada, was dismayed that none of the new funding for health care would make it into child services. In a letter to the prime minister's office, Blackstock outlined the bleak realities of Aboriginal children in care: 'There are more First Nation children and youth in institutional care in Canada than there were at the height of the residential school operations in the 1940s' (*Windspeaker*, Nov.). Aboriginal children represent 30 to 40 per cent of children in child-welfare care but make up only 5 to 6 per cent of Canadian children (ibid).

One of the biggest impediments towards effectively managing First Nations child-welfare agencies is that their funding comes from INAC, which does not consider itself a children's ministry. First Nation child-welfare agencies are expected to maintain the same standards as their provincial counterparts, with 22 per cent less funding per child (ibid.). Blackstock asserted that children are included in INAC's mandate and that, accordingly, the department should make the welfare of children in its care a priority (ibid.).

The federal government also allocated 'new found' money to the creation of a $120-million trust fund for the north. Each territory was to have access to $40 million designed to encourage development and buttress Canadian sovereignty in the region (*National Post*, 13 Dec.). Prime Minister Martin said that his long-term goal was to make the territories provinces.

Residential schools

The *Blackwater* decision of the British Columbia Court of Appeal in 2003 ruled that the federal government was vicariously liable for the abuse that took place at the Port Alberni Indian Residential School. The court argued that the federal government was responsible because it was ultimately in control of every aspect of the school's operation. The ruling had significant implications for the liability of non-profit organizations which helped establish and run residential schools for almost half a century, by absolving them of any responsibility for the actions taken by the people they employed to work with children and shifting that burden onto the federal government.

On 17 November the AFN released a report evaluating the alternative dispute resolution process (ADR), the vehicle through which the federal government endeavoured to resolve claims of abuse made by the former students of residential schools. The ADR assigned two categories of harm: categories A and B. Category A was for survivors claiming physical abuse with injuries that lasted more than six weeks or required hospitalization – including sexual abuse. Damages were capped at $25,000. Category B claims involved 'less serious' injuries and were capped by the government at $1,500 or, if there were aggravating factors, $3,500 (*Windspeaker*, Dec.). The ADR created a situation where, even though abuse was proven and compensation paid, no action was taken against the people who committed the abuse. The report offered several recommendations, including the abolition of the current system which allocates points for the nature of the abuse, and the adoption of a new definition of child abuse (*Windspeaker*, Jan.).

The AFN regarded the ADR as unworkable for most residential-school survivors. Under it, critics pointed out, it would take fifty-three years to settle all of the claims – in the interim, many of the survivors would pass away from old age without ever getting the chance to have their stories heard (ibid.). According to the AFN, the ADR process was a complete waste of money because the government spent three times more on overhead than it did on compensating victims (ibid.). Calgary lawyer Vaughn Marshall described the ADR process 'as a compensation program for bureaucrats, not residential school survivors' (*Windspeaker*, Dec.).

Elder Elmer Courchene joined the AFN in criticizing the government's dealings with residential-school survivors because the ADR was not survivor-driven. Courchene asserted that the government's definition of abuse is too limited: 'The way the government is looking at physical abuse is only that you've been hit and there's a mark on you for the rest of your life' (*Windspeaker*, Jan.). The official position of the federal government was that it would not compensate for the loss of language and culture. In 2004 a group of residential-school survivors in southern Alberta was working to challenge this position.

Provincial and territorial developments

British Columbia

Natural-resource development. A constant refrain in the history of British Columbia and its relations with First Nations people concerns the province's failure to recognize and participate in the treaty-making process. British Columbia negotiated only a few treaties during the nineteenth century, and the majority of reserves have been reduced to the size of small towns. Indeed, the province has pursued a particularly restrictive land-claims policy, going so far as to pass legislation that caps the total percentage of land that can be allocated to First Nations people, a policy not pursued by other federal or provincial governments in Canada. As a result, the province has been and will continue to be a site of contestation around definitions of Aboriginal rights and access to land and natural resources.

The reluctance of the B.C. government to negotiate has forced Aboriginal groups increasingly to use the courts in order to resolve land claims. Unfortunately, using the legal system to deal with land claims is a frustratingly slow process, often taking several decades. Accordingly, there is a great deal of concern among First Nations groups that the resources on disputed lands will be extracted and exhausted by private companies before land claims can be resolved.

In 2004 two events occurred that may help to allay some of the concerns expressed by First Nations regarding the development of natural resources on disputed lands. The first was a memorandum signed by B.C.'s mining and tourism interests. In January the Council of Tourism Associations, the B.C. and Yukon Chamber of Mines, and the Mining Association of B.C. signed a memorandum calling for all groups to work together to settle land-use issues. Essentially, the agreement appealed to all the parties involved in resource development to consider the rights of First Nations people when pursuing deals on crown land. This agreement was made in response to a particular land-claims case then under review by the British Columbia Court of Appeals. In that case, the initial court ruling held private companies jointly responsible for development on crown land under dispute.

The second event was a landmark decision of the B.C. Court of Appeals. Aboriginal groups have typically been opposed to economic development because they believe that such development does not respect their interests (*Globe and Mail*, 24 Nov.). In the case of *Haida v. British Columbia*, the Appeals Court ruled that governments must consult Aboriginal groups before allowing development on disputed lands. The Haida were trying to stop the provincial government from renewing the logging giant Weyerhaeuser's lease on a tree farm located on the Queen Charlotte Islands. The tree farm comprised approximately one-quarter of the Islands, land that has been under dispute for some time. Although the B.C. court recognized the government's obligation to consult First Nations people, third parties like Weyerhaeuser were not found to be liable for the crown's failure to discharge title.

The court's decision that governments must deal with Aboriginal groups in such situations had the potential to affect the pace of resource development across the country, particularly in the burgeoning north. The federal government appealed the ruling, and the Supreme Court of Canada limited the judgment by saying that although the government had an obligation to engage 'in meaningful consultation with Native groups,' this did not mean that Aboriginal people could veto resource development on disputed land (ibid.). First Nations groups were unhappy with the decision, saying that it did not go far enough to protect their rights (*National Post*, 19 Nov.).

The politics of water. The year 2004 continued to see water being shipped to Gilford Island from Fanny Bay at great cost to the Kwicksutaineuk First Nation, and the provincial and federal governments continued to flounder in its search for a solution to the problem. Access to adequate services and infrastructure remains a serious problem for many First

Nations people living in British Columbia, especially in remote areas. The community of Kwicksutaineuk, located on Gilford Island, is accessible only by float plane or boat. It is facing serious health problems directly related to living conditions and a dearth of adequate or properly maintained services. By 2004, the community's water system had been in disrepair for the past ten years, and for the preceding five years drinking water had been shipped into the community. Additionally, all of the homes in the community were infected with mould and no housing alternatives existed. The mould was causing serious health problems among the children, some of whom had to be flown to outside hospital facilities on a biweekly basis. Lack of access to clean water is not an unusual situation for Aboriginal communities.

The prairies

Treaties and economic development. Although the three prairie provinces are covered by the numbered treaties, the original intention and parameters of these treaties, cross-border jurisdiction, and economic development continue to be serious sources of dispute. In 2004 three First Nation groups from Alberta joined forces with the Southern Peigan (or Blackfeet) of Montana to dispute the expropriation of tribal lands by the U.S. government and mining companies. The territory in question covers 52,000 hectares of parkland in northwestern Montana, known as Badger-Two Medicine (*National Post*, 17 Nov.). In 1855 the U.S. government signed a treaty with the Blackfeet which recognized Badger-Two Medicine as Blackfeet territory; however, an 1895 land deal altered aspects of the 1855 treaty. The Blackfeet contend that the land was never transferred. By 2004, the land under dispute was threatened by oil and gas development, and in order to block this Blackfeet leaders in the United States and Canada entered into negotiations with Washington in March. This dispute raised questions about the significance of borders and their application to First Nations people.

The manner in which individual bands have chosen to use the unique status of reserve lands to expand and develop their local economies came under fire in 2004. The Siksika (Blackfoot) Nation of southern Alberta was involved in negotiations with a U.S.-backed hospital to establish a private facility on urban reserve land near the Calgary International Airport. This was one of several projects under consideration by various First Nation groups to offer health services to paying customers on reserve land where federal and provincial laws that prohibit the application of fees for medical services under the Canadian Health Act cannot be enforced (*National Post*, 22 April). In a similar case, a First Nation band in Saskatchewan planned to build a for-profit diagnostic imaging clinic on reserve land that falls within the eastern portion of Saskatoon. The efforts of these two groups were reflective of a broader attempt by bands to create economic opportunities and generate more revenue in order to provide better services for their communities.

'Starlight Cruises.' For the last several decades, Saskatchewan police officers have been taking Aboriginal men on rides (also known as 'starlight cruises') in police vehicles and abandoning them in remote locations with terrible consequences (Windspeaker, Nov.). In November 1990, seventeen-year-old Neil Stonechild was found frozen to death in an industrial part of Saskatoon. The last time Stonechild was seen he was being forced into a police car by two officers. Then, in January and February 2000, the bodies of four more Aboriginal men were found frozen to death in isolated areas of the city. Later that same year, Darrel Night came forward and alleged that two police officers had dropped him outside the city and forced him to walk back in below-freezing temperatures. Fortunately, Night found shelter and did not suffer the same fate as Stonechild and the 2000 victims. The two police officers who 'picked up' Night were found guilty of unlawful confinement and dismissed from the police force in 2001.

A Commission of Inquiry, headed by the Honourable Mr Justice David Wright, into the death of Neil Stonechild was held in 2004. Although the inquiry did not find sufficient evidence to charge anyone formally for Stonechild's suspicious death, Wright criticized the Saskatoon City Police for supporting and perpetuating a system of justice that is racist, unresponsive, and dangerous to members of its community (*Windspeaker*, Nov.). Saskatoon Police Chief Russell Sabo fired constables Larry Hartwig and Bradley Senger for their conduct in the Stonechild case. Sabo said that he fired the two officers for 'not diligently and promptly disclosing information that Stonechild was in their custody as it was their duty to do so' (*Windspeaker*, Dec.).

Precipitated by the international furore caused by the so-called starlight cruises, an investigation into the Saskatchewan police force and justice system was initiated in 2002. Called the Commission on First Nations and Métis Peoples and Justice Reform, this $2.8-million investigation reported in June 2004 that 'anti-Native racism exists in the police system and contributes to an environment of distrust' (*Globe and Mail*, 22 June). The commission tabled 122 recommendations – the most important ones calling for the establishment of an independent provincial investigation agency to handle allegations of police abuse and excessive force and placing an Aboriginal liaison officer at every police station. Wilton Littlechild, the chairman of the commission, commented that the abuse seemed widespread and suggested that a national study would find similar results. The degree to which the commission's report would lead to significant and meaningful change remained to be seen. Saskatchewan Justice Minister Frank Quennell indicated that, under the province's current budget, there were insufficient funds to implement any of the report's more significant recommendations (*Globe and Mail*, 22 June).

Stolen Sisters. Further revelations regarding the endemic nature of violence towards First Nations people were contained in an Amnesty International report in 2004 entitled *Stolen Sisters*. The report focused on the stories of Aboriginal women, predominantly from western Canada, who had gone missing over the last several decades. Sadly, in western Canadian cities and towns, posters asking for help locating missing Aboriginal women are not uncommon. In fact, Aboriginal women between the ages of twenty-five and forty-four are five times more likely than other Canadian women of the same age to die from violence, and over the past three decades more than 500 Aboriginal women have gone missing or have been murdered.[1] Most of these cases remain unsolved and forgotten. An infamous example is the Robert Pickton case, where over twenty Aboriginal women went missing in the same area over several decades and the authorities failed to act.

Regrettably, the release of *Stolen Sisters* coincided with the Stonechild inquiry and the Commission on First Nations and Métis Peoples and Justice Reform and thus received little attention. Critics of the commission said that, despite the breadth of the commission's mandate, nowhere did its report grapple with the violence Aboriginal women face at the hands of white men in the larger community (*Globe and Mail*, 24 June). Indeed, given the very disturbing statistics revealed by *Stolen Sisters,* it is surprising and perhaps revealing that this information did not make national headlines or raise a public outcry. The absence of consideration paid to *Stolen Sisters* and the status of Aboriginal women more generally expose a deeply rooted problem in Canadian society.

1 Amnesty International Canada, *Canada: Stolen Sisters – A Human Rights Response to Discrimination and Violence against Indigenous Women in Canada* (Ottawa: Amnesty International 2004).

Another Walkerton? The politics of access to clean water are becoming increasingly important in Canada as elsewhere. In 2004 the Yellow Quill First Nation of Saskatchewan, a community of 1,000 people, had been under a boil-water advisory since 1995 (*Windspeaker*, Feb.). This situation was rectified only after the newly appointed environmental health officer with the Saskatoon Tribal Council insisted that something be done. When the health officer learned of the situation at the Yellow Quill reserve, she immediately contacted the volunteers at the Safe Drinking Water Foundation (SDWF). Founded in 1997, SDWF is dedicated to making safe drinking water a basic human right, and works towards making that goal a reality. Following three years of negotiations, the federal government agreed to help find a solution to the community's unsafe drinking water. After almost ten years, the Yellow Quill First Nation was finally to have access to safe drinking water.

Safe drinking water is a basic human right guaranteed under the Geneva Convention, and Canada fails to ensure that this right is observed in First Nation communities. The federal government is trying to devolve most of its responsibilities to provincial governments. As a result, many First Nation communities are left without access to adequate funding, proper equipment, and the technical capacity necessary to properly regulate and protect their drinking water. At the close of 2004, over one hundred Aboriginal communities across Canada remained under boil-water advisories – a situation that seemed unlikely to change in the near future.

Métis Nation Saskatchewan (MNS). The MNS held elections on 26 May 2004 and Dwayne Roth was elected president. However, the Saskatchewan and federal governments refused to recognize the newly elected president and his provincial council owing to allegations of irregularities at polling stations. Keith Lampard, former chief electoral officer for Saskatchewan, reviewed the election results. In October, Lampard's report revealed that there were grounds to the allegations. In fact, Robert Doucette, another one of the presidential candidates, was initially declared the winner after the election in May but the decision was later overturned when uncounted ballot boxes were discovered.

From June 2004, the provincial and federal governments withheld funding for the MNS. Funding would not resume until after another election. Roth announced that he would take legal action against Lampard and the provincial government, seeking compensation for damages incurred. Ralph Kennedy, secretary of the provincial council of the MNS, condemned the actions of the government because they interfered with First Nations sovereignty and self-government (*Windspeaker*, Dec.).

Ontario

Treaty rights and land claims. In March 2004 an Ontario court ruled that legislation requiring status Indians to pay for licences under the federal gun registry is unconstitutional because it violates long-held treaty rights. The case involved two Ojibwa partridge hunters who had been charged by the Ontario Provincial Police (OPP) for the illegal possession of firearms. Judge Diane Petit-Begg found that their arrest violated rights guaranteed to members of the Whitesand First Nation under the Robinson Treaty of 1850. Aboriginal groups have opposed the Firearms Act because, in their view, it violates extant treaty rights and First Nation groups were not consulted when the legislation was drafted (*National Post*, 4 March). Chief Bill Erasmus of the AFN expressed his desire for a gun registry controlled by First Nations, where public safety and registration would be monitored at the band level (ibid.).

In May, the Rainy River First Nation won a ninety-year struggle to regain land the provincial government had expropriated without compensation and sold to white settlers. The agreement, worth $71 million, returned 18,600 hectares of land in northwestern Ontario to the band and made provision to help the Rainy River First Nation buy back some of the original land from the individuals who then owned it (*Globe and Mail*, 18 May).

Court decisions. In a landmark decision, the Ontario Court of Appeal certified Canada's first residential-school class-action lawsuit. This ruling reversed the decision of a lower Ontario court which rejected the claim made by residential-school survivors on the basis that the varied experiences of the students were not sufficiently universal for the claimants to constitute a class (*National Post*, 4 Dec.). The decision made it possible for former residential school students to bypass the ADR process instituted by the federal government to deal with claims of abuse in Native residential schools. Court of Appeal Judge Gould believed that the trial route would prove more effective than the ADR, a system conceived and managed by the same bureaucracy that established and ran residential schools (ibid.).

Also in 2004, the Ontario Superior Court was forced to decide whether Aboriginal children had a constitutional right to grow up with Aboriginal families. The Pikwakanagan First Nation contested the adoption of three children born to an Aboriginal father and a Chinese-Canadian mother. The Toronto Children's Aid Society removed the children from their homes and arranged three separate adoptions: to an Aboriginal family headed by the birth father's aunt, to a family that included a Chinese-Canadian and another non-Native parent, and to a non-Chinese family (*Globe and Mail*, 4 May). The band had the right to challenge the adoptions under Ontario law. According to Ontario law, Aboriginal children taken from their families must be placed within their band or with an Aboriginal family, unless a substantial reason exists for not doing so (ibid.).

Madam Justice Ruth Mesbur of the Ontario Superior Court upheld the adoptions, stating that 'time is of the essence in proceedings concerning the welfare of children ... children's emotional well-being always trumps concerns regarding the importance of nurturing their native heritage' (ibid.). Mesbur further asserted that the Pikwakanagan community should have organized itself better if it wanted its right to control adoptions to become a reality. Aboriginal groups greeted this ruling with tremendous disappointment. (It remained unclear whether the agency had made any effort to place the children with Aboriginal families.) The case was still under review by the Superior Court at the end of 2004.

A similar case regarding the adoption of two girls by white foster families was challenged by the Squamish Nation of British Columbia. Interestingly, the Hamilton Children's Aid Society, despite the fact that it had placed the girls with their current foster families, supported the claims of the Squamish Nation. The Squamish wanted to place the children with a member of the community who fostered children for the band. In 2004, after several years of acrimony and thousands and thousands of dollars in legal fees, the band withdrew its application after the woman with whom the Squamish intended to place the children moved away from the community. The foster/adoptive families stated their intent to seek reimbursement for legal fees from the Squamish Nation.

These cases raised very real fears among Aboriginal communities that what Aboriginals refer to as 'the scoop' of the 1960s might recommence. In that decade, thousands of First Nation children were removed from their homes for specious reasons. The AFN passed a motion in 1999 condemning the 1960s scoop and the adoption of Aboriginal children by non-Aboriginal families, indicating how seriously First Nations leaders take this perceived threat.

The injustice system? The inquiry into the shooting death of unarmed protestor Dudley George began in July. George's family, supporters, the United Nations, and Amnesty International fought long and hard for this investigation into the events that took place the day he was killed. In 1995 George and approximately thirty unarmed protestors decided to expand their two-year occupation of an abandoned military base into the adjacent Ipperwash Provincial Park. The parkland had been confiscated from the Chippewa of Kettle and Stoney Point First Nation by the military during the Second World War.

Two days later, the OPP moved into the park and George was shot and killed. In 2003 Sergeant Kenneth Deane was found guilty of criminal negligence and resigned from the OPP. Allegations were levelled against former premier Mike Harris about the nature of his involvement in the operation. Initially, the OPP had remained at a distance, content to watch the non-violent protest. However, after several top-level meetings and urgent phone calls, the police were ordered into the park to eject the non-violent protestors. The inquiry was to review confidential materials in order to ascertain whether this tragic incident was politically motivated, a consequence of racism in the OPP, or simply the result of OPP incompetence.

The year 2004 witnessed another inquiry into the treatment of First Nations people by police authorities. An OPP special tactical unit stationed in Barrie was disbanded and eight of its members were charged with discreditable conduct and deceit after an investigation was held into an incident that had taken place earlier in the year. In January, the OPP special tactical unit was called in by the Chippewa of the Thames First Nation's police to help deal with an armed man who had barricaded himself in a residence (*Globe and Mail*, 12 March). After entering the house, members of the unit defaced the owner's property. Several large Xs were drawn through the homeowner's warrior's flag with a ballpoint pen, and another large X was drawn through the picture of an Aboriginal protestor facing off against a Canadian soldier at Oka. This incident was the first time the OPP had been allowed onto Chippewa First Nation territory since the execution of Dudley George.

Band elections. The Six Nations of Grand River held their election in November. Chief Roberta Jamieson, the incumbent, announced that she would not run for re-election. Jamieson stated that she believed she had accomplished her objectives in office and did not need to run again (*Windspeaker*, Nov.).

In December, Jamieson was appointed chief executive officer of the Board of the National Aboriginal Achievement Foundation. She was the first Aboriginal woman to earn a law degree in Canada and was the founding chair of imagineNative, an international media-arts festival.

A first. Harry Laforme was appointed to the Ontario Court of Appeal. The first Aboriginal man to hold this position, Laforme said that he brought an important and underrepresented perspective/voice to the court (*Globe and Mail*, 23 Nov.).

Quebec

Land claims. In October an Innu band near Baie-Comeau filed an injunction in Quebec Superior Court to prevent the forestry company Kruger Inc. from cutting trees on Île René-Levasseru. The 2,000-square-kilometre island was created during the 1960s when Hydro-Québec dammed the Manicouagan River (*National Post*, 28 Oct.). It lies within the band's traditional territory and the Innu wanted their land claims settled before Kruger was allowed to go in and exploit the natural resources.

Band governance. The residents of Kanesatake have long been divided over the direction and practice of policing and crime within their community, and incidents in 2004 reflected these rifts. In the fall of 2003, the federal government allocated $900,000 to help fight organized crime at Kanesatake after Grand Chief James Gabriel signed an agreement with the solicitor general's department to bring in an interim police force (*Windspeaker*, March). This police force was comprised of officers drawn from the RCMP, the Sûreté du Québec, and Aboriginal constables from over twenty reserves (ibid.).

Gabriel, along with three other chiefs, made the decision to replace the current acting police chief, Terry Cross, and bring in the joint police force. His action was opposed by other members of the band council because neither they nor the community-appointed police commission had been informed. Following the arrival of the new police force, a crowd of protestors surrounded the police station, and Gabriel's house and car were set on fire. Gabriel and his family fled the community. The twenty-four-hour stand-off ended after the Sûreté du Québec signed an agreement with the Kanesatake protestors allowing the interim police force to leave the station.

There has been a long history in the community of political interference in police matters. Kanesatake's independent police commission had been established in response to residents' demands. However, the work of this commission was impeded by the chief and council, who refused to release the money necessary to operate the force.

Atlantic Canada

Treaties and self-government. For those communities that lived through the resettlements of the 1950s, the agreement that the Inuit of Labrador signed with the provincial and federal governments in 2004 was a tremendous milestone for the region. The Inuit in Labrador, much like other Inuit across Canada, never signed a treaty with the Canadian government. However, when southern governments became interested in the area's rich natural resources, the Inuit forced governments to address their land claims and demands for self-government. As a result, an agreement was signed in 1997 by the government of Newfoundland and Labrador and Ottawa which gave the Inuit the right to establish their own government.

In 2004 a plebiscite was held by the Inuit to determine whether or not they would go forward with the agreement. At the end of May, the Inuit of Labrador voted overwhelmingly in favour of self-government. The agreement gave the Inuit control over an area of land larger than the Republic of Ireland, and the power to enact laws dealing with education, health, and social services (*Globe and Mail*, 23 May). The new government was to be called Nunatsiavut and those companies that wanted to explore and develop resources in the region would have to deal with the Nunatsiavut government.

The Labrador Métis Association, representing approximately 6,000 people, announced its intention to challenge this agreement in court on the basis that half the land ceded by the government was still claimed by the Métis. Originally, the Métis tried to negotiate their land claims in conjunction with the Labrador Inuit Association, but the federal government rejected the rights of the Métis to do so. The federal government does not recognize the Aboriginal rights of Métis people. As a result, the Métis launched a lawsuit in order to have the agreement declared invalid.

The Miawpukek First Nation's small reserve in southern Newfoundland is the only Mi'kmaq reserve recognized in the province. In 2004 the band was involved in negotiating a self-government agreement with the provincial government. Of the negotiations, Chief Misel Joe said: 'We have long sought to assert our autonomy and self-determination [and] although there is still a lot of negotiating work to come, I am glad that we have reached this milestone' (*Globe and Mail*, 11 May).

The First Nations of Newfoundland did not negotiate treaties with the British and when the province joined Confederation in 1949 no consideration was paid to First Nation groups.

The north

Land claims and the politics of energy. During the 1970s, an inquiry led by Justice Thomas Berger halted the construction of the Mackenzie Valley Natural Gas Pipeline until Aboriginal land claims in the region were settled. In 2004 construction of the pipeline was halted once again as a result of the federal government's failure to settle Aboriginal land claims. The Deh Cho First Nations filed an injunction in the Supreme Court of the Northwest Territories in September to stop the project until their land claims were resolved. The Deh Cho believed that they had been unfairly excluded from discussions around the pipeline, and they regarded the pipeline and their land claims as directly linked (*Globe and Mail*, 3 Sept.). When finished, the Mackenzie Pipeline would bring gas and oil from the Arctic to the south, and had the potential to open up the north for gas exploration. The injunction came just as the oil companies involved in the pipeline project were seeking regulatory approval.

The Deh Cho Nations is one of four First Nation groups affected by the pipeline and was the last group to settle its land claims with the federal government. The Deh Cho have been negotiating with the federal government since the 1970s. Forty per cent of the pipeline would cross Deh Cho territory, and before they agree to construction of the pipeline on their land the Deh Cho want their land claims settled, a measure of self-government, and a resource-sharing agreement with the federal government (ibid.). Negotiations with the federal government stalled and in late October the Deh Cho amended their demands: they would drop the lawsuit if they were given one seat on the regulatory panel and progress was made in their land-claims dispute.

One of the companies participating in the project is the Mackenzie Valley Aboriginal Pipeline LP (APG), Canada's largest Aboriginal enterprise. APG is a limited partnership between three of the four Aboriginal communities (the Inuvialuit, Gwi'chn, and Sahtu) with lands adjacent to the Mackenzie valley. The APG has the potential to include the equal participation of Aboriginal people in one of North America's largest energy enterprises, while earning APG $21.2 million a year (*National Post*, 26 July).

Implementing the Nunavut Land Claims Agreement. The auditor-general, Sheila Fraser, criticized the management of Indian and Northern Affairs Canada in a 2004 report. In particular, Fraser focused on the failure of INAC to implement measures set out in the Nunavut Land Claims Agreement. Indeed, Fraser's report underscored INAC's failure over the preceding decade to ensure the agreement's success. James Eetoolook of Tunngavik commented: 'Indian Affairs deserves the rap it will get from the Auditor-General. It's done a bad job with a good agreement' (*Globe and Mail*, 10 Feb.).

In order to gauge the success of the agreement, Fraser measured the progress achieved by the objectives laid out in the original text, focusing in particular on those provisions intended to increase Inuit self-reliance. For example, the agreement guaranteed that, after a period of training and transition, 85 per cent of all government jobs would be held by Inuit (ibid.). Instead, as Fraser uncovered, the percentage of Inuit occupying government jobs at the time of her audit had decreased 5 per cent over the previous four years (ibid). To fill the 60 per cent of government jobs not occupied by Inuit, INAC employed people from southern Canada. It cost INAC $65 million every year to recruit non-Aboriginal people from outside the region, and pay the costs of an unemployed Inuit workforce. INAC exacerbated the problem by failing to make the necessary investments in education and training that would enable the Inuit to take over the jobs occupied by southerners. INAC employees were reluctant to implement an agreement that would make their jobs redundant.

Control over natural resources. Joe Handley, the premier of the Northwest Territories, where approximately half the population is Aboriginal, spent much of 2004 trying to acquire some control over the natural resources in the territory, specifically over who gets the revenue from the territory's diamond mines. Two diamond mines in the area are worth over $2 billion in exports every year, making Canada the third-largest diamond exporter in the world (*National Post*, 7 Dec.). A third mine was to go into production later in the year. All revenue from these mines goes south to Ottawa to be distributed at the federal government's discretion.

Initially, the NWT were governed by a commissioner appointed by Ottawa. Today, the territories have their own governments with jurisdictional responsibilities similar to those of other provinces, with one significant exception – the territories exercise no control over their natural resources. Ottawa has always been reluctant to relinquish control over its provinces' rich resources. For example, although Alberta and Saskatchewan were made provinces in 1905, they did not have control over their natural resources until the 1930s. Acquiring control over its own resources allowed Alberta to benefit from the discovery of oil at Leduc in 1947. Handley sought a revenue-sharing arrangement similar to the provinces' – with the federal government, territory, and Aboriginal groups each receiving one-third of the monies generated. This agreement would almost double the income of the NWT, which operates under serious financial constraints. The territories do not control the revenue from the development of their own natural resources and transfer payments are stretched to the limit trying to meet the proportionally higher costs of housing and health care.

Electoral controversy in Nunavut. Nunavut's nineteen-seat legislature operates on a consensus basis without the interference of political parties, and the MLAs choose their leader and cabinet from among themselves. However, political controversy infected Nunavut's elections when Tagak Curley chose to challenge incumbent Premier Paul Okalik for the position. Curley decided to enter the race after Okalik's government passed a Human Rights Act which included protection for such things as sexual orientation. If elected, Curley said that he would amend the Human Rights Act because he felt certain provisions were clearly against the law of God (*Globe and Mail*, 16 Feb.). Okalik won his riding and was re-elected premier by the MLAs.

As a fundamentalist Christian, belonging to a growing evangelical Christian movement sweeping the north, Curley thinks that Nunavut's Human Rights Act is contrary to traditional Inuit values (*National Post*, 6 March). Ironically, fundamentalist Christianity has become closely associated with the traditional Inuit way of life. Jim Bell, editor-in-chief of the *Nunatsiaq News*, declared: 'It's a real culture war that's going on and a real sort of battle over what the Inuit identity consists of and what should the role of the Nunavut government be in asserting that identity' (*Globe and Mail*, 5 March).

The cost of environmental change. Climate change in the north has increasingly become a serious concern, particularly for indigenous peoples. First Nations people in the Arctic have teamed with environmental groups to urge the United States to join other nations in cutting greenhouse-gas emissions. Cutting greenhouse-gas emissions would slow down the thaw of the polar ice caps. Hunting cultures are especially at risk from global warming; several hunters have fallen through the ice while pursuing hunting and trapping activities (*Globe and Mail*, 13 Nov.).

In November, during the same week as the foreign ministers of the eight northern nations were scheduled to meet to discuss issues of trade and sovereignty, 250 scientists released the Arctic Climate Impact Assessment Report in Reykjavik. The report revealed that the Arctic heats up faster than the rest of the globe because the dark ground and water, once exposed, absorbs far more heat than snow and ice. The scientists called upon the United States to join other nations in cutting greenhouse-gas emissions to slow down the thaw of the polar ice. The United States opposes caps on greenhouse-gas emissions.

In December several Inuit groups announced their intention to file a claim against the United States with the Inter-American Commission on Human Rights. They claimed that the United States, by contributing substantially to global warming, threatens their existence (*Globe and Mail*, 15 Dec.).

The politics of housing. The government of Nunavut and the territory's land-claims organization turned to Ottawa for help to deal with their housing crisis. The cost of building houses in the north is tremendous and the federal government has failed to invest in the north's infrastructure. Indeed, the housing problem has become increasingly worse since 1993, when the federal government stopped funding social housing. The housing situation in the north contrasts starkly with that in the south, where the federal government continues to fund housing on reserves.

In September a request was made for $1.9 billion over ten years to address the housing crisis (*Globe and Mail*, 30 Sept.). Peter Kilabuk, Nunavut's housing minister, said that the money was needed for catchup: 'We find ourselves in more of a shocking situation than what a lot of officials had anticipated' (ibid.). A recent report showed that 54 per cent of Inuit (or 12,000 women, men, and children) lived in substandard housing (ibid).

Although an aura of optimism marked the beginning of 2004, following the promises made by the federal government in the Speech from the Throne, First Nations people across the country would continue to face the same challenges in 2005 – lack of clean drinking, inadequate housing, poor services, and systemic racism.

CAREY HILL

British Columbia

British Columbia's Liberal finance minister, Gary Farrell-Collins, made headlines several times in 2004. In February, he introduced a balanced budget and by year's end the economy appeared to be in good shape even though it had suffered the challenges of the avian flu epidemic, the mountain pine beetle, and considerable labour strife. However, at the close of the year, Farrell-Collins surprisingly announced his resignation on what might be perceived as a high note yet amidst controversy surrounding charges that his former aide committed fraud and breach of trust regarding the B.C. Rail deal.

While the newsmaker was probably the finance minister, the story of the year was labour relations. Labour unrest was so significant that it nearly led to a general strike. Striking Hospital Employees' Union (HEU) workers were legislated back to work by Gordon Campbell's Liberals. Other labour disputes also took place throughout the year.

In addition to labour unrest, British Columbia suffered plagues in 2004. It was reported that the pine beetle ravaged four million hectares, or the size of Denmark, in 2003, with more damage in 2004. Another epidemic, the avian flu, led to the culling of many chickens and other fowl and the federal government's commitment of $60 million for farmers' losses.

The year included a federal election in which all parties tried to woo B.C. voters (the federal Liberals were the most obvious suitors, choosing five high-profile candidates). Another well-known local politician, Svend Robinson, suffered a major setback in 2004. He was found guilty of theft and decided not to run in the federal election.

While British Columbia suffered calamities and strife in 2004, it performed well economically. The province balanced its budget and was predicting a surplus of more than $2 billion by year's end.

Cabinet shuffle

The year began with a cabinet shuffle in late January, a first for Campbell since he was elected in 2001. Seventeen ministers were dropped or reassigned and six new ministers were appointed (*Nanaimo Daily News*, 27 Jan.). Notably, the finance minister, Gary Farrell-Collins, remained in his position. Earlier, following an internal audit, the minister of children and families, Gordon Hogg, had resigned (*National Post*, 24 Jan.). The ministers who were dropped from cabinet included Hogg, Judith Reid, Ted Nebbeling, Lynn Stephens, Katherine Whittred, and Greg Halsey-Brandt.

Kevin Falcon replaced Judith Reid as transportation minister. His new portfolio included the task of privatizing B.C. Rail. Formerly, as the government's deregulation czar, he had overseen the elimination of some 80,000 regulations since June 2001. Other new ministers included John Les as small business and economic development minister, Ida Chong as minister of state for women's services, Susan Brice as minister of state for mental health, Pat Bell as minister of state for mining, and Roger Harris as minister of state for forestry operations. Sindi Hawkins moved from Health Planning to Intergovernmental Relations.

A year of labour unrest

While there was an early shakeup in the government's cabinet, other shock waves reverberated through the labour sector as unrest was common, especially in April, when striking Hospital Employees Union workers almost led the province in a general strike. Early in the year, the government's problems with labour relations surfaced as B.C. doctors demanded an 11 per cent raise (*Vancouver Sun*, 29 Jan.), with the minister, Colin Hansen, vowing they would get nothing. Hansen argued that the doctors were the costliest in the country based on per-capita spending. By March, he was optimistic that the doctors would accept a two-year wage freeze (*Prince George Citizen*, 6 March).

Among health employees, the greatest challenge for the government was from those who did the cooking, cleaning, and clerical tasks along with the licensed practical nurses at 330 hospitals, clinics, and long-term-care facilities across the province. The members of the Hospital Employees' Union went on strike on 25 April. Their main aim was to end contracting out of their services. Between 30 April and 3 May, 6,000 surgeries were cancelled as a result of the dispute as well as tens of thousands of diagnostic tests including CT scans, MRIs, and X-rays (*Kimberley Daily Bulletin*, 3 May).

In order to get the 43,000 striking HEU workers to return to work, the government introduced back-to-work legislation, Bill 37, on 29

April. The bill offered no cap on contracting out and was retroactive to 1 April, meaning that the workers owed up to ten days' pay. Moreover, the legislation resulted in a 15 per cent wage rollback (*Province*, 11 May). The labour minister noted that the government would save $400 million though the wage rollbacks. The workers would have sixty days to decide with an arbitrator how the wage rollbacks would occur. For example, they could reduce their sick days or work an extra ninety minutes per day.

The *Globe and Mail* (6 May) wrote that Campbell 'went too far.' Protests against the government's actions were British Columbia's biggest since 1983, when a provincial government restraint program had sparked political unrest that nearly became a general strike. For their part, the B.C. Teachers' Federation (BCTF) and the Greater Vancouver transit workers were off the job for one day in support. Northland Pulp and Paper and B.C. Hydro were both on the picket lines for one day as well (*Windsor Star*, 3 May).

Eventually, the Campbell government backed down: the two sides brokered a deal to avert the general strike of teachers, transit drivers, municipal and provincial employees, and some private-sector staff. The deal involved Campbell offering a cap on contracting out of 600 more full-time jobs over two years in addition to 1,300 already served notice, $25 million for enhanced severance, and the elimination of the bill's retroactivity. The wage-and-benefit rollback was also reduced to 14 per cent (*Toronto Star*, 8 May). Even after the deal was struck, sporadic picketing continued. For example, pickets held up ferry terminals at Schwartz Bay and Departure Bay but were eventually cleared and sailings resumed.

On 2 May, Justice Robert Bauman provided his decision on the HEU's having violated the back-to-work order. He fined the HEU $150,000, the highest fine ever for such activity (*Times Colonist*, 26 June). Previously, the highest fine went to a strike by Brinks guards in 1984 that had involved violence and intimidation (*Vancouver Sun*, 18 May).

That same month, the British Columbia Nurses' Union (BCNU) agreed to a bargaining framework. The 28,000 members of the BCNU accepted zero per cent increases over two years with no rollbacks in hourly rates, benefits, or time-off provisions (*Times-Colonist*, 27 May). The BCNU president, Debra McPherson, noted a need for an increase in the number of full-time nurses, greater shift flexibility and choice, longer retention of senior nurses through phased retirement, and more jobs for new graduate nurses (ibid.).

After the stand-off with hospital employees, the Campbell Liberals also successfully negotiated with the doctors. The government's negotiating mandate with doctors was zero, zero, and zero over three years. The B.C. Medical Association rejected zero in year three and the province and doctors eventually settled on a two-year contract of zero and zero (*Province*, 11 May).

In other labour news, in March Justice David Tysoe, who had been appointed to head an inquiry into the film and television industry, released a report. Among his recommendations was a new grievance procedure regarding the B.C. Council of Film Unions, if the council was in agreement, to provide faster and less formal resolution with arbitration (*Barrie Examiner*, 6 March). Moreover, the report noted that labour strife had turned into a disincentive to conduct films in British Columbia. For example, the report compared B.C.'s situation with that of Ontario and noted that the Teamsters, who were responsible for most of the grievances, were not as involved in Ontario as they were in British Columbia (*National Post*, 5 March).

Other labour strikes in 2004 included a beer strike by Brewers Distributors that affected Molson and Labatt, which are responsible for 90 per cent of the beer sold in the province. A deal was reached in mid-May (*Prince George Citizen*, 14 May). Also, in the fall, the B.C. Teachers' Federation began bargaining. It said that it would not accept zero per cent wage increases since the government was reporting a surplus. First Vice-President Irene Lanzinger declared that teachers would seek improvements to working conditions and a raise: 'They [the government] certainly aren't going to be able to make the argument that they don't have the money, which is the argument they made to everyone else' (*Times-Colonist*, 22 Sept.). Finance Minister Gary Farrell-Collins reported that in 2006 the mandate for bargaining would not be zero per cent increases but that the teachers were expected to support zeros over two years.

Balancing the budget

In February, British Columbia balanced the budget and called for balanced budgets for the following three years. The government's budget papers noted: 'Achieving balanced budgets will complete the shift to a stable and sustainable fiscal policy – a basic requirement to build and reinforce consumer and investor confidence' (*Province*, 18 Feb.). The balanced budget did not involve any tax cuts, and some organizations, including the Canadian Federation of Independent Business, were critical of this (*Province*, 18 Feb.). NDP opposition leader Joy MacPhail stated that the cuts over the past three years had been mean-spirited (*Prince Rupert Daily News*, 18 Feb.). Other critics noted that tax cuts in 2001 of $2.2. billion had led to the current deficit which was being filled through cuts to services (*National Post*, 18 Feb.).

The B.C. Business Council's Jock Finlayson lauded the budget, as did Kevin Evans of the Retail Council of Canada. Finlayson explained: 'The stars are lining up quite favorably for B.C.'s economy' (*Province*, 18 Feb.). Growth of 2.8 per cent in 2004 and 3.1 per cent in 2005 was forecast in the budget's Economic Review and Outlook (*Province*, 18 Feb.).

Public-private partnerships

Part of the government's strategy to reduce costs involved engagement with public-private partnerships or P3s. In June, the government signed its first public-private partnership agreement with Ledcor Projects of Vancouver to redesign and rebuild the 188-kilometre Sierra Yo Yo Desan road in northwestern British Columbia.

The Liberal government's P-3 agency, Partnerships B.C., also outlined what kind of information would be released to the public regarding the P3s. The CEO of Partnerships B.C., Larry Blain, noted that the final project agreement, the value-for-money report, and a statement from the fairness auditor would be made public. The role of the fairness auditor is to sit in on the negotiations and decision-making meetings and determine whether the process is fair. Blain also noted that Partnerships B.C. would never make proposals from other bidders public because losing firms do not want their details provided (*Vancouver Sun*, 21 June).

Another public-private partnership of some controversy involved the Vancouver General Hospital's academic ambulatory care centre. The centre was to be built as a public-private partnership under the auspices of Partnerships B.C., which had nine P3s in the works, including Fraser River Crossing, Okanagan Lake Bridge, Brittani Mine Water treatment facility, and Sea-to-Sky Highway improvement project (*Province*, 12 April).

Pine beetle epidemic

Besides labour strife, the B.C. government and its citizens had to deal with the continuing impact of the mountain pine beetle on the forests of the province. As the year closed, the B.C. government expected to advertise 300,000 cubic metres of salvage timber for sale in an effort to control the beetle infestation (*Province*, 9 Dec.). As noted above, the government reported that the spread of the pine beetle infestation in 2003 included four million hectares, about the size of Denmark and double the amount of 2002 (*Vancouver Sun*, 1 Dec.).

Moreover, the B.C. pine beetle epidemic was recognized by NASA scientist Chris Potter as one of the biggest North American ecosystem disturbances ever observed (*Vancouver Sun*, 18 Dec.). According to Potter, the infestation had been visible from satellite images since 1998 and should be considered a possible cause of greenhouse-gas levels. Potter explained: 'In the northern hemisphere, it is what looks to be the biggest warming-drying event' (*Vancouver Sun*, 18 Dec.). Insects contribute to an increase in carbon-dioxide levels by killing plants and trees. However, others, including UBC forest sciences professor Bart van der Kamp, suggested that while pine beetles are indeed responsible for increasing carbon dioxide, 'it is smaller than what you would get from a fire that size' (*Vancouver Sun*, 18 Dec.).

At the same time that the forest industry, government, and citizens were becoming increasingly concerned about the pine beetle plague, a report from the Sierra Club came to light which explained that the B.C. Forest Service had been gutted. Ben Parfitt and Kerri Garner examined the number of jobs cut from the provincial ministry of forests – 800 over three years including 304 scientific technical officers (*Vancouver Sun*, 4 Dec.). Moreover, the report compared the human resources to manage forests in British Columbia with those of the U.S. Forest Service. It found that each Forest Service employee in the United States is responsible for managing a forest area equivalent to five and a half Stanley Parks while each Forest Service employee in British Columbia is responsible for managing a forest area equivalent to forty-five Stanley Parks (*Vancouver Sun*, 4 Dec.), a considerable difference.

Avian flu epidemic

Another epidemic, that of the avian flu virus, had its origins on a Matsqui farm on 19 February. It quickly spread to twenty-three nearby farms in the Fraser valley, the centre of the $1-billion poultry industry in British Columbia (*Toronto Star*, 10 April). The Fraser valley outbreak was believed to have originated with wild ducks that are carriers but not necessarily affected by the avian flu (ibid.). As a result of the avian flu, the industry expected to see layoffs of over 5,000 employees along with some secondary job losses related to the transport and sale of the birds (ibid.). It was expected to take six months for poultry farmers to resume their operations. The strain known as H7 was not as deadly as the H5N1 strain which killed about two dozen people in Asia earlier in the year. Ailments were limited to a few Fraser valley poultry workers who got sick with the flu and conjunctivitis.

As a result of the avian flu, it was estimated that some nineteen million domestic birds, including chickens, ducks, turkeys, and geese, would have to be slaughtered (*Edmonton Journal*, 17 April). Those birds that tested negative for the virus would be put into the food chain (*Toronto Star*, 10 April). Disposal of the birds was not without controversy. Protesters opposed to the dumping of chicken carcasses at an interior landfill at Cache Creek blockaded the entrance to the facility. Cache Creek mayor John Ranta and Ashcroft Mayor Andy Kormendy had warned that citizens might blockade the facility since it was not equipped to deal with hazardous waste (*Kimberley Daily Bulletin*, 13 April). The blockade closed the dump site for seven hours (*Vancouver Sun*, 14 April).

Following this blockade, John van Dongen, the minister of agriculture, said that landfills would be used only as a last resort. He made the announcement after holding a meeting with thirty mayors and government officials in Abbotsford (*Edmonton Journal*, 17 April). Other options included disposal on government land, private property, unused barns, and open-air gravel pits.

In June, the federal government stated that it would pay $60 million to B.C. farmers to compensate them for losses due to the avian flu epidemic. Only farmers who lost chickens would be compensated (*Trail Times*, 9 June).

Politician theft caught on camera

While poultry farmers suffered huge setbacks in April, a well-known local MP was involved in his own tragic incident. Svend Robinson, then NDP MP for Burnaby-Douglas, stole a diamond ring from an auction market. The auctioneer valued the ring at $64,000 while the RCMP set its worth at $21,500. Robinson was caught on camera and charged with theft of a diamond ring (*National Post*, 22 June). He decided not to run in the federal election. Bill Siksay, his former assistant, ran in his place and won the seat.

Robinson pleaded guilty to the charge and the crown prosecutor, Len Doust, claimed that Robinson turned himself in only because he knew he had been caught. A provincial court judge handed Robinson a con-

The 38th Federal Election – Results for British Columbia

Party	Seats	Popular Vote*
Liberal	8	28.6%
Conservative	22	36.3%
NDP	5	26.5%
Green	0	6.4%
Independent	1	
Total	36	

* Popular vote percentages available only for the major parties.
Source: CTV News, Election 2004, http://www.ctv.ca/mini/election2004/.

ditional sentence with no criminal record and 100 hours of community service. At year's end there was some speculation that Robinson would return to his law career. In the meantime, he worked for the B.C. Government Employees' Union (BCGEU) on some grievance files (*Toronto Star*, 26 Dec.).

Federal election

The 38th federal election took place on 28 June 2004. Once again, the results were decided before residents in British Columbia had finished voting. The Liberals won a minority government and a fourth straight mandate. In British Columbia, the Conservatives lost six seats while the Liberals gained two and the NDP also gained two. One independent, Chuck Cadman, was elected. He had previously been elected to the Canadian Alliance Party but had lost his nomination bid and opted to run as an independent.

Paul Martin's Liberals had appointed several 'star' candidates to run in British Columbia including former NDP premier Ujjal Dosanjh, union president David Haggard, Bill Cunningham, president of the B.C. wing of the federal Liberals, former forestry executive David Emerson, and community activist Shirley Chan (*Globe and Mail*, 8 May). Of these, Dosanjh and Emerson were successful. The loss by Cunningham was a particular surprise since he challenged the NDP candidate Bill Siksay, who ran in Svend Robinson's former seat after Robinson admitted to stealing jewellery at an auction. The Liberals also won the Esquimalt-Juan de Fuca riding with Keith Martin, who had previously run as a Reform and Alliance member.

Tobacco damages and earthquake assessments

In May two political events occurred that addressed British Columbians' quality of life, one surrounding tobacco control and the other regarding earthquake assessments for schools. The B.C. Court of Appeal ruled that the Tobacco Damages and Health Care Recovery Costs Act, which the Supreme Court of the province had struck down, was constitutionally valid (*Daily News*, 20 May). British Columbia was pursuing a $10-billion claim, based on the estimate that treating B.C. residents for smoking-related illnesses costs $500 million annually (*Star-Phoenix*, 22 May).

Furthermore, British Columbia allocated $2 million to assess school risks from earthquakes, with upgrades to follow (*Times-Colonist*, 29 May). Tracy Monk's organization and the B.C. Confederation of Parent Advisory Councils pushed for a ten- to fifteen-year upgrade of all schools and were successful in having the Liberal government agree to assessments for schools to determine their earthquake risks.

British Columbia and Alberta cooperate on trade issues

May was a busy month for the B.C. Liberals as the Alberta and B.C. cabinets also held a joint meeting. The two provinces signed off on eight issues including harmonizing environmental and energy regulations, sharing medical facilities during emergencies and times of extremely heavy use, increasing cooperation in the development of distance-learning programs, and creating better information systems for highway travellers between the two provinces (*Vancouver Sun*, 27 May). Among the other issues discussed during the five-hour joint cabinet meeting was the need to develop the Prince Rupert corridor as a port for Alberta's goods and a gateway to the far east (ibid.). The B.C. premier also promised that Alberta would have a say regarding B.C. Hydro's plans to develop new hydroelectric facilities on the Peace River.

B.C. Rail

In July the B.C. government's transportation minister, Kevin Falcon, announced that the deal to sell B.C. Rail to CN Rail for $1 billion was finalized (*Province*, 15 July). The government would use some of the $1 billion to pay off a $500-million B.C. Rail debt (*Vancouver Sun*, 15 July). The deal was not without controversy, including a police investigation regarding two aides, one to the finance minister and the other to the former transportation minister, Judith Reid. Charges against the aides, David Basi and Robert Virk, included breach of trust and fraud and were laid in December. Moreover, CN Rail announced that it would cut a third of the unionized workforce, resulting in job losses of 400 (*Vancouver Sun*, 30 July).

Safe Streets Act

In late October, the B.C. Liberal government closed the legislative session by making Bill 71 law (*Vancouver Sun*, 27 Oct.). B.C. Liberal MLA Lorne Mayencourt had introduced a bill to outlaw 'aggressive panhandlers and squeegee kids' a year earlier. The Safe Streets Act makes squeegeeing for money, aggressive panhandling, and soliciting cash at captive sites such as bank machines against the law. The law defines aggressive behaviour as including obstructing someone's path, using abusive language, following somebody, physically approaching someone in a group of two or more people, or continuing to solicit somebody after he or she has already declined to give money. In order to commit these offences, a panhandler would have to be within five metres of a person being solicited (ibid.).

The law did not immediately go into effect since Attorney General Geoff Plant desired to consult with police, the Union of B.C. Municipalities, the Safe Streets Coalition, and anyone who wanted to provide input in developing the regulations, specifically the penalties (ibid.). NDP members Joy MacPhail and Jenny Kwan voted against the bill, as did Paul Nettleton, an independent. Kwan argued that the bill was a 'publicity stunt' and that the activities specified were already addressed under municipal by-laws and the Criminal Code (ibid.).

Offshore oil and gas development

As the year closed, the B.C. premier explained that he was optimistic regarding the possibility of oil and gas development off the Queen Charlotte Basin. He said that the Priddle Report on the issue was only 'passingly interesting,' that British Columbia was still building the knowledge-base on offshore development, and that the federal government was willing to work with the province on the issue (*Times-Colonist*, 12 Dec.).

The Priddle Report, authored by Roland Priddle, former chair of the National Energy Board, was released in November and offered two main findings. First, 75 per cent of people who made submissions to the panel wanted the moratorium on offshore oil and gas exploration to remain in place. Second, the report suggested that views were polarized and there was not 'a ready basis for any kind of public policy compromise' (*Times-Colonist*, 23 Nov.).

It appeared that offshore oil and gas might become a federal election issue as Federal Environment Minister and Victoria MP David Anderson sent letters to Liberal candidates indicating that the party supported the thirty-three-year moratorium on offshore oil and gas drilling in the province (*Nelson Daily News*, 20 May). Anderson explained that the moratorium would stay until 'knowledge gaps on the risks involved, the resources at stake and the economic and social factors that might have a bearing on the decision are filled' (*Vancouver Sun*, 29 May). Premier Campbell dismissed the letter, noting that he had spoken with cabinet ministers and the prime minster and that they were encouraging concerning offshore oil and gas (*Daily Townsman*, 18 May).

For their part, the Coastal First Nations noted that, until efforts are made to include their meaningful participation, the moratorium must stay. The Coastal First Nations include Wuikinuxv Nation, Heiltsuk, Kitasoo/Xaixais, Gitga'at, Haisla, Metlakatla, Old Massett, Skidegate, and Council of the Haida Nation (*Prince Rupert Daily News*, 18 May).

Forestry

New forest regulations were passed in 2004. The Forest and Range Practices Act replaced the Forest Practices Code. These results-based regulations reduced the paperwork related to the regulations to 500 pages from over a metre high (*Alberni Valley Times*, 27 Jan.). The regulations shifted accountability for forest management and environmental protection from government to companies and the foresters who work for them (*Vancouver Sun*, 24 Jan.). The chief forester, Larry Pedersen, noted that greater accountability would now be placed on the licence holder. The forest industry lauded the new regulations while environmental groups argued that companies now had license to do what they want on the lands. For example, West Coast Environmental Law's Jessica Clog expressed concern that environmental objectives were to be achieved 'without unduly affecting the timber supply' (*Vancouver Sun*, 24 Jan.). The chief forester explained that forest companies must present plans as to how they will achieve objectives and the forests ministry now has the ability to step in to prevent damage from happening, which it could not do under the old code (ibid.). The forest industry did not speculate on how much money would be saved as a result of the reduced paperwork burden. The old code was to remain in effect until 31 December 2005, when companies were required to complete their transition to the new regulations.

Citizens' Assembly on Electoral Reform

The Citizens' Assembly on Electoral Reform issued its final report in December, after holding fifty public hearings and receiving 1,603 written submissions. The Citizens' Assembly was an independent, non-partisan, representative group of British Columbia citizens who were randomly selected for the purpose of learning the values, hopes, and desires that should underlie the electoral system in British Columbia and recommending an electoral system for the province to adopt. An electoral system translates votes into seats. The Citizens' Assembly recommended what it called the British Columbia – Single Transferable Vote (BC STV), a form of proportional representation.

In its press release the assembly explained: 'A main feature of this "single transferable vote" (STV) system is that rather than marking an "X" beside one name, voters number candidates from most favourite to least favourite (1,2,3,4, etc.). If a voter's favourite candidate is not elected, or has more votes than are needed to be elected, then the voter's vote is moved to his or her next most favourite candidate (#2). The vote is transferred rather than wasted. The aim of this system is to make all votes count.' Furthermore, the assembly suggested that this system offered effective local representation and greater voter choice and incorporated the values of fair election results. Voters were scheduled to vote on the new electoral system in the provincial election to be held on 15 May 2005. If approved by the voters, the government was to introduce legislation so that the 2009 election would use the BC STV system.

Economy

The economy was a good news story for British Columbia in 2004. There were gains in tourism, improvements in the technology sector, and significant increases in GDP and disposal income per capita. Retail sales also increased considerably over the previous year.

Tourism rose 28 per cent, to 667,000 visitors, during the first nine months of 2004 compared with the same period the previous year (*Vancouver Sun*, 17 Dec.). Tourism B.C. President Rod Harris pointed to re-emerging Asia-Pacific economies, strong foreign currencies, and greater comfort about international travel since the SARS scare of the previous year. In particular, numbers from Japan (45 per cent increase), Taiwan (69 per cent increase), and China (28 per cent increase) were strong. However, U.S. travel to British Columbia dropped 0.2 per cent during the first three quarters of the year, while European travel increased 12 per cent. U.S. travel was affected by security issues and the rising Canadian dollar.

In the technology sector, the slump that began in 2001 appeared to end in 2004. According to B.C. Stats, GDP in the tech sector was up 2.9 per cent or $838 million during the first quarter of 2004 compared with the last quarter of 2003 (*Vancouver Sun*, 26 Jan. 2005). Things started improving in 2003 and 2004 showed strong growth, with figures of $1.7 billion in the first quarter, a $160-million gain over the same quarter in 2003. In particular, an increase in revenues in the high-tech manufacturing sector was encouraging, as revenues totalled $557 million in the first quarter of 2004, an almost 10 per cent increase over the last quarter of the year before. As the year closed, Ipsos-Reid conducted a poll suggesting that industry executives were optimistic about the future: 55 per cent of technology-company CEOs believed that the sector would be doing better by late 2005, up from 13 per cent in 2003.

In November, Labour Minister Graham Bruce expressed 'a little bit of excitement' as the unemployment rate in B.C. dropped to 6.4 per cent, the lowest since 1981 (*Vancouver Sun*, 4 Dec.). Statistics Canada cautioned that some of the decrease in the rate was due to people leaving the workforce. Since the beginning of 2004, the number of jobs overall had grown by 1 per cent. Labour economist Rosalyn Kunin explained: 'The economy has made a spectacular turnaround in the past year or so. The economy is doing better than it has for the past 10 years' (ibid.). She pointed to residential construction and recent investments in mining and resources in addition to job growth from the Olympics, including the convention centre, the RAV line, and the Sea-to-Sky Highway.

GDP for 2004 was up and at its highest rates since 2000 for several indicators, including GDP at market prices, up 8.3 per cent over the previous year, and GDP per capita, up 7.4 per cent from 2003 (*Statistics Canada*, 2008). Moreover, disposable income per capita was up 5.1 per cent over the previous year, and also at its highest since 2000.

As the year closed, consumer confidence was high, evidenced by strong holiday retail sales leading to a 7 per cent overall increase in B.C. retail purchases in 2004 or $45 billion in sales for the year (*Vancouver Sun*, 14 Jan. 2005).

Alberta

The year 2004 was uncharacteristically busy for Alberta's citizens, as they were called to vote not once, not twice, but three times in federal, municipal, and provincial elections. With the possible exception of the municipal election in the city of Edmonton, none of the elections returned especially surprising results. Nevertheless, each had its own particular twists and turns, and each had implications for the way politics would unfold in the province over the next few years.

The federal election: Paul Martin's Alberta dreams

By the end of 2004, it was hard to imagine that as the year dawned, Prime Minister Paul Martin had dreams of establishing a significant Liberal presence in Alberta. Martin's ascendancy to the Liberal leadership and prime minister's position in late 2003 had re-energized Alberta's federal Liberals, since his record of fiscal responsibility during his tenure as finance minister was popular in the province. Consequently, Martin was successful in attracting some relatively high-profile candidates to seek election under the Liberal banner. The biggest coup was Ken Nicol, who abruptly stepped down as leader of the provincial party in January to seek the Liberal Party nomination in Lethbridge. Edmonton Ellerslie MLA Debby Carlson left provincial politics to run for the Liberals in the competitive Edmonton Strathcona district. Doug Faulkner, the mayor of Fort McMurray, ran for the party in the northern district of Athabasca.

Although the Liberals were successful in attracting high-quality candidates, the improved prospects for the party meant that Martin and the Liberals waded into some messy nomination contests. Carlson narrowly defeated Jonathan Dai for the Strathcona nomination, amid allegations that some of Dai's supporters were unable to cast votes in the contest. In Edmonton East, Martin appointed John Bethel as the candidate, sparing Bethel a nomination showdown with former Liberal

MLA and former provincial leadership aspirant Sine Chadi, a move that angered Chadi and his supporters. These stories, however, were minor compared to the mess in Calgary South Centre where Julia Turnbull had quit her job as a lawyer and had been campaigning for two years for the 2004 election. The Liberals asked Turnbull to step aside so that Martin could appoint former Calgary police chief Christine Silverberg to the nomination. Turnbull refused to step aside and Silverberg ultimately decided not to seek the nomination. These incidents made Martin and the Liberal Party appear heavy-handed and violated the tradition of local party democracy at the electoral district association level.

The early hopes for the Liberal Party in Alberta soon evaporated as Martin and his government became increasingly mired in the sponsorship scandal. As it became clear that the federal election would not be the easy romp to a majority government the Liberals first envisioned, the party shifted its focus to shoring up its electoral base in Ontario and Quebec; incremental gains in Alberta became a lower priority. Meanwhile, the newly created Conservative Party of Canada coalesced around the leadership of Calgary's Stephen Harper. Because the Progressive Conservative vote had largely collapsed in Alberta with the creation of the Reform Party in 1993, the transition at the local level from the Canadian Alliance to the Conservative Party of Canada was relatively seamless. The Conservatives were thus campaigning from a position of strength.

Although the Conservative dominance in Alberta made the June federal election a relatively low-key affair in the province, the final days of the federal campaign saw Alberta leap to national prominence. At issue was the news that Alberta would announce a dramatic overhaul of its health-care system two days after the federal election. The reforms, Premier Ralph Klein had warned, might put Alberta at odds with the Canada Health Act. Prime Minister Martin seized on the news and accused Klein and Harper of having some sort of secret plot to dismantle health care. Although the provincial government quickly backpedalled from the proposed reforms, the issue put Harper and the federal Conservatives on the defensive during a period in the campaign that saw the party losing ground after being ahead in the polls. Many federal Conservative activists were angry at Klein for the intervention, accusing him of ultimately costing them the election.

In the end, the election results in Alberta were almost identical to those of 2000. Despite the bright early prospects, the Liberals only managed to re-elect the two MPs they returned in 2000: David Kilgour and Anne McLellan. The Liberals' vote share was 22 per cent (up only slightly from the 20.9 per cent they earned in 2000). None of the party's high-profile recruits managed to win seats. The Conservatives, meanwhile, romped to victory, taking almost 62 per cent of the vote and the other twenty-six seats from Alberta. Although the NDP did not win a seat, the party increased its vote share from 5.4 per cent to 9.5 per cent. The other interesting story on election night was the performance of the Green Party, which took an astonishing 6.1 per cent of the vote, the party's second- best performance in any province in Canada.

As usual after a federal Liberal Party victory, many in Alberta were frustrated with the election result, since the overwhelming majority of Albertans had voted Conservative in a bid to change the government. There was some comfort for these voters in that they had at least contributed to reducing Martin to a minority government. They wondered, however, what it would take to finish the job.

The municipal elections: change in Edmonton, chaos in Calgary

After a welcome summer respite from the campaign trail, attention turned to the province's municipal elections, held on 18 October. Edmonton provided most of the drama, as incumbent mayor Bill Smith sought a fourth term as mayor. Smith faced two primary challengers. Former city councillor Robert Noce was taking his second stab at unseating Smith, having finished second to him in 2001. Stephen Mandel, who had been elected as a Ward 1 councillor in 2001, also challenged Smith. Throughout the campaign, Mandel faced an uphill battle; he was the last of the challengers to declare his candidacy and trailed Smith and Noce in polls during the election. Nevertheless, Edmonton voters warmed to his combination of fiscal conservatism and emphasis on smart social spending. In the end, Mandel won a stunning victory, taking 41 per cent of the vote compared to 33 per cent for Smith and 25 per cent for Noce.

The close race in Edmonton was in sharp contrast to the mayoral contest in Calgary, where incumbent Dave Bronconnier won 79 per cent of the vote; his nearest competitor took only 5 per cent. The only real surprise of the night came in Ward 10, where two-term incumbent Diane Danielson was defeated by Margot Aftergood in a close contest. The Ward 10 results were thrown into question two days after the election when city election officials asked police to investigate possible fraud. Over 1,200 mail-in ballots for Ward 10, intended for voters who would be gone on election day, were sent to the same post office box. Aftergood admitted her campaign requested the ballots, but noted that they were never counted. She continued to insist that her campaign had done nothing wrong. Aftergood was sworn in as an alderman, but she received a cold reception from most of her new City Council colleagues, many of whom were donating money to support Danielson's legal challenge of the results. The police investigation even led to the seizure of a computer at the home of Calgary MLA Hung Pham. Although there were no indications that Pham had any personal involvement in the scandal, the investigation raised further questions about ties between the Aftergood campaign (particularly David Aftergood, Margot Aftergood's husband) and the provincial Conservatives. Lawyers for the city, Aftergood, and Danielson were gearing up for a legal showdown when the city reached a settlement with Aftergood at the end of November. She agreed to resign her seat in return for the city paying some of her legal bills. Although the settlement dealt with the more immediate question of the Ward 10 election, it left many Calgarians wondering how such abuse of the electoral process was possible. City Council asked the province to hold a public inquiry, but the province opted for a scaled-down investigation into the Ward 10 affair, raising questions about whether the Aftergood's Conservative ties led the party to be scared of what a public inquiry might uncover. Premier Klein insisted, however, that cost was the major reason for the decision not to pursue a public inquiry. Regardless, both the investigation and the Ward 10 by-election would be held in 2005.

Fort McMurray also saw a shake-up as Councillor Melissa Blake defeated incumbent mayor Doug Faulkner, who had unsuccessfully run for the Liberals in the federal election. In other Alberta communities, the election results were far less dramatic. In Lethbridge, Mayor Bob Tarleck won a second term, as did Medicine Hat's Garth Valley. Morris Flewwelling became mayor of Red Deer after four-term incumbent Gail Surkan chose not to seek another term.

The provincial election: referendum on Ralph Klein

The ink was barely dry on the municipal election results when on 25 October Premier Klein, after three years in office, called an election for 25 November. This election call was a deviation from the usual cycle of spring elections every four years. The Conservatives justified the early election call by claiming they did not want a provincial election during the province's centennial celebrations in 2005. When calling the election, Klein framed the election in terms that would be very familiar to any Alberta premier: Albertans needed a strong provincial government to stand up to an intrusive federal government. The campaign was also noteworthy in that Klein had indicated that this would be the final election of his political career.

Despite the Conservatives' attempt to run a safe, 'boring' campaign, as Klein described it (*Calgary Herald*, 30 Oct.), campaign events quickly went in a different direction. In the first week of the campaign, the premier complained about abuses to the Assured Income for the Severely Handicapped (AISH) program, noting that two women who had been complaining to him about the low levels of AISH benefits did not appear handicapped to him. The story quickly became Klein's apparent insensitivity to the plight of AISH recipients and his lack of awareness that some disabilities are not readily apparent. Klein backtracked from those remarks, but this early campaign event quickly turned the election into a referendum on Ralph Klein and his personality.

Klein's larger-than-life persona had been central to the Conservative government and its electoral success since he became premier in 1992. However, since his 2001 re-election, there had been signs that his folksy charm was not what it used to be. In late 2001 he had made a drunken visit to a homeless shelter where he berated its residents. In May 2004 Klein made his first ever appearance before the legislature's Public Accounts Committee in order to answer questions about the cabinet's travel habits. While there, he complained that the Liberals were accusing him of lying when they asked for receipts for some travel expenses. These were taken as signs that Klein was increasingly out of touch with public opinion and not interested in transparent and accountable government. His offhanded remarks during the campaign simply added to these fears.

Things on the campaign trail got worse for Klein on a personal level when he had to leave the campaign for a couple of days to tend to his mother, who had been taken off life support and was dying in a Calgary hospital. Deputy premier Shirley McLellan stepped in to fill in for the premier on his scheduled campaign stops. After a few days to deal with this family crisis, Klein returned to the campaign trail.

Part of the reason the election focused so heavily on Klein's personality was that the Conservatives had little in the way of policy initiatives to announce. The party was banking on the province's robust economy and healthy fiscal position as the key to re-election. This let the opposition parties take some of the policy initiative and kept all of the attention on Klein and his quirky personality. Despite the fact that the Conservatives seemed poorly prepared for the campaign, they enjoyed a significant advantage in being the incumbent party and being able to outspend significantly all of the other parties combined in Alberta's largely unregulated system of campaign and political party finance.

For their part, the Liberals were led in this campaign by Kevin Taft, who had become leader after Ken Nicol made the jump to federal politics. The Liberals announced a fairly detailed set of policies, including the elimination of health-care premiums, diverting 35 per cent of annual surpluses to the Heritage Savings and Trust Fund, reforms to municipal taxation, the transformation of Calgary's Mount Royal College into a university, and a package of democratic reforms, including fixed election dates and a citizens' assembly on electoral reform. Although not as flamboyant as Klein, Taft waged a reasonably effective campaign with limited resources.

The New Democratic Party was led by Brian Mason, campaigning in his first election as party leader. The NDP promised the elimination of health-care premiums, increased spending on health care and education, a province-wide prescription-drug purchasing plan, and a revamped energy royalty system that would increase the province's share of oil and gas revenue.

A number of smaller parties also contested the election. The newest entrant was the Alberta Alliance, the latest in several parties trying to outflank the governing Conservatives on the right. The Alliance was led by Randy Thorsteinson, who in the 1997 election, as leader of Social Credit, had led that party to an impressive finish, with almost 7 per cent of the vote. Thorsteinson's Alliance fielded a complete slate of eighty-three candidates. The Alberta Greens fielded forty-nine candidates in an effort to promote environmental causes in the province.

On 22 November, voting day, there was not much doubt that the Conservatives would win the election. There were only two questions about the election results. The first had to do with how many voters would actually show up at the polls. In the end, only 44.7 per cent of registered voters bothered to cast a ballot in the election, a result that surpassed the previous record low of 47.25 per cent in 1986. Undoubtedly, after three elections in one year, voter fatigue was a factor, but several observers interpreted this low turnout as a sign that many Conservative supporters were frustrated with the direction of the government but could not bring themselves to support an opposition party.

The second question was how large the Conservatives' margin of victory would be. As the election results rolled in, it quickly became apparent that this election would not be a repeat of 2001, when the Conservatives absolutely crushed the opposition. The NDP took just over 10 per cent of the vote (up from 8 per cent in 2001) and doubled its seat total to four by taking two additional seats in Edmonton, including one by former leader Ray Martin. The Liberals more than doubled their seat performance in 2001, taking sixteen seats. The Liberals' popular vote, however, was up only 2 per cent over their total in 2001. They retook some of the seats they had lost in Edmonton in 2001 and retained their seat in Lethbridge East, but the most encouraging sign for the party was that it had managed to establish a beachhead in Calgary, taking three seats. Harry Chase took Calgary Varsity, radio personality Dave Taylor took Calgary Currie, and David Swann, the former chief medical officer of Medicine Hat, who had been fired from that position in 2002 for his public support of the Kyoto Accord, took Calgary-Mountain View. The Alberta Alliance took close to 9 per cent of the vote and elected Paul Hinman in Cardston-Taber-Warner.

The losses blunted the celebration for the Conservatives in what would have been considered a remarkable landslide in almost any other province. The Conservatives took sixty-two seats with 47 per cent of the vote. Although victorious, the party had dropped more than 15 per cent of the vote and lost twelve seats. The party had lost votes and one seat to the Alliance in the rural areas, where that party performed very well. The Liberals and the NDP took vote share and seats in the urban areas. The government looked for answers. One issue that had come up during the campaign had been the relative lack of availability and affordability of post-secondary education in Alberta, a situation that drew criticism from students, parents, and the province's business community. The fact that the losses in Calgary had come in districts with or near post-secondary education institutions reinforced the perception of the government's vulnerability on that issue. Inevitably, though, the result raised questions about Premier Klein's leadership. In the past, his populist persona had helped to carry the party to victory; the campaign and results of the 2004 election suggested that his personality was becoming a liability. Late in the campaign, Klein had signed a pledge that he would stay on as premier until 2008 but would not take the party into the next election. Election night on 2004 marked the unofficial start of the race to replace him.

Dar Heatherington's trial and its aftermath

Besides the string of elections, one of the events that held the province's attention in 2004 was the trial and sentencing of Lethbridge alderman Dar Heatherington, who had made national headlines in 2003 when she disappeared during a civic visit to Great Falls, Montana. Heatherington was later found in Las Vegas, claiming she had been drugged and sexually assaulted. Under questioning from Great Falls police, she later admitted to having lied about the incident. After returning to Lethbridge, police there charged her with public mischief for events preceding her trip to Montana.

The trial began in late January and heard details of a series of increasingly sexually explicit letters that Heatherington claimed she received from a stalker. The court heard that police had become frustrated with the fact that, despite extensive surveillance of the Heatherington residence, they never managed to catch the alleged stalker dropping off the letters. Heatherinton's story unravelled further when she later told a police detective that she had lied about the letters and when evidence from Heatherington's computer showed fragments of correspondence that resembled the letters from the stalker. For its part, the defence alleged that her husband, Dave Heatherington, was the author of the letters, but that the police did not carry its investigation far enough to uncover the truth.

On 29 June, provincial court judge Peter Caffaro found Heatherington guilty of the charge of public mischief and ordered her to undergo psychiatric evaluation prior to her sentencing on 10 September. According to the province's Municipal Government Act, an elected municipal government official convicted of a crime that carries a sentence of five or more years must immediately resign; a public mischief charge carries with it a maximum sentence of five years. Heatherington initially refused to resign her seat. On 9 August, however, she abruptly did so, saying that the time she needed to devote to clearing her name would render her unable to carry out her duties as alderman. On 10 September, the judge sentenced Heatherington to twenty months, eight of which would be served as house arrest and the last twelve under strict curfew conditions. Heatherington was also ordered to seek counselling and perform community service.

Although this appeared to be the end of the story, Heatherington's case simply would not recede from the public eye. On 8 October, Heatherington filed her appeal of her conviction at the provincial court. Later that month, there were allegations that Heatherington had violated the conditions of her house arrest. In mid-December, she was back in court to face those charges, where the court heard that maintaining the conditions of her house arrest was taxing the resources of her probation officer. The hearing on the alleged breaching of her house-arrest conditions would continue in early January, guaranteeing that this story would make news in another calendar year.

The BSE crisis enters year two

Another story that began in 2003 but carried through the year was the BSE (bovine spongiform encephalopathy) or mad cow crisis. In May 2003 the Canadian beef industry was shattered when it was announced that a Canadian Black Angus cow from Alberta had tested positive for BSE. Almost immediately, the United States shut the border to all Canadian beef and live cattle imports. Given the close integration of the two countries' industries, the American import ban devastated the Canadian beef industry. As the centre of Canadian beef production, Alberta felt the impact of the BSE crisis most profoundly. Prices for cattle plummeted, with a ripple effect through the agricultural economy of the province. Provincial and federal compensation packages helped to sustain the industry, but ultimately the focus was on convincing the United States to reopen the border. The United States had allowed the resumption of imports of boneless meat from young cattle but was still not allowing live cattle from Canada to be imported into the country.

Shortly before Christmas 2003, it appeared that the Americans had discovered their own case of mad cow disease in a dairy cow in Washington. Early in January 2004, however, it was confirmed that the dairy cow had in fact originated in Alberta and had been exported to Washington. This announcement set back the progress towards reopening the border and reinforced the perceptions that Alberta's beef industry was rife with BSE and that imports of Canadian cattle into the United States were increasing the vulnerability of the American industry to the disease. The net impact was that the United States would not accept Canadian cattle for 2004.

This development continued to hurt Alberta's cattle industry. Ranchers were facing a horrendous combination of large herds with no markets and dwindling income because of the low prices. This was demonstrated in a concrete way in two high-profile seizures of cattle by the Alberta Society for the Prevention of Cruelty to Animals. The organization had to intervene to rescue hundreds of neglected cattle in two separate ranches.

The question of what to do to get cattle moving across the border again was front and centre in the province. Many, including Premier Klein in mid-January, suggested that Alberta might have to institute a system of mandatory testing of all cattle for BSE in an effort to restore confidence in Alberta's beef industry. Such a move was steadfastly resisted by many officials and by industry, who argued that this would be prohibitively expensive and unnecessary, given the low risk of any given cow being infected by BSE and the even slimmer chance that this could be transmitted to the human population.

As the crisis dragged on, more and more questions were being raised about Alberta's beef industry and the province's response to the crisis. One question centred on what to do with the glut of cattle awaiting shipment to markets. Simply put, there was not enough slaughtering capacity to deal with the millions of cattle. Many in industry proposed a massive cull of older cattle. Others suggested the development of new slaughterhouses and packing plants in Alberta, but investors were reluctant to risk building plants that might be uncompetitive once the border reopened. There were also questions over why beef prices in Canadian grocery stores remained high, even though ranchers were getting record low returns for their cattle. This led to suggestions that meatpackers were engaged in illegal behaviour such as price fixing or were making windfall profits on the backs of ranchers and consumers. The biggest question of all was who had benefited from the millions of dollars in bailouts given by the provincial and federal governments: ranchers or packing plants. Although both packers and the provincial government insisted that the bailouts kept the industry alive, Agriculture Minister Shirley McClellan bowed to public pressure and asked Provincial Auditor General Fred Dunn to expedite his audit of the bailout programs. On 3 August, Dunn reported that the BSE crisis led packers' profits to almost triple. Dunn also concluded that the bailout program may have contributed to the huge industry profits by encouraging more farmers to get their cattle to market, contributing to a decline in prices. He did, however, clear the packing industry of doing anything wrong, saying that it simply responded to market conditions. Dunn also concluded that the packers received a reasonable share of the bailout program, given their stake in the industry. The report raised some serious questions about how well the aid program was conceived and administered and led McClellan to promise that the government would never repeat that mistake again (*Calgary Herald*, 4 Aug.).

Ultimately, the resolution of the crisis lay with the United States government. For most of the year, progress on this front was slow, largely because of the vagaries of the U.S. presidential election. The beef industry got a brief ray of hope on 30 April when U.S. President George W. Bush met with Prime Minister Martin and publicly committed his administration to ending the ban on Canadian beef imports. President Bush stressed his commitment to free trade, which distinguished him from the more protectionist sentiment among the Democrats in the United States. In fact, Senator John Kerry, the Democratic nominee for the presidency, had signed his name to a letter calling for the border to remain closed to Canadian beef imports. Despite the president's commitment, there was little concrete action. By the end of the year, however, the situation improved dramatically. In October, Japan announced that it would likely start accepting beef imports from the United States in 2005, removing one of the major roadblocks to reopening the border. The best news of all came out of a mid-November summit meeting between President Bush and Prime Minister Martin, when President Bush announced that he would begin the regulatory process to reopen the border. On 29 December, the U.S. Department of Agriculture announced that it would be lifting the ban on Canadian cattle imports and that cattle could be flowing across the border as soon as March. Canadian ranchers reacted with cautious optimism, but there was still a lingering concern that court actions by protectionist groups in the United States could delay the border opening. Furthermore, on 30 December, another suspected case of BSE was discovered in a ten-year-old Alberta dairy cow. Although officials argued that it should not derail the reopening of the border, Alberta ranchers could be forgiven for feeling somewhat nervous about their future.

The legislature

The provincial legislature sat for only one sitting, lasting from February through May in 2004. Because of the provincial election, there was no fall sitting of the legislature. This may have been just as well, since the government had little in the way of new legislation to propose in the session. The opposition Liberals were also somewhat preoccupied as their ranks were depleted owing to the decisions of Nicol and Carlson to run in the federal election and a leadership-selection process that saw Kevin Taft crowned as leader in March. The Throne Speech had little new to announce, other than increased spending and the opening of a new Alberta government office in Washington, D.C.

On 24 March, provincial Finance Minister Pat Nelson unveiled the budget. The province's booming oil revenues meant that the government could direct some more money to the provincial debt, which would be reduced to $2.7 billion by the end of the 2005–6 fiscal year. The budget's projections of energy pricing, critical to predicting provincial government revenue, were very conservative, however, leading many to predict that the province would eliminate the accumulated debt by the province's centennial celebration in 2005. Other than that, there were few exciting announcements in the budget. The budget contained modest cuts in corporate taxation rates and increased spending for the Learning Ministry and the Health Ministry, as well as some funding for capital projects.

With little in the way of legislative initiatives, the opposition had some opportunities to seize the agenda, and they did so on two fronts. The first was the debate over the BSE compensation packages. NDP MLA Brian Mason went after the government over the effectiveness of the programs and potential profit taking by packing companies. As discussed earlier, the government ultimately had to call the auditor general to investigate. The second was the use of government aircraft by the premier and other cabinet ministers that led to Klein's infamous appearance before the Public Accounts Committee in May.

One of the more noteworthy episodes started as a debate over automobile insurance and ended up raising questions about the autonomy of the province's universities from political interference. The Conservatives announced a plan that would see insurance rates cut by 5 per cent overall. The opposition parties called for a government-run insurance program, such as the ones in place in neighbouring British Columbia and Saskatchewan. In the legislature, Premier Klein compared this proposal to Chilean President Salvador Allende's nationalization of mining in 1973, which led to a coup by General Augusto Pinochet. Faced with criticism of his insensitivity towards a brutal period in Chile's history, the premier tabled a term paper he had written for a course he was completing by correspondence from Athabasca University. What had started as an offhand remark turned into a question about Klein's academic honesty when it became apparent that passages from the paper bore a striking resemblance to text on the Internet, raising charges of plagiarism against the premier. Learning Minister Lyle Oberg called up the presidents of Alberta's four universities to discuss matters that arose from the incident, including confidentiality of student records and academic freedom. In the phone calls, he also asked the presidents to write letters supporting the premier's commitment to lifelong learning. This led Alberta's opposition leaders to call for Oberg's resignation, charging that he bullied officials from institutions that were heavily dependent on provincial government funding.

In August, the province received the report from the MLA Committee on Strengthening Alberta's Role in Confederation. The committee of nine government MLAs had been struck in 2003 to deal with the 'firewall' ideas that had become popular among many small-c conservatives in the Conservative Party. The 'firewall' concept originated in a letter written by Stephen Harper and others after the 2000 federal election. In the letter, they urged Premier Klein to take advantage of as many areas of provincial jurisdiction as possible, including setting up an Alberta pension plan and a provincial police force and ending the tax-collection agreement with Ottawa. Although Klein was not particu- larly supportive of these ideas, their popularity required a response and the committee, chaired by Edmonton Rutherford MLA Ian McClelland, was a way to provide it. The report concluded that, although Albertans had understandable frustrations with their place in Canada, they wanted to see Alberta positively engage the federation. To this end, the committee rejected the idea of withdrawing from the Canada Pension Plan, saw Alberta collecting its own taxes as too expensive, and called for a study of renewing the mandate of the RCMP before 2012. The report's defence of the status quo disappointed firewall advocates and may have helped to drive some to the Alberta Alliance, which was championing those ideas.

All told, the provincial government looked listless throughout 2004. A policy-bare session of the legislature and a platform-free provincial election that returned a diminished majority left the government with little momentum. Premier Klein looked to his post-election cabinet to revitalize his government. Most of the faces in cabinet were not new ones, although many were shuffled to new jobs. Shirley McClellan became finance minister, replacing the retiring Nelson. The Learning super-ministry was split back into Education (with Gene Zwosdesky as minister) and Advanced Education (with Dave Hancock as minister), reflecting the greater priority being given to the latter in the aftermath of the election. Lyle Oberg was moved to Infrastructure and Transportation. The biggest demotion came for Gary Mar, who lost the Health Ministry and went to Community Development. The most significant change, however, came in the backrooms, where Rod Love returned to be the premier's chief of staff. Love had been Klein's chief political adviser for much of his career, but left in 1997. His return seemed to be a sign that the government wanted to be more focused and disciplined in 2005 than had been the case in 2004.

The economy

The only appropriate word to describe Alberta's economy in 2004 is 'booming.' Alberta led all provinces in Canada with a 4.4 per cent real increase in GDP in 2004. Its unemployment rate declined in 2004, averaging 4.6 per cent for the year, also the best performance in the country. Wages increased by an average of 6.5 per cent and retail sales increased by 11.3 per cent. Remarkably, however, despite the overheated economy, inflation remained relatively negligible at 1.4 per cent.

The engine for this blistering pace of economic growth was, of course, the energy sector, as both oil and gas had banner years. In 2004 the price of oil shot up from just over $30 a barrel to $55 a barrel, a record high, before easing off to around $45 a barrel by the end of the year. Natural gas, too, averaged around $6 per gigajoule for most of the year, also a record annual high. Not surprisingly, this led to a modest increase in conventional oil drilling and exploration, which were up almost 5 per cent in Alberta over the previous year. The real action, however, was in the oil sands, as the high prices justified the higher production costs there. There was over $6-billion worth of investment into the oil sands over the course of the year.

The high prices helped to offset the impact of the surge in the value of the Canadian dollar. Surprisingly, despite the fact that the high Canadian dollar made Alberta's products less competitive internationally, Alberta's exports increased substantially over the previous year. Real exports were up by 4.7 per cent, with manufacturing exports outpacing energy exports.

Alberta's ranchers continued to struggle with the effects of the BSE crisis, as the total losses to the industry since the crisis began topped the $5-billion mark. However, the effects of this on the agricultural sector were mitigated by a reasonably good harvest, stronger crop prices, and governmental support programs.

In Alberta business, the biggest story was Calgary-based WestJet airlines, which was in its ninth year of operations. Over the years, it had built a sterling reputation as a friendly, efficient discount carrier that treated its employees well and was an outstanding member of the corporate community. Developments during 2004 would tarnish that reputation. Rising fuel prices put huge pressure on the bottom line for all airlines, requiring them to raise fares. WestJet expanded capacity, including flying into destinations in the United States for the first time. Although this was obviously a sign that the airline was doing well, the increased capacity meant that a lower proportion of the airline's seats were filled, reducing its efficiency. WestJet also faced a new player on the discount airline scene in Montreal-based Jetsgo. Finally, in the fall, a leaner Air Canada emerged from bankruptcy protection in a better position to compete with its arch-rival.

It was a development in this rivalry between Air Canada and WestJet that kept the airline in the news. In April, Air Canada filed a suit against WestJet for lost profits and revenue and $5 million in punitive damages, alleging that the company had used a former employee's access to a private Air Canada website that had sensitive data that gave WestJet an unfair advantage in planning routes and fares. In July, the lawsuit became much more serious when Air Canada increased its claim for damages to $220 million in compensation and punitive damages. In October, discount rival Jetsgo filed its own lawsuit against WestJet for $50 million, alleging that it too had been a victim of corporate espionage. The suit took its toll on WestJet's reputation and executive offices, as a vice-president at the centre of the dispute resigned. Over the summer, WestJet's chief executive officer, Clive Beddoe, apologized to employees and shareholders for his handling of the incident. This did little to mollify Air Canada, which added Beddoe to the suit in December. That same month, WestJet filed a counter-suit of its own, accusing Air Canada of abusing the court process to drive it out of business. The legal twists and turns were expected to continue into 2005.

Miscellaneous

The city of Calgary was completely preoccupied by the improbable playoff run of the National Hockey League's Calgary Flames. The team had made the playoffs after a mediocre regular season, finishing sixth in the Western Conference and twelfth overall. Led by the inspirational leadership of captain Jarome Iginla and goaltender Miikka Kiprusoff, the Flames caught fire during the playoffs and made it all the way to the Stanley Cup finals, defeating the Vancouver Canucks, Detroit Red Wings, and San Jose Sharks on the way. In the final, the Flames came up one game short against the Tampa Bay Lightning, losing the final series by four games to three. After every Flames victory, fans would pour into a stretch of Calgary street that became known as the 'Red Mile,' celebrating into the early hours of the morning. The excitement over the Flames' success spread through the province and even had some people cheering in Edmonton, the home of the Flames' traditional rival, the Edmonton Oilers.

The other development that had Albertans cheering was Medicine Hat's Kalan Porter's victory on the second season of the popular television reality show *Canadian Idol*. Porter defeated a field of ten finalists to win the crown in September, sending Medicine Hat into a frenzy.

Lieutenant Governor Lois Hole continued her battle with cancer in 2004. In the spring, Premier Klein wrote Prime Minister Martin to ask that the very popular Hole's term be extended at least to the end of 2005, so that she could preside over the province's centennial celebrations that year and greet the queen; the prime minister quickly agreed. As always, Hole was a vigorous advocate for increased funding for the arts and culture and education as well as for greater efforts to eliminate poverty. Her efforts were rewarded in October when she announced the Lieutenant Governor of Alberta Arts Awards which would be awarded biannually. The awards were funded by a variety of private benefactors, whose contributions were matched by the provincial government. Sadly, Hole's illness got the better of her late in the year and she was unable to officiate at a number of important events, including the swearing in of the new cabinet. As testament to Hole's impact on Alberta society, the city of Edmonton named a library after her and the new women's hospital at the Royal Alexandra Hospital was named the Lois Hole Hospital for Women.

JOSEPH GARCEA

Saskatchewan

The year 2004 was a relatively positive one for Saskatchewan in which provincial pride received a boost from the results of two different national talent contests. In one contest, Tommy Douglas, a former premier of the province, was voted the greatest Canadian in the national competition conducted and televised by the CBC for his role in laying the foundations of the country's universal health-care system (*Saskatoon StarPhoenix*, 30 Nov.). This result provided the surviving stalwarts of the Co-operative Commonwealth Federation with confirmation that history would recognize the greatness both of Douglas and of the party that he had led. Clearly, Douglas's vision had not been forgotten by the country. In the other contest, Theresa Sokyrka, a young musician from Saskatoon, finished in second place in the second instalment of the *Canadian Idol* competition held by CTV. Only having a Saskatchewan team win the national football and curling championships would have meant more to the people of this province. Saskatchewanians' success in those two contests served a broader purpose than buoying the pride of residents in the province. It provided evidence for them that, despite the odds, they could make notable contributions to the public good and compete with the rest of the country. It was also a morale boost for them to know that good things had happened, were happening, and could continue to happen in the province. At least for a brief moment, some wondered whether they were already living in the proverbial 'greener pastures' wherein they could achieve greatness and excellence without leaving the province.

Elections

Provincial election

Among the major political stories of 2004 were three that emerged from the narrow election victory by the New Democratic Party in the 2003 provincial election. The first of these stemmed from a controversy regarding potential electoral irregularities surrounding the election results for the Lloydminster constituency, where the Saskatchewan Party candidate defeated the NDP candidate by sixty-four votes. The uncertainty as to whether a by-election would have to be held ended when the NDP candidate decided to withdraw the application for an official review of the election process and results (*Saskatoon StarPhoenix*, 24 Aug.).

The second story that flowed from the provincial election was a proposal by the NDP premier, Lorne Calvert, for a modification of the provincial electoral system. The proposal, which was heavily criticized by the Official Opposition, was that by-elections would not be required for any seat vacated thirty-six months after the preceding election. This meant that, in a regular four-year term, the seat could remain open for twelve months, and if the term was extended to the five-year limit, it could remain open for twenty-four months. The government's rationale – that it wanted to avoid the situation which had occurred in the Carrot River Valley constituency where voters had to go to the polls twice in the span of six months – was not convincing politically and the government abandoned the proposal (*Moose Jaw Herald*, 1 June).

The third story was the replacement of Elwin Hermanson as Saskatchewan Party leader. After his party lost the 2003 election, he stepped down as leader of the party and Brad Wall became the new leader by acclamation. One of Wall's first objectives was to conduct a review of party policy in an attempt to shift the Saskatchewan Party from the right to the centre of the political spectrum, thereby broadening the party's base of support.

Federal general election

The federal election of 2004 proved to be quite interesting in Saskatchewan. The Conservatives won thirteen seats and the Liberals won one in Regina as Ralph Goodale, the former finance minister, held his seat. The election saw the NDP shut out of the seat count as the Conservatives won by very slim margins of just over 100 votes in two seats (Regina-Lumsden, Lake Centre and Palliser) that were previously held by the NDP. The lawyers for both defeated candidates insisted that there had been irregularities in the voting processes, but ultimately both withdrew their complaints on the grounds that investigating them would be too costly and time-consuming (*Saskatoon StarPhoenix*, 8 Sept.). Among the notable defeated candidates was the outspoken and controversial independent MP Jim Pankiw (Saskatoon-Humboldt), who had been banished from the Conservative caucus, and Chris Axworthy, a former NDP MP and provincial MLA and cabinet minister, who had run under the Liberal banner. The other noteworthy event in the election was that former Tory premier Grant Devine was forced to run as an independent after being rejected as a candidate by the Conservative Party, which was worried that it could be adversely affected by the tarnished image of his government resulting from the illegal activities of some of his cabinet ministers and MLAs (*Saskatoon StarPhoenix,* 20 and 21 Feb.).

The legislature and government

The provincial legislature entered a new era in 2004. In a joint press conference held in May, the NDP and the Saskatchewan Party announced a new legislative schedule that institutionalized a fixed spring and fall session, rather than only a spring session. The legislative process would start in the fall with a Throne Speech and be followed by a spring session to wrap things up. The rationale cited for the change was that, in the past, the time between sittings had been too long and new problems and issues that arose could not be dealt with in a timely manner (*Saskatoon StarPhoenix*, 27 May).

Spring session of legislature

On 18 March Lieutenant Governor Lynda Haverstock opened the 25th legislature of Saskatchewan with a Speech from the Throne entitled 'Making Saskatchewan Ready for the Next Generation' (Saskatchewan Government, *Speech from the Throne 2004*, 18 March). Its main emphasis was on three areas: education, opportunity for the province's youth, and building a green and prosperous economy through diversification and innovation. Towards those ends, the provincial government committed itself to hosting annual public summits to focus on common efforts in achieving economic, environmental, and social progress.

Major promises in the field of education included: the implementation of Career Start, designed to prepare students for and link them to career opportunities in the province; the expansion of the existing 'School-plus' program, intended to enhance the capacity of schools to meet the needs of students and their families; and the establishment of the Post-Secondary Graduate Tax Credit program. The provincial government made a point of issuing a clarion call for young graduates to stay in the province by declaring that 'our future is wide open and your future is here!'

The provincial government also made several commitments to foster economic development, including: expanding the Saskatchewan Immigration Provincial Nominee Program to meet the needs of an expanding economy and to increase the size of the population; and devoting more attention to the needs of the agricultural sector, through, among other things, assisting those involved in agri-business and continuing efforts to expand the livestock industry and open up the American border for Saskatchewan cattle. For the forestry industry, the government promised a new forest centre in Prince Albert. For other parts of the resource sector, it promised further development in the uranium industry and further expansion of the potash industry; enhancement of the royalty and incentive structures to increase exploration for diamonds and other types of minerals; expansion of CO_2-injection projects in the oil patch to extract more of the heavy oil reserves; greater use of clean coal for power generation; and increased exploration and utilization of alternative energy sources such as wind, ethanol, bio-fuels, solar, and hydrogen.

Other major commitments in the Throne Speech were: entrenching in legislation the principle of government ownership of crown utilities; finding ways to ensure that the province would have the cheapest utility bundle (electricity, natural gas, phone service, auto insurance) on an annual basis; seeking a private-sector management company to manage the assets of the crown corporation known as Investment Saskatchewan; and building a pool of private- and public-sector capital to expand further the Saskatchewan economy. Another major initiative was to establish the Young Entrepreneurs of Saskatchewan program, which would make funds available to young entrepreneurs and community-based enterprises under the stewardship of highly qualified business and community leaders and a pool of experienced business mentors.

The commitment to the greening of the provincial economy and the province as a whole included an agenda of energy conservation consisting of the establishment of the Office of Energy Conservation, the Energy Star appliance rebate program, the retrofitting of public buildings across Saskatchewan, and Energuide for Houses. The government also promised that, during its term in office, it would unveil a broader-based Green Strategy.

Another government promise was that, during that session, it would introduce a plan to continue to balance the provincial budget without adversely affecting the provision of health services. Towards that end, it would do the following: promote a preventative approach to health care; introduce legislation to ban smoking in public places across Saskatchewan in 2005; establish and provide financial resources for a five-year housing strategy designed to provide adequate housing for the less fortunate, a major factor that affects health; assess how health dollars are used and how they can be used most effectively; explore how to reduce waiting times for surgery and diagnostic imaging; and introduce a strategy to assess and support people with cognitive disabilities, including Fetal Alcohol Spectrum Disorder. As well, to ease the pressures on the health system and on families, the government indicated that it would introduce amendments to the Labour Standards Act to allow people to take advantage of compassionate-care benefits when caring for gravely ill family members, as well as a comprehensive disability strategy to help people with disabilities so that they could be included in the social and economic life of local communities and the province as a whole. The provincial government also committed itself to starting to implement the second phase of the Voluntary Sector Initiative, with the goal of strengthening and supporting Saskatchewan's volunteers, communities, and families. Additionally, it would work with the Council of the Federation and the federal government to improve funding arrangements for health care and the equalization program while also addressing the vertical fiscal imbalance.

Shortly after the presentation of the Speech from the Throne, the focus shifted from policy to politics as the spring session proved to be highly politicized. The reason for this was that the slim two-seat electoral win by the NDP government in 2003 left the door open for the possibility of an early election. The prospect for such an election was increased when NDP member Myron Kowalsky was appointed Speaker and Clay Serby announced that he would have to undergo cancer treatments (*Saskatoon StarPhoenix,* 27 Feb.). Kowalsky's appointment as Speaker and Serby's medical leave meant that the NDP and the Saskatchewan Party each had twenty-eight seats in the legislature. The Official Opposition considered bringing the government down and forcing another election by accusing it of breaking election promises related to tax increases and job cuts in the public service (*Regina Leader Post*, 10 April). Ultimately, however, it decided not to do so. In fact, it actually helped the government pass the budget rather than trying to block it and force an election. The government and the Official Opposition reached a compromise on the budget wherein the estimates for agriculture, health, learning, environment, and the Executive Council (70 per cent of the budget) would be considered by the Finance Committee, and all the rest would be considered in the standing committees (*Saskatoon StarPhoenix*, 24 April).

This compromise allowed the NDP to continue governing but allowed the Official Opposition to get more details on, and offer more criticism of, the government's fiscal framework. Not everyone was happy with the budget. Among those unhappy was the leadership of the Saskatchewan Association of Rural Municipalities, which was hoping for more tax breaks and financial supports for farmers (*Saskatoon StarPhoenix*, 1 April). But delivering what it claimed to be the eleventh balanced budget was more important for the NDP government than appeasing certain constituencies that sought increased expenditures for their respective sectors. Another major budgetary imperative for the provincial government was to make the claim that Saskatchewan had the lowest-priced utility bundle in the country (*Saskatoon StarPhoenix*, 30 June).

Fall session of legislature

Given the political machinations during the spring session, much of the legislative business was left for the fall session. Unlike the spring session, which had been particularly hard on the government, the fall session went relatively smoothly. It commenced with the release of the government's mid-year financial report, which showed an additional $899 million beyond what had been projected. The extra money allowed the government to keep its election promise of providing the cheapest provincial utility bundle in the country by offering a $137 rebate to all Saskatchewan households (*Saskatoon StarPhoenix*, 30 Dec.). The government also passed legislation ensuring public ownership of crown corporations. The Calvert government tried to pass 'available hours legislation' but this was met by very strong resistance not only from the opposition Saskatchewan Party but also from the Saskatchewan Business Council, a consortium of thirteen business organizations. Collectively, the members of the council threatened a boycott of the provincial economic summit planned for early 2005 if its concerns were not met (*Saskatoon StarPhoenix*, 7 Dec.).

The provincial budget

The provincial budget address presented in the spring sitting of the legislature provided the provincial government with an opportunity to demonstrate whether there would be continuity or discontinuity either in its priorities or in its general approach to fiscal management, and to provide taxpayers with some perspectives on its record of fiscal management. The budget address consisted of three major sections devoted, in turn, to financial accountability, revenues, and expenditures.[1]

In the first major section of the budget address, the minister of finance, Harry Van Mulligan, noted that over the past decade the government had greatly enhanced accountability and transparency in its fiscal operations by introducing the following documents and the requirement that they be submitted in the legislature within 120 days of the fiscal year-end: balanced budget legislation; interim financial reporting; summary financial statements with the public accounts; and department performance plans and reports. The budget address also noted another major initiative to increase transparency and accountability: a Summary Financial Plan, which provided a consolidated financial overview of all government departments, crowns, agencies, and boards.

The finance minister stated that he was presenting the 11th consecutive balanced General Revenue Fund budget. However, he acknowledged that to do this the government had to rely on a $158-million transfer from the Fiscal Stabilization Fund for expenditures on health care, education, agriculture, and highways. Although this constituted a 40 per cent reduction from the transfer of the last fiscal year, it was by no means insignificant. The minister also acknowledged that, over the most recent three years, the government had accessed over $400 million from that fund to produce balanced budgets.

The 2004–5 provincial budget was also balanced by reducing the operating budgets of twelve departments. The only two departments that did not have their budgets reduced were those responsible for health and education, which accounted for almost two-thirds of government expenditures. Other budget-balancing measures included holding overall government spending increases to $15.6 million, or .7 per cent of the total budget; holding the line on salaries in government departments and crown corporations; cutting approximately 500 seasonal, temporary, and permanent staff; reducing the operating costs, though not the overall budget, of the Department of Health; reorganizing extension services offered by the Department of Agriculture by consolidating thirty-one offices into nine and adding a new call centre; and redeploying staff within the Department of the Environment.

The minister of finance took a considerable amount of time during the budget speech to explain that the province was not being treated fairly under the national equalization program. In making the case, he

---

1 http://www.gov.sk.ca/finance/budget/budget04/2004papers.htm.

cited a paper by economist Thomas J. Courchene which indicated that Saskatchewan's natural resources were still being treated inequitably under the equalization-funding formula used by the federal government, and that at times the province was penalized at rates exceeding 100 per cent of its energy revenues. Courchene referred to this phenomenon as 'confiscatory federalism' and called for a return to the previous mining tax base and for the same treatment of the province's oil and gas revenues as that provided to Atlantic Canada.

The major changes to the revenue budget included the following: increasing the Provincial Sales Tax (PST) rate from 6 per cent to 7 per cent, an increase that would yield $138 million in the first year, but not expanding the tax base, and providing a slight increase in the PST rebate to minimize the adverse effects of the increase to lower- income families; increasing the mark-up on bottled beer by twenty-six cents per litre; increasing several fees and licences to reflect more accurately the actual service costs; increasing the tobacco tax by one and a half cents per cigarette; limiting the fuel-tax exemption on farm gasoline to 80 per cent of all bulk purchases and eliminating the annual farm rebate for retail gasoline purchases; and modifying the indexation of personal income-tax brackets and credits annually starting in 2005.

Among the major expenditures noted in that budget address were those for the agricultural and health sectors. For the agricultural sector, the budget promised over $1 billion over the next five years to implement various aspects of the Agricultural Policy Framework. For the health sector, it promised $2.7 billion, which amounted to an increase of $160 million or 6.3 per cent over the previous year. This particular increase constituted 72 per cent of the overall increase in operating expenses over the previous year. Of the $160 million in new health funding, $115 million was targeted for salaries, benefits, and medical fees-for-services. The minister of finance noted that health-care costs had increased at an average of 6.6 per cent each year since 1999 and that if the trend continued it would not be sustainable because within a few years health care would consume more than half of the annual operating budget. The minister also observed that, to ensure that the health-care system was financially sustainable, special initiatives would be required, including: detailed expenditure and program assessments; debates of key issues and options related to services, management, and funding; and more equitable funding arrangements from the federal government.

For the social-welfare sector, the budget contained additional expenditures for both new and enhanced program initiatives. The most notable of these were the following: expanding prenatal services under the

KidsFirst program for sixty additional families; adding over 200 new childcare spaces for needy families; increasing the Saskatchewan Child Benefit payments for single-parent households; increasing support through the Saskatchewan Employment Supplement for low-income working parents; and investing $12.6 million into affordable housing construction under the Provincial Housing Policy Framework.

The budget also included substantial expenditure increases in various other sectors. For the municipal sector, it included $10 million for the municipal revenue- sharing program, an increase of approximately 13 per cent, and additional funding for the 'safe communities' initiative designed to fight organized crime. For the transportation sector, the budget provided $295 million for construction and maintenance of some of the major highways, including the twinning of some parts of the Yellowhead Highway. For the education sector, there were increases both for the K-12 system and for the post-secondary system. For the K-12 system, it included $527.9 million in operating grants and $24 million for capital projects to school divisions. For the post-secondary sector, it included $425.4 million in operating grants and $16 million for capital projects to institutions and an additional $9.8-million increase to the Innovation and Science Fund. It also increased the Post-Secondary Graduate Tax Credit from $350 to $500 for 2004 and ultimately to $1,000 within the following three years.

For the youth sector, the budget allocated nearly $3 million for youth employment and entrepreneurship programs. Of this, $2.2 million was devoted to the creation of approximately 600 employment opportunities for students; $500,000 was added to the Aboriginal Employment Development Program to promote Aboriginal training and employment; and $500,000 was directed to the Young Entrepreneurs of Saskatchewan program to provide approximately 150 youth entrepreneurs with business-development loans of up to $15,000.

Other expenditure measures designed to contribute to economic development were the following: $211 million in job training and job creation; $10 million for the Small Business Loans Association, which effectively doubled the amount of funds at its disposal; and an investment of $50 million by Investment Saskatchewan, a government-owned but privately managed investment fund.

Finally, the budget included some incentives designed to contribute to making the province more environmentally friendly and sustainable. For that purpose, it provided a PST rebate program for Energy Star-compliant appliances and $860,000 for the Ethanol Fuel Tax Rebate program.

The economy

In 2004 Saskatchewan officially became a 'have province' again after many years of being one of Canada's 'have-not' provinces. This happened despite the fact that the farm economy was hit hard by mad cow disease, which resulted in the closing of U.S. border to Canadian beef exports and low prices (*Saskatoon StarPhoenix*, 15 July). Similarly, grain farmers' hopes of a bumper crop were dashed when an early frost hit the province in August, which, according to estimates, cost the Saskatchewan and Manitoba farm economies $1 billion. By the end of the year, the farm economy had started to hope for a better year ahead as the U.S. government indicated that the border would be reopened to young cattle the following spring.

The strong economic performance for the province was based largely on the boom in the energy sector, which gave the province one of the highest growth rates among Canadian provinces for the year. It was also based on a relatively strong performance by crown corporations, which did not post any major losses such as those that had happened the year before for Sasktel and SaskWater totalling approximately $64 million (*Saskatoon StarPhoenix*, 8 and 15 April).

The year ended on a cautionary note for the province as economic forecasters projected only 2.2 per cent growth for the following year (*Saskatoon StarPhoenix*, 17 Dec.).

The judiciary

In 2004 the Saskatchewan government was in court in a continuing legal battle regarding the failed Spudco investment. After dealing with a legal suit for some time, it launched a countersuit of $10 million alleging that partner companies had misrepresented the economic potential of the joint venture. Within months the countersuit was dismissed, but a settlement was reached in the lawsuit levelled against the government. The settlement included a payment of $7.9 million, bringing the total cost of settlements to $34.4 million (*Saskatoon StarPhoenix*, 16 Oct.).

Saskatoon's policing system continued to deal with cases of wrongful accusations and inadequate investigations in which it had been involved over the previous fifteen years. The provincial government appointed Alberta's Court of Queen's Bench Justice Edward P. McCallum to head an inquiry into the wrongful-murder conviction of David Milgaard for which he had spent twenty-three years in jail (*Saskatoon StarPhoenix*, 21 Feb.). Later that year, Saskatoon's chief of police also apologized to the family of Neil Stonechild, the Saskatoon teen who had been found frozen to death more than fourteen years earlier. A provincial inquiry into the case conducted by Judge David Wright described the original investigation by the Saskatoon police as 'superficial and totally inadequate' (*Saskatoon StarPhoenix*, 24 Nov.).

Saskatoon's chief of police, along with the premier and the minister of justice, apologized to approximately one dozen people who had been wrongly accused of being involved in satanic rituals involving sexual abuse of children in the early 1990s in the town of Martensville (*Saskatoon StarPhoenix*, 8 Jan., and 6 and 20 Feb.). The malicious-prosecution case was settled out of court, with the government of Saskatchewan and the Saskatoon and Martensville police forces paying $1.3 million (*Saskatoon StarPhoenix*, 16 Nov.).

At the same time as it was grappling with past problems, the Saskatoon police force along with other police forces across the province and provincial politicians were trying to find ways to deal with the increase in the use of the drug 'crystal meth.' This was becoming the new scourge in the illegal drug trade, which, according to some, was reaching crisis proportions and constituted a threat to the lives of individuals and the well-being of families and communities.

On another legal front, four same-gender couples made history in the Saskatchewan context as they won their case for legally marrying within the province. When the judge declared the traditional definition of marriage unduly restrictive and unconstitutional, Saskatchewan became the seventh jurisdiction in Canada to legalize gay marriage (*Saskatoon StarPhoenix*, 6 Nov.).

Intergovernmental relations

Federal-provincial relations

The year 2004 was an important one in federal-provincial relations on at least two fronts. The first concerned the premier's signing of a $41-billion 'First Minister's Health Care Accord' described as a ten-year plan to strengthen health care (*Saskatoon StarPhoenix*, 17 Sept.). The second concerned equalization payments. Although Saskatchewan had become a 'have' province again, Premier Lorne Calvert was able to convince Ottawa that it was entitled to two equalization-adjustment payments of $120 million and $367 million (*Saskatoon StarPhoenix*, 28 Oct.).

While the provincial government was happy to receive this money, it had several concerns. One was that it was $2 billion less than what it would have been entitled to if there had not been any changes to the funding formula. A second concern was that the agreement did not preclude further cutbacks in the future, and a third was that reforms to the federal equalization program failed to address the issue of equitable treatment of provincial resource revenues. Finance Minister Van Mulligan indicated that, under the existing equalization formula, higher resource royalties could result in a loss in equalization payments of over 100 per cent through what he referred to as a claw-back mechanism. He added that any cutbacks in equalization payments would have an adverse effect on the province's ability to fund escalating costs in health care, agricultural support, and education (*Saskatoon StarPhoenix*, 3 Feb.).

Provincial-municipal relations

Provincial-municipal fiscal relations were again prominent on the political landscape. This was in part due to the 'New Deal for Cities' that Prime Minister Paul Martin had promised in 2003. The president of the Saskatchewan Urban Municipalities Association, Mike Badham, suggested that, given that promise, special consideration should be given to the implementation of the 'New Directions' proposal involving Saskatchewan's municipalities and the provincial government (*Saskatoon StarPhoenix*, 2 Jan.).

Representatives of the municipal sector hoped that a significant part of New Directions would be the implementation of the recommendations of the Commission on Financing Kindergarten to Grade 12 Education (known as the Boughen Commission). That report recommended a reduction in the dependency of school boards on the property tax base, something that municipalities had been requesting for many years. Although the municipalities favoured the commission's recommendations, school board representatives were concerned that making the school system more dependent on provincial transfers was potentially problematic in that they would become more vulnerable to the fiscal imperatives of the provincial government for a greater proportion of their funding (*Saskatoon StarPhoenix*, 9 Jan.). In the spring budget, the provincial government continued its policy of subsidizing farmers for a portion of their education/property-tax bill, but it did not implement the recommendations of the Boughen Commission.

In May the minister responsible for learning, Andrew Thomson, announced that in an attempt to save money and reduce the number of smaller school closures, the government would press for amalgamation of the province's eighty-one school divisions into thirty-three. This initiative was part of its efforts to lay the organizational framework upon which it could then implement the recommendations of the Boughen Commission. But there was no movement on the commission's recommendation for education/property-tax relief beyond a promise that 30 per cent of any new money the province would get from the federal equalization program would go to tax relief (*Saskatoon StarPhoenix*, 14 May).

This approach angered representatives of the municipal and farm sectors, especially the executive of the Saskatchewan Association of Rural Municipalities. It maintained that the NDP government had betrayed its promise to provide a substantial reduction in Saskatchewan's education/property taxes, which it claimed were among the highest in Canada. Some of those representatives threatened a tax revolt whereby they would not collect or turn over taxes for education purposes. The provincial government was worried about such brinkmanship, but it reminded the municipalities that they had a statutory responsibility to collect and transfer those taxes and that if they did not do so they would be held responsible for their actions.

In August, Learning Minister Andrew Thomson released a map that was to be used as the basis for consultations that were to be conducted by the Task Force on Educational Equity with school division officials and other education stakeholders during the fall on the boundaries of a consolidated system. The map depicted the consolidation of the province's existing school divisions. Upon completion of its consultations, the task force was to make recommendations for the provincial government to consider for producing an amalgamation map that would go into effect in January 2006 (*Saskatoon StarPhoenix*, 7 Aug.).

Aboriginal affairs

The provincial government gave conditional approval for the creation of a casino on the Whitecap Dakota First Nation, approximately twenty kilometres south of Saskatoon, to be operated by the Saskatchewan Indian Gaming Authority (SIGA). Some of the conditions included reforms to SIGA's model of corporate governance and the implementation of the internal controls recommended by the provincial auditor, Fred Wendel. The Calvert government indicated that the province would hold casino revenues until those conditions were met (*Saskatoon StarPhoenix*, 10 Aug.).

Another major Aboriginal story in 2004 was the Métis Nation Saskatchewan (MNS) election held on 26 May which featured a three-person race for the presidency involving Alex Maurice, Dwayne Roth, and Robert Doucette. The election was marred by accusations of election irregularities and lax controls of the ballot boxes. Following the initial recount, Doucette was declared the winner. However, later the same day, Roth was declared the winner because a ballot box was brought in from North Battleford containing ballots that were considered legitimate by some but had not been counted (*Saskatoon StarPhoenix*, 14 Oct.). The change in winner created a controversy that ultimately led the Saskatchewan government to appoint Keith Lampard, a former chief electoral officer for the province, to review the allegations and electoral procedures. His final report, released in the fall of that year, stated that there had been irregularities and that the election was not fair and transparent. However, neither the federal nor the provincial government was authorized to force another election. Roth launched a defamation lawsuit against the provincial government, while Doucette formed a so-called provisional Métis council as an alternative voice for Métis people, which had a symbolic rather than a governance role.

With the Lampard report in hand, the federal and provincial governments decided to cease funding to the MNS until the election issue was resolved. For its part, the provincial government put a halt to the $410,000 in annual funding it paid to the MNS, while, at the federal level, Indian and Northern Affairs Canada (INAC) put on hold more than $1.2 million which it had announced in the March federal budget as part of Ottawa's response to a Supreme Court decision on Métis rights, and Canadian Heritage froze the second half of a $517,227 payment it had been transferring to the organization annually (*National Post*, 27 Nov.). As the year came to an end, this unfortunate saga was not resolved and the MNS essentially ground to a standstill.

One of the most interesting news stories involving Aboriginal governments was the announcement by the Muskeg Lake Cree Nation that it was using a $15,000 grant it had received from INAC to explore the feasibility of establishing a comprehensive health-care centre on its urban reserve in Saskatoon, just one kilometre from the Royal University Hospital in Saskatoon. The proposed centre included a primary health-care centre, a laboratory for medical tests, and medical imaging using X-ray, ultrasound, and MRI machines. The Muskeg Lake Cree Nation leaders overseeing the initiative argued that such a centre would not contravene the principle of not allowing the operation of privately owned MRI machines in the province because it would be owned and operated by a First Nation government and not a privately owned business (*Saskatoon StarPhoenix*, 22 Jan.).

Other major issues and events

One of the major events in 2004 was the grand opening of the Canadian Light Source 'synchrotron' project at the University of Saskatchewan. This is only one of seventeen such facilities in the world. Its establishment placed the university, the city, and the province at the centre of an international research hub that would use that particular technology (*Saskatoon StarPhoenix*, 23 Oct.). The project cost $174 million and has a multi-million-dollar annual operating budget. The contributors to the construction costs included federal research funding agencies, the provincial governments of Saskatchewan, Alberta, and Ontario, Saskatoon's municipal government, and some private-sector companies. No other recent development has created the same type of buzz within the so-called town-and-gown network as this particular project. The grand opening was marked by a set of light beams projected high above the city into the dark night sky, a spectacle that some viewed as a symbolic gesture of knowledge shedding light on darkness and others as an effort to recreate the extraordinary celestial event that, according to the Bible, was witnessed approximately two thousand years earlier over Bethlehem.

For some, however, the more exciting event of the year was the national Brier curling championship. In a province where curling is a 'sacred sport,' the Brier attracted the devout both as volunteers and spectators. Although the Saskatchewan team did not win the championship, the city of Saskatoon garnered considerable respect from the national curling community for its ability to put on a national event that attracted a record number of spectators.

The year closed with anticipation for an exciting year to come as Saskatchewan finalized the plans to usher in its centennial year in 2005. The announcement that the queen would be visiting the province for the celebrations was welcome news for those who hoped that it would be a truly memorable royal and historical event.

GEOFFREY LAMBERT

Manitoba

The New Democratic government of Premier Gary Doer maintained a low profile in 2004. The economy did quite well, if not perhaps as well as in previous years. The main focus of public and media attention at mid-year was the federal election, one that had important ramifications for the province and, in particular, its capital. Later in the year, attention shifted to all the excitement generated by the opening of a new arena on the site of the former Eaton's building on Portage Avenue in downtown Winnipeg.

The legislature

It was a complaint of the small Liberal caucus (with only two seats, they did not constitute an official party) that the legislature did not meet very often. This was true, since the house sat for only fifty-three days in 2004, which was a marked increase over the 2003's total of thirty-seven days – and that was an election year. This may be a sign of a government running out of ideas, or of one that mercifully wished to spare the community any more 'government' than is necessary. In any event, the incumbent NDP government did not seem to suffer any significant loss of support through not calling the legislature into session.

The budget was presented on 11 April by Finance Minister Greg Selinger, who was completing five years in the role. His budget was less expansive and optimistic than it had been in previous years, the fault, he explained, of a slower economy (a condition exacerbated by the higher value of the dollar), the BSE crisis, and diminished transfer payments from the federal government. Nonetheless, he claimed, the government had been able to deliver on most of its promises to invest in areas of crucial need. For example, the government had paid particular attention to health care, which had been for some years (including, one might add, the last couple of years of the Gary Filmon Conservative government) the largest item in the budget, and close (at 41.9 per cent) to being the highest percentage of the operating budget anywhere in the country.

The new tax changes introduced by Selinger were few (some mentioned in the budget had already been announced) but important. They included a cut in the corporate tax rate; an enhancement of the film and video tax credit (the previous year had been Manitoba's best year in this regard); an odour-control tax, designed to deter 'nuisance odours,' such as those emanating from pig farms; and a provision for income-tax-credit carryovers. In other areas, the sales tax was to be broadened to apply to certain professional services (legal, accounting, and so on). There was to be an adjustment of the land-transfer tax, the education support levy was to be reduced, and there was the inevitable raising of taxes on tobacco and alcohol. But income tax, at least, was not touched.

Overall, the finance minister proposed total spending of $7.233 billion on programs, with a further $138 million to be spent on capital projects. The main beneficiary was health care, with a budget increase of around 4 per cent and a budget appropriation of nearly $3 billion. There were some losers in that some departments were held to the same budget as before, or were expected to manage on one a little reduced. Moreover, the government also announced that it intended to cut four thousand jobs in the civil service, to save $30 million in wages. Also, there was to be some consolidation of departments, starting with the merger of Vehicle Licensing and Testing with Autopac, the government's motor-insurance arm. Departments were also told to not go beyond the rate of inflation in setting their day-to-day operating-expense budget.

The government estimated its revenues at $7.38 billion. Its revenue estimates for the next four years (2005–9) were very positive, and the NDP obviously believed that it would be able to keep its promises, pay off debt, and govern with no deficit without reaching into the Fiscal Stabilization Fund (better known in some quarters as the 'sunshine fund'). It appeared that the government would end the 2003–4 financial year with a surplus of about $5 million, but only after dipping into the Stabilization Fund to the tune of $143 million.

This, the fifth budget of the Doer era, was typical of the rest in that it incorporated social reform and fiscal prudence. Many detected a hint of the Third Way or Blairism in the package, not a good thing in the eyes of some observers. Clearly, Doer could not be easily or accurately characterized as either a radical or a socialist big spender.

The new lieutenant governor, John Harvard, read the Throne Speech on 22 November. Harvard, a former MP, had been appointed only a few months previously, as a means of opening up a parliamentary seat for Glen Murray, at the time the mayor of Winnipeg. Before entering politics, Harvard had worked for the CBC, both TV and radio, as an interviewer and anchorman.

There was a sort of 'sameness" about the Throne Speech if compared to one or two of its immediate predecessors. But, as they say, if you are on to a good thing, or if it ain't broke, don't fix it. Essentially what the speech did was reiterate some of the government's commitments and clarify its version of what its key achievements had been. For instance, there was a renewed commitment to elevating the status and increasing the opportunities for Native people, who constitute more than a tenth of the province's population. There was a further commitment to defend Medicare as well as 'continuing to support post secondary education.'

This was an area where the New Democrats took particular pride in their record. They felt that the freeze on tuition rates (now four years old) as well as the student tax rebates they offered had been perhaps the primary reasons for the substantial increases in college and university enrolments over the 2000–4 period. The fact that other provinces had seen equivalent increases while still significantly increasing tuition fees never punctured the government's conviction in this regard. Moreover, continuing the policy was important as a means of showing the government's concern and understanding. The fact that the colleges and universities in Manitoba found it increasingly difficult to cope, since the government did not compensate them for the tuition revenue foregone, also failed to have much impact on the government's policies.

Finally, one must mention the Throne Speech's emphasis on affordability, security, the sacredness of Manitoba's water supply, the government's clench-jawed commitment to raising the level of opportunity and the quality of life for seniors, young people, and those living in rural areas, and the centrality of hydro in the province's (post-Kyoto) economic development.

There was a cabinet reshuffle, as some of the more overburdened ministers sought relief. David Chomiak, the country's longest-serving minister of health (he had held the position ever since the NDP was elected to office in 1999), stood down from that arduous portfolio, assuming instead the responsibility for Energy, Science and Technology (or EST as it became known). However one judges his performance, his integrity and commitment were never in doubt. He was succeeded at Health by the outgoing EST minister, the Reverend Tim Sale, a former social worker and Anglican minister who had been one of the premier success stories of this government. Mary Ann Mihaychuk, who had left Intergovernmental Affairs (and the legislature) to run for the mayoralty of Winnipeg, was replaced by Scott Smith. Jim Rondeau was promoted to Industry, Economic Development and Mines (Smith's previous portfolio) from Healthy Living, which went to newcomer Theresa Oswald, elected to the legislature in 2003. Healthy Living was a small-budget operation designed to enable its minister to discover, initiate, and promote programs of preventative health.

Little new legislation of any significance was introduced this year. This may have reflected the fact that there was a federal election (which resulted in some losses by the Liberals to both their principal rivals) and a series of federal-provincial meetings over such issues as equalization and support for Medicare.

The economy and economic developments

Although lacking some of the gusto of previous years, 2004 was still an excellent one for Manitoba's economy. The economy was hurt by the BSE crisis, and the rising dollar was not good for exports. Yet unemployment was low by national standards, averaging around 5 per cent over the year. Moreover, unemployment among fifteen- to twenty-four-year-olds also compared positively, at just over 11 per cent, with other provinces. The real GDP rose by about 3 per cent, and there were healthy increases in the amount of both public and private investment, 15 per cent and 8 per cent respectively. And Manitoba enjoyed a substantial increase in population.

Immigrants and people moving within Canada were among the factors pushing the population, as of 1 July, to 1.07 million. The province's own sponsorship program played a major role, too, while some groups in the community (such as the Jewish community, who brought in core-ligionists from Argentina) were notably active.

Most of the major sectors of the Manitoba economy showed growth, the exceptions being some sectors of manufacturing (such as power tools) and parts of agriculture. Although the total volume of activity in agriculture as a whole was higher than the year before, a cold summer and the unnecessarily dragged-out BSE-induced ban on exports of beef and cattle to many countries played a negative role in rural fortunes. Perhaps the booming pork industry was agriculture's saving grace.

Income rose somewhat (2 per cent), retail spending was active, and the housing market, regarded by many as a litmus test of the economy as a whole, remained strong. Indeed, over the last four years, the number of permits issued for house building increased by 70 per cent, and prices for existing homes reached all-time highs. Indeed, it looked as if Winnipeg was losing its advantage over other cities in this respect.

Much of the province's economic surge was fuelled by major construction projects, with more still to come. These included a major renovation and expansion of the Engineering Building at the University of Manitoba, the drawing up of plans for the new downtown headquarters of Manitoba Hydro, and the proposal for a Human Rights Museum by the Forks in Winnipeg. The latter was a project dear to the heart of the late Izzy Asper, kept alive by members of his family. (However, there seemed to be a discrepancy in the Aspers' and the government's version of what exactly had been promised financially.) Other important projects were undertaken in Brandon, including an extension to Brandon General Hospital.

The main event, however, was the opening, on 22 November, of the new downtown Manitoba Telecommunications Services building (the MTS Centre, or 'phone booth,' as it became known.) From the beginning, the new structure proved a valuable addition to the city. It represented an economic boom to people running businesses close to the new facility and symbolized (many thought) what the city could do if it made up its mind to do it. The opening also kept alive, indeed stimulated, the dreams of all those who thought it would be possible to revive downtown Winnipeg. It certainly needed a facelift.

A casualty of this building boom was the old, venerable Winnipeg Arena, which opened for the last time on 6 November. The space it occupied was to be dedicated to more retail space (it is right next door to Polo Park, said to be one of the three busiest malls in the west). The old arena went out with style, the major tenant, the Manitoba Moose hockey club of the American Hockey League, inviting some popular former players from the still beloved Winnipeg Jets, who had left in 1996. Thus, for one last time, local fans could see on the Arena ice Teemu Selanne, Thomas Steen, and various, less celebrated, others.

Towards the end of the year, the Crocus Fund, a labour-sponsored venture-capital fund, suspended trading, with the justification that some considered its stock overvalued. It was not clear when, if ever, shareholders would be able to divest themselves of unwanted shares. Before the end of 2004, there were resignations, accusations, and a lot of confusion. This issue was not destined to die with the close of the year.

Politics and political parties

The federal election had a significant impact on provincial and Winnipeg municipal politics. Winnipeg mayor Glen Murray had been under strong pressure from the Liberals to throw his hat in the federal ring.

He had a national profile, and a lot of admirers locally. He was at first somewhat reluctant to enter the fray, since it was apparently made clear to him by Reg Alcock, president of the federal Treasury Board and the Liberals' patronage boss and campaign manager for Manitoba, that he (Murray) should expect to have to fight for a nomination and could not expect to have anything handed to him on a silver platter. (This was perhaps not the best signal to send your star potential candidate. But the massive Alcock, 6'7" tall and heaven knows how many hundred pounds, is not noted for subtlety.)

The most obvious seat for Mayor Murray was Winnipeg South Centre, which contained his former City Council ward. However, the incumbent MP, Anita Neville, reputedly made it quite clear that she would make a fuss if she were to be forced out. In the end, John Harvard, the member for Charleswood-St James-Assiniboia in the House of Commons for eleven years, proved willing to accept the job of lieutenant governor, which had fortuitously become vacant. So Murray ran in Charleswood-St James-Assiniboia, not perhaps his 'natural area' but a winnable seat nonetheless. And he was to receive all kinds of help.

Under existing law, he had to resign as mayor of Winnipeg as soon as he became a candidate. Anyone wishing to run for the vacant mayoralty and who held public office also had to resign their positions. Hence, Murray's resignation set off a process requiring by-elections at both municipal and provincial levels, which had to be scheduled for a date not long before the federal general election. In fact, they were held only a week before the national election on 28 June. No doubt this caused confusion in some quarters.

There was a certain unexpected element to the results. The most significant was Murray's personal defeat. He lost a close race to the Conservative candidate, Steven Fletcher. Fletcher is a quadriplegic, the first ever to serve in Parliament, who has risen above the challenges of his medical condition to chart a successful career. In 2004 he was only thirty-two years of age and had served two active if controversial terms as president of the University of Manitoba Student's Union, acquired degrees in engineering and business, and been president of the provincial Progressive Conservative Association.

A number of city councillors resigned their seats to run for mayor. The irony was that they all lost, to a political newcomer but brilliantly successful businessman, Sam Katz, impresario and owner of a baseball team, the Winnipeg Goldeyes of the Northern League. Many felt that he could be relied upon to maintain Murray's vigorous pursuit of the public's business.

Murray himself found it hard to re-establish himself in the private sector, though he did sign a book contract. He ended the year as a resident fellow of Massey College at the University of Toronto. A controversial mayor but, in the eyes of many, an inspiration too, he appeared to have been able to shake Winnipegers out of their 'mediocre is good enough' mentality. To some, he had been one of the great mayors of Manitoba's capital.

There were also two consequential by-elections for the provincial house. Mary Ann Mihaychuk (the member from Minto in Winnipeg) resigned from the provincial cabinet and the legislature to run for mayor. Meanwhile, Mervyn Tweed, previously the PC member of the legislature for the rural seat of Minnedosa, near Brandon, was elected as a Conservative to the House of Commons. The resulting provincial by-elections reaffirmed the status quo.

The provincial parties had fluctuating fortunes this year. The Liberals struggled for attention most of the time. They had done quite well in the polls, the year before, but a poll published late in this year in the *Winnipeg Free Press*, and conducted by the local company Probe Research, suggested that the Liberals were losing ground provincially to the PCs. The Tories were clearly improving, but there remained some sentiment that their leader, Stuart Murray, lacked the qualities a party leader is expected to possess. For some people, that meant he was simply too nice a fellow to make himself grubby by stooping into the gutter of provincial politics. To others it meant 'Stu must go.'

At the head of the pack was the NDP and its leader Gary Doer. It is almost startling to realize that Doer entered his seventeenth year as party leader in April 2004, no doubt putting him in very select company as far as leadership of a provincial party, anywhere, was concerned. Although there had been occasional grumbling, he had never faced serious opposition within his party. And, according to national polls, he remained among the most popular, if not the most popular, premier in the country. No doubt this was due to his assiduous avoidance of political risk.

Other events

A number of other issues commanded attention in the course of the year. One was the continued saga of James Driskell, who had served a decade in prison for a murder he had not committed. An analysis of DNA evidence and other material by the Department of Justice in Ottawa cast doubt on the verdict. Driskell was not quite out of the woods but was getting closer when the federal minister of justice, Irwin Cottler, ordered a new trial. However, the province more or less declined to go any further, so it looked as if Driskell might soon have that particular incubus off his shoulders. It had been a long wait.

Not for the first time, public sentiment and general water-cooler discussion expressed a lack of confidence in the legal system, since three men with Winnipeg connections – David Milgaard, Thomas Sophonow, and now James Driskell – had served several years of their lives in prison for murders of which they were innocent. All three had been the victims of poor police work, as well as some people's incapacity to admit that they were wrong.

The city of Winnipeg became one of the first jurisdictions in the land to place a complete ban on smoking in public places; previously, there had been a partial ban. Huddling next to the entrance to one's workplace in mid-January while trying to keep warm at the same time was not to be allowed either, since a distance of twenty-five feet (eight metres) from the building was required. There was pressure on the province to follow suit, but the government seemed reluctant to annoy people any further.

Life in small-town Manitoba continued on its accustomed path, namely, varied economies (depending on the nature of the local economy) and stable, secure societies. For some small towns, the future looked bleak; they saw their young disappear to the cities, along with the professional people who provide leadership in such settings. Yet other communities were thriving. For the most part, such places offered the advantages of small town life but were located not too far from 'the city,' as Winnipeg is commonly referred to, and close to the American border. Thus, the fastest-growing communities in the province were places like Winkler and Steinbach, which were beginning to experience something of a housing shortage. Preferring a more conservative culture to what they expected to find in Winnipeg, a number of small firms located in these towns or others like them. They were also the favoured destinations of many of the international immigrants who had recently immigrated to Manitoba.

Winnipeg became the home of the national public health officer and in theory home of the Public Health Agency of Canada Laboratory. The location of the officer and the lab had been the subject of a lot of heavy politicking in the period before Dr David Butler-Jones got the appointment. There was considerable opposition to locating the office in Winnipeg, many people motivated by the usual dreary and self-serving objections to Winnipeg. It took every resource possessed by the formidable Reg Alcock to subdue the objections of colleagues such as Dr Carolyn Bennett, who was the cabinet member supposedly making the ultimate decision. As it turns out, no career scientists in Ottawa or Toronto (God forbid!) had to move. The new chief quickly got used to life on the plane, commuting between Winnipeg, Ottawa, and elsewhere.

KEN COATES AND GREG POELZER

The Territories

For decades, the Canadian north attracted little national attention and seemed locked in a permanent place on the political and economic margins of the nation. Yet, through the early years of the twenty-first century, northern Canada continued to evolve and develop in important ways, altering the long-standing colonial relationship with the government of Canada, emerging at the forefront of several critical global debates, and demonstrating the resilience and creativity of Indigenous peoples, communities, and governments in a constantly changing political environment. While the region still struggled to assert its presence in national affairs, widespread concern about climate change altered global interest in the region and provided the territorial north in Canada with an unexpected – and unwelcome – entrée into international affairs.

Developments in 2004 continued along a path of regional stability and steady improvement in economic prospects. Social challenges remained acute, with such areas as Indigenous housing receiving neither the attention nor the resources needed to address severe problems. The most substantial transitions in the area, including the implementation of land claims, self-government, and co-management agreements, attracted almost no national attention, although the arrangements were, in form and substance, of considerable long-term significance. For most Canadians, the territorial north had appeared to fall off the national radar; in the territories, public affairs were largely without controversy and rancour, but with several very promising signs of regional unity, national recognition, and growing global significance.

The north in national and international affairs

The north's perennial challenge – attracting national and international attention – remained in evidence in 2004, albeit with several very significant developments. The most dramatic change related to the growing international concern about the pace and impact of climate change and global warming. For the previous decade, scientists had been warning about rapid climate change, related to the release of CO_2 into the atmosphere. Arctic scientists were particularly concerned, given the region's environmental sensitivity and the likely impact of increased temperatures on the Arctic icecap, animal habitat, and Inuit reliance on the northern ecology. Northern residents had reported significant changes over the years, including sightings of unusual insects and birds, subtle shifts in animal migrations, and the growing instability of Arctic ice. While environmentalists outside the region paid heed to the early warnings, the gathering worries had not yet coalesced into a significant political movement.

Then came the release of the Arctic Climate Impact Assessment (ACIA) Report in 2004. The ACIA combined a comprehensive scientific review of the impact of global warming on the Arctic with a policy report outlining options for regional mitigation and adaptation. The report, prepared for the Arctic Council (an inter-state forum with representation from all eight circumpolar nations, Indigenous peoples, observer states, non-governmental organizations, and inter-parliamentary organizations), was presented in November. Previous reports about northern climate change had garnered little external attention; the seriousness and political acuity of the ACIA report ensured that it received international media coverage. As the report concluded:

Despite the fact that a relatively small percentage of the world's greenhouse gas emissions originate in the Arctic, human-induced changes in arctic climate are along the largest on earth. As a consequence, the changes already underway in arctic landscapes, communities, and unique gestures provide an early indication for the rest of the world of the environmental and social significance of global climate change. As this report illustrates, changes in climate and their impacts in the Arctic are already being widely noticed and felt, and are projected to become much greater. These changes will also reach far beyond the Arctic, affecting global climate, sea level, biodiversity, and many aspects of human social and economic systems. Climate change in the Arctic thus deserves and requires urgent attention by decision makers and the public worldwide.[1]

The core message – that one of the world's most vulnerable ecological zones faced serious threats due to industrial expansion and pollution in the south – linked north and south together in a manner not hitherto

1 Jim Berner et al., *Arctic Climate Impact Assessment – Scientific Report.*

seen. Media attention was strong, providing Indigenous representatives from across the territorial north, particularly Sheila Watt-Cloutier and Mary Simon, with an opportunity to raise Arctic concerns with international audiences. The response to the report was immediate; what separated this issue and this document from others was that it gave every indication of becoming the foundation for a long-term and comprehensive debate. Uniquely, the issue of climate change thrust the Canadian north into the forefront of one of the most important global debates in history, with the Arctic coming to symbolize the impact of industrial excess and the interconnectivity of humanity and the environment.

The north in the 2004 federal election

Arctic environmental concerns did not have an immediate impact on Canadian national politics. Indeed, in the chaos surrounding the sponsorship scandal, the Gomery Inquiry, and the weakened government of Prime Minister Paul Martin, northern issues seemed to register not at all at the national level. Prime Minister Martin called an early summer election, held on 28 June 2004, with the national campaign focusing largely on accusations of Liberal corruption and incompetence and the 'hidden agenda' of Stephen Harper's Conservative Party. The results were decidedly inconclusive, with the Liberals reduced to a minority government, albeit one buttressed by three Liberal members of Parliament from the territorial north. The Nunavut riding reflected the unique importance of personality and local support in the thinly populated constituency. Nancy Karetak-Lindell, the incumbent Liberal MP, won re-election easily over rivals Manitok Thompson (independent), Bill Riddell (NDP), and Duncan Cunninghman (Conservative). Karetak-Lindell received over 3,800 votes, more than three times the total of her closest rival, Thompson. Manitok Thompson had long been a significant force in territorial politics, elected to represent Aivilikin in the NWT legislature in 1995. She held high-level cabinet posts and later won the Rankin Inlet/Whale Cove riding in the first Nunavut election, held in 1999. She was the only woman to win her seat and subsequently held cabinet posts in the Nunavut government. A former Liberal, Thompson opted to run as an independent in the 2004 federal election, defeating her Conservative and NDP rivals but falling well short of Karetak-Lindell.

In the Northwest Territories, long-serving Liberal MP and cabinet minister Ethel Blondin-Andrew faced a substantial challenge. While she was highly regarded nationally – she was the first Aboriginal woman elected to the House of Commons – she had been facing progressively stiffer re-election contests. She won her seat in 2004 by only fifty-three votes over Dennis Bevington of the New Democratic Party. She was rewarded, subsequently, by maintaining her seat at the Liberal cabinet table, shifting from the Ministry of State (Children and Youth) to the Ministry of State (Northern Development), both minor positions in the Martin administration. The Yukon seat held to form as well, with Liberal MP Larry Bagnell winning easily over the second-place finisher, Pam Boyde of the NDP. Bagnell had a reputation for solid constituency work and ready accessibility, but he still represented a major change from the Yukon's long-standing tradition of sending prominent national politicians to Ottawa, including Eric Nielson, deputy prime minister and cabinet heavyweight, and Audrey McLaughlin, former leader of the NDP. Boyde tried to draw attention to Bagnell's inability to make a mark on Ottawa – 'Nice guy is not all an MP is about' – but Yukoners felt comfortable with their representative (*Whitehorse Star*, 25 June).

The north in national politics

Given the lack of attention to northern affairs in the 2004 election, and the absence of a powerful national figure from the region in Ottawa, many anticipated that northern issues would stay off the national agenda in 2004. That turned out not to be the case. Indeed, because of the steady increase in the power, ability, and presence of territorial political leaders, the focus had shifted from the federal arena to the more nuanced world of federal-territorial relations. The three northern leaders – Paul Okalik from Nunavut, Dennis Fentie from the Yukon, and Joe Handley (who replaced the very effective Stephen Kakfwi in December 2003) from the Northwest Territories – had been working collaboratively on a pan-northern agenda, focusing on such issues as the implementation of land-claims agreements, devolution of federal responsibilities, northern health-care funding, and long-term development strategies. Presenting a more coordinated front helped get the attention of the government of Canada.

Prime Minister Martin, with a long-term interest in northern and Aboriginal affairs, was open to a more comprehensive approach to territorial issues. The prime minister and the territorial leaders announced in mid-December 2004 that they were going to prepare a comprehensive Northern Strategy for Canada, with Indian and Northern Affairs Canada (INAC) in the lead role. The intention was to consult widely on the best means of developing the region, in accordance with local wishes and with the goal of addressing some of the most serious problems facing the north and its residents. The government leaders gave themselves less than a year to come up with a comprehensive strategy. The government of Canada allocated $120 million, split equally between the territories, towards the development and implementation of the Northern Strategy.

The idea got fairly strong reviews across the territorial north, where it was greeted as being the logical extension of the quarter-century-long devolution of responsibilities to territorial governments. As Premier Fentie stated in a video conference between Whitehorse and Gatineau (National Capital Region): 'It is obvious that that vision is about a whole Canada, a Canada from sea to sea to sea.'[2] Not everyone was unequivocally enthusiastic, however. As the Inuit Tapiriit Kanatami, which was generally quite supportive of the federal government initiative, pointed out: 'In the stated principles of the Northern strategy the government writes that it is "pan-Northern and comprehensive in scope." Much of the focus of this Northern Strategy Framework is on devolution of powers to Territorial governments. It ignores the imminent formation of Inuit-self government assemblies in Nunavik, and Nunatsiavut (Labrador). The $120-million commitment uniquely to three existing territories ignores over a third of the Inuit populations who live in these two Northern regions.'[3] For most Canadians, and indeed for the government of Canada, there was an assumed equivalence between the territorial north and the Canadian north, once again.

Territorial politics

Of the three territories, only Nunavut had an election in 2004. In the Yukon, the Yukon Party government led by Dennis Fentie remained in office, buttressed by a substantial majority (twelve of eighteen seats) in the Legislative Assembly. The Northwest Territories had hosted a territorial election the previous year and, in the style of the consensus government, had replaced Stephen Kakfwi, one of the most effective northern politicians of his generation, with Joe Handley. Kakfwi left territorial politics at that point. A minor scandal of sorts also hit Roger Allen, a NWT cabinet minister, who was already under criminal investigation when the accusation surfaced that he had given up resi-

---

2 'Northern Strategy Framework,' Remarks by Premier Dennis Fentie, 15 December 2004, Whitehorse, Yukon, and Gatineau, Ont., via videoconference.

3 Inuit Tapiriit Kanatami, 'Inuit Respond to Northern Strategy Framework,' 15 December 2004, http://www.itk.ca/media-centre/media-releases/inuit-respond-northern-strategy-framework.

dence in the Northwest Territories. Although living in northern Alberta, he had claimed to have a residence near Inuvik, making him eligible for a housing allowance from the government. He was forced to repay $10,000 and, in October 2004, stepped down from his seat in the Legislative Assembly.

Even in a year with no election, the Yukon did not suffer for want of political drama. Audit reports relating to the management of the municipal finances in Dawson City raised major concerns about the management of the community's affairs. Beginning in the 1990s, Dawson City Council had gone on a fairly extensive building program, adding a swimming pool, an improved recreation complex, and a city-wide television cable system. The town ran up debts well in excess of the limits set by the Yukon Municipal Act and had a cash shortfall of close to $1.5 million. Accusations circulated that Mayor Glen Everitt and Chief Administrative Officer James Scott Coulson had spent money unwisely, had not kept Dawson council properly informed, and had run up major expenses, including on the mayor's credit card, without attending to standard accounting measures. The details were not available in full in 2004, but the government of Yukon had learned enough. The mayor and the entire council were relieved of their duties and Dawson was put under the control of a public trustee. The conflict had sharp political overtones as well. Everitt was a well-known Liberal and sometimes-Liberal candidate in territorial elections. The governing Yukon Party represented a more conservative perspective and there was no love lost between the mayor and the local member of the Legislative Assembly.

The Nunavut election, only the second in the short history of the territory, involved the selection of the nineteen members of the Nunavut legislature. Nunavut's political environment remained highly contentious but not particularly volatile. There were major issues on the table, including the contentious plan to decentralize government services away from Iqaluit (as a means of revitalizing the economies in smaller centres), Nunavut's aggressive Inuvialuit-first language and hiring practices, and the need to improve educational outcomes in the territory, then among the very lowest in the country. Votes were held in eighteen of the nineteen ridings; long-time Inuit leader Tagak Curley was acclaimed in Rankin Inlet North, replacing John Anawak. As in the first election, Nunavut eschewed formal political parties and ran the election on a constituency basis. While Premier Peter Okalik ran again, as did many of his cabinet ministers, the territorial vote was not a standard ballot-box test of the popularity of the government of the day.

Election day results saw a sizable shift in the composition of the House. Eight of eighteen sitting members were re-elected; five incumbents, including Kevin O'Brien, Speaker of the legislature, lost their seats. Premier Okalik won his riding but was not assured of retaining the premiership. Indeed, following the election, he faced a substantial challenge from Tagak Curley but was narrowly returned to the premiership. Significantly, the non-partisan nature of the Nunavut electoral process resulted in some interesting patterns. The number of candidates up for election ranged from a low of one in Rankin Inlet North to seven in Uqqummiut. In the latter case, James Arreak won the constituency with only 27 per cent of the vote. At the opposite extreme, two candidates – Ed Picco and Paul Okalik – secured over 70 per cent of the votes in their ridings. The elected representatives were overwhelmingly Inuk in ethic background, Keith Peterson, the former mayor of Cambridge Bay, being a notable exception. Only two of the eighteen elected territorial representatives were female; long-serving member of the territorial assembly Manitok Thompson opted not to run in the election.

In the Nunavut election, almost everyone turned out to vote (81 per cent in total) – these are community contests in the main – but the number of electors is, by Canadian standards, extremely low. In the seven-candidate riding of Uqqummiut, for example, James Arreak won with slightly more than a quarter of the votes – but only 148 total ballots. The biggest vote getter in the territory – Edward Picco in Iqaluit East – secured the backing of only 569 voters. Peter Kattuk won the riding of Hudson Bay with almost 43 per cent of the vote, but only 127 ballots marked with his name. The Nunavut legislature was, like those across the territorial north, an exercise in very direct democracy, where family and personal connections and ties to the local community played a major role in determining electoral success.

A post-election review of the 2004 contest conducted by the chief electoral officer revealed significant problems with the conduct of elections in Nunavut. The absence of professionally run political parties meant that candidates and their managers, financiers, and advisers did not fully understand territorial requirements. There were consistent problems with getting financial reports completed in a timely fashion, even though the sums involved were typically very small. The chief electoral officer suffered from a shortage of a trained and readily available staff and had to cope with the formidable logistics of delivering ballots to and collecting them from a vast territory; indeed, residents in several remote communities were actually permitted to vote by telephone. The CEO also recommended that winter elections be avoided, since the prospect of severe storms was so high as to represent a significant threat to the ability to complete the election in a timely manner.

Public affairs in the Yukon Territory

Stability and gradual improvement remained the dominant characteristic of the Yukon in 2004. The population of the territory increased marginally from the previous year, up from just fewer than 30,000 to over 30,600. Whitehorse, with almost 22,800 people, accounted for almost all of the growth. The Yukon's unemployment rate fell markedly, from 9.3 per cent to 5.8 per cent; government employment made up a comparatively small portion of the increase in jobs while still representing one-third of all of the employed workers in the territory. With wage increases slightly above the national average – 3.0 per cent compared to 2.2 per cent nationally – and with inflation about half that of Canada as a whole (1.0 per cent compared to 1.9 per cent), the territory appeared to be in fairly good shape.

Solid economic signs could be seen across the Yukon, especially in the near doubling (from $33.6 million to $62.6 million) in resource production, most of it in gold. There was also a significant increase in building permits, resource prices, and the number of travellers visiting the territory, the latter a key indicator of the strength of the crucial tourism industry. Rental vacancies had fallen to slightly more than 5 per cent, one-quarter of what they had been five years earlier. The number of employment-insurance claims dipped in 2004, as well. Costs remained significantly higher in the outlying communities than in Whitehorse, with Dawson residents paying a full 20 per cent more than in the capital city. Housing prices in Whitehorse, at an average of $188,000 in 2004, continued to increase sharply, a further sign of consumer confidence in the territorial economy. The territory's GDP jumped from $1.3 billion in 2003 to $1.4 billion the following year, solid if unspectacular growth.

The Yukon appeared, on a statistical level, at least, to have found equilibrium by the early part of the twenty-first century. The wild economic swings of the previous three decades had been replaced, in general, by stability. The Yukon Party government was well entrenched in office and had not implemented the strong conservative measures its opponents had feared. Government remained the backbone of the economy, aided by a strong seasonal tourism sector and an ever resilient gold mining industry. Aboriginal land claims had largely been settled, with attention now focused on the difficult, but less flashy, task of implementing the agreements and the self-government accords. While social challenges remained, particularly in the outlying communities and within the Aboriginal population, general conditions in the Yukon seemed to be improving. For example, life expectancy for Aboriginal males stood at sixty-three years in 1994 and had risen to sixty-seven a decade later. For non-Aboriginal males, life expectancy had gone from seventy-three to seventy-five years. A major gap remained, but the margin had closed significantly. The changes in Yukon life lacked profile and drama, but they represented a steady improvement in social and economic conditions across much of the territory.

The Yukon remained pretty much at steady state through 2004, save for the major conflict between the government of Yukon and Dawson council. The government continued to lobby for the construction of a natural gas pipeline along the Alaska Highway, a project at odds with the Mackenzie Valley Pipeline project but with substantial Aboriginal support in the territory. Mineral exploration activity continued on a modest scale, but without major discoveries or new operations. The placer gold operations remained active, as did the summer tourist operations. But, if there were no great reasons for celebrate in 2004, there were no reasons for panic either. The economy maintained its course, as did public affairs generally. The Yukon Party administration led by Dennis Fentie was successful without being overwhelmingly popular – it had more support in the communities than in the government-dominated centre of Whitehorse. Aboriginal politics had turned substantially internal, focusing more on claims implementation than on major battles with government, and federal-territorial relations emphasized the internal mechanisms of devotion more than high-level constitutional wrangling.

Public affairs in the Northwest Territories

The Northwest Territories, much like the Yukon, appeared to have settled into a pattern of incremental change. In previous decades, the opening of new mines, like the major diamond mines developed east of Yellowknife, would have resulted in a spike in population. Now, with the mines flying their personnel in and out of the NWT and with greater than ever reliance on the regional workforce, population growth remained very limited. Indeed, the territorial population of 31,940 in 2004 represented an increase of only 300 over the previous year, accounted for almost entirely by the Aboriginal population's very high birth rate. Births over deaths in the NWT in 2004 were roughly 7,000 over 150 and net out-migration was close to 500 people. As in Nunavut, the population was predominantly young and, as in the Yukon, concentrated in a handful of cities, with Yellowknife accounting for more than 19,000 of the territory's residents (and with Fort Smith, Hay River, and Inuvik adding another 6,800 people). With a birth rate a full 60 per cent higher than the national average, it was clear that natural increase would ensure a steady growth in the territorial population.

The economic conditions in the NWT continued to change, largely in a positive direction. For example, federal government support payments for NWT residents stood at $9.3 million in 2004, an increase of $300,000 from the previous year but a full $3.6 million lower than in 1998, a peak year for the territory. The number of income-support cases, likewise, had fallen from over 1,700 in the last three years of the previous decade to slightly more than 1,100 in 2004. Average income stood at $44,080, an increase of $1,500 on the previous year. Personal incomes ranged widely, however, from a low of $23,500 in Wrigley to over $52,000 in Yellowknife. Labour-force activity remained relatively strong, with 76 per cent of the population working and with an official unemployment rate dropping a full percentage point to 6.0 per cent. Prices had increased by some 2 per cent over the previous year, roughly in keeping with the increase in income. The high cost of living in the smaller and remote communities remained a major problem. In the small settlement of Paulatuk, food prices were 222 per cent higher than in Yellowknife. Even Fort Simpson, at 145 per cent, was significantly more expensive, as was Fort Resolution, at 131 per cent. Building permits spiked dramatically in 2004, related largely to the growth of Yellowknife and the diamond sector. Non-residential permits exceeded $100 million, up significantly from the previous two years, which averaged close to $89 million. Crude oil production remained steady, although there was a significant drop – from 988,000 to 739,000 thousand cubic metres – in natural gas production. Diamond production, on the other hand, soared from $1.6 billion in 2003 to over $2 billion in 2004, helping to offset a dramatic decline in gold shipments (from $42 million to $8.8 million). Overall, the GDP for the NWT jumped from $3.7 billion in 2003 to $4.3 billion in 2004.

On the opposite side of the ledger, major social problems remained in evidence. Crime rates, for example, continued to be exceptionally high, with over 19,500 cases recorded in 2004 – up from around 11 per cent a decade earlier. Of these, over 2,900 were crimes of violence. The overall crime rate was staggeringly high, at 45 per 100 people, which was higher than Nunavut (38/100) and the Yukon (25/100) and well in advance of the 8/100 rate for the country as a whole. The same was true of such unfortunate indicators of underlying social pathology as spousal abuse, alcohol and drug abuse, and suicide, particularly among the young. Problems related to sexuality, including teenage pregnancy, incest, and sexual assault, remained persistent. Housing also remained an important challenge in the NWT. Among the 13,902 households in the territory, 4,015 (29 per cent) had some type of housing problem, and 2,260 (16 per cent) were in core need. Core need is defined as a household with a housing problem but without with sufficient levels of income to address it.[4]

Dreams for a better future continued to dominate public affairs in the Northwest Territories. For more than a quarter-century, promoters and governments had been debating the desirability of constructing a natural gas pipeline down the Mackenzie River valley. The issue remained on the table throughout 2004, seeming to move slowly towards a decision to proceed. When the pipeline project had surfaced in the 1970s, Aboriginal groups opposed the plans vociferously, demanding comprehensive protection of the environment and the northern way of life. By 2004, Aboriginal governments, companies, and individuals provided strong – but far from unanimous – support for the pipeline project. The fact that Indigenous organizations were going to benefit directly through partial ownership of the pipeline, and from royalty agreements associated with land-claims settlements, was behind the change of heart on this crucial matter.

The Northwest Territories economy continued to expand, enjoying near boom conditions in 2004. The continued development of the diamond sector spurred the economy. With two diamond mines in operation and several more in development, the NWT seemed poised for a prolonged period of prosperity. Furthermore, the continued development of the Beaufort Sea oil and gas fields underlined the continued strength of the Inuvik region and promised further expansion in exploratory and productive activity. Aboriginal groups were increasingly engaged in the regional economy, largely through commercial joint ventures, government and corporate training programs, and land-settlement royalty arrangements. While the economic circumstances for many Indigenous peoples remained largely unchanged, greater opportunities for the growing number of young Aboriginal people completing high school, college, and university programs established a very different base for employment and development at the community and regional level.

4 Government of the Northwest Territories, *2004 NWT Community Survey*.

Land-claims negotiations continued, albeit with a steadily declining number of Aboriginal groups. In December 2004 the Tlicho/Dogrib and the territorial and federal governments reached an agreement on land claims and self-government rights. The accord provided the Tlicho with control over some 39,000 square kilometres of land and gave them a share of royalty revenue from the NWT's diamond mines. The tripartite agreement ended a long-running negotiation and provided the communities with a radically different legal and financial foundation for the governance of community affairs. As Dogrib Grand Chief Joe Rabesca commented, 'I worked at it for so long – all the travel, the work people done. I'm used to speaking in public, but I don't know what to say. I'm so happy. Everybody here is ready to go to dance.'[5] By 2004, most of the outstanding claims in the NWT had been resolved, leaving the Deh Cho in the southwest part of the territory to complete an agreement with the government of Canada.

Public affairs in Nunavut

Nunavut faced formidable challenges in 2004, primarily those of a weak, government-dependent economy, a youthful and socially challenged Indigenous population, widely scattered and small communities, a ferociously high cost of living, and numerous health and other pathologies that affected the safety and stability of the territory. The territorial population continued to grow, reaching 29,900 in 2004, a function of one of the highest birth rates in the industrial world. There were 24 births per 1,000 people in Nunavut in 2004, much more than double the Canadian average of 10.6 and much higher than the NWT's 16/1000. The death rate, in contrast, was around 4/1000 people, well under the national average of more than 7/1000.

Nunavut was, as a consequence, a very young jurisdiction, the youngest in Canada, with a rapidly expanding school population, overcrowded housing, and severe pressures on social and community services. Iqaluit remained by far the largest community, with close to 6,000 people, more than one-fifth of the Nunavut total. The other settlements were very small, with the next nine largest communities ranging from Rankin Inlet's 2,200 residents to Pond Inlet's 1,200. Crime rates, as in the NWT, remained shockingly high, with approximately 39 offences per 100 people in 2004, up sharply from 20/100 in 1999 (Canada's rate

5 'Diamond Royalties Part of N.W.T. Land Claims Bill,' CBC News, 8 December 2004.

stood at a comparatively small 9/100). Other measures – including the fact than well over 40 per cent of Nunavut residents over twelve years of age smoked, against a national average of 16.5 per cent – pointed to a territory that was young, poor, and facing severe health problems.

The challenges in Nunavut were daunting, with no obvious resolution. The small and scattered population of Nunavut placed immense pressures on the government of the territory. In addition, the social, economic, and cultural crises that affected most communities added to the geographic and climatic difficulties. Over 60 per cent of the Nunavut population was under twenty-five years old. Substance and sexual abuse and the extremely serious and widespread challenge of fetal alcohol syndrome only added to rapidly expanding educational, social work, and medical costs. Community infrastructure lagged well behind accepted Canadian standards, with urgent needs for additional housing, safe water and sewage systems, schools, medical facilities, and the like. By 2004 Clyde River had experienced a decade-long wait for a government-funded home; Iqaluit had over 100 families on the list of those needing social housing. The reality that there were few economic prospects beyond fishing and diamond mining gave the territory a sense of being unable to escape its fundamental fiscal difficulties.

The Nunavut economy continued to expand, albeit largely through increased government expenditures. The territorial GDP stood at $991 million in 2003 and increased to slightly more than $1 billion the following year. Inflation had been held in check, reaching only 1 per cent a year, which helped a little to address the very high cost of living. Personal incomes were perhaps higher than expected, with a median family income of $49,900 in 2004, as against a national median income of $58,100. This figure, however, masks two important realities: the extremely high cost of living in Nunavut communities and the fact that a disproportionate number of the best-paying jobs in the territory (police officers, senior civil servants, teachers and principals, and company officials) were held by non-Inuit people. Nunavut family income was well below that in the Yukon ($67,800, the second-highest in the country) and the NWT ($79,800, the highest in Canada).

The contours of public affairs in Nunavut did not change significantly in 2004. The newness of the Nunavut political experiment meant several things: that the costs of government remained very high and a focus for public debate, that the growing rivalry between Iqaluit and the other communities would remain highly contentious and fuel demands for decentralization of government services, and that the effort to make the political and administrative systems in Nunavut more Inuvialuit in nature would consume a great deal of public attention. Northern politicians knew that the effort to transform the territory would take time, displaying a patience that was not generally shared by southern politicians and members of the Nunavut public. Still, for a political undertaking that was only five years old in 2004, Nunavut had made some impressive strides.

One of the most controversial public issues of the year involved the firing of Harbir Boparai, hired into a short-term position in Panniqtuuq. Boparai, of South Asian descent, alleged that he had been subject to racial discrimination and was fired from his job unfairly. Subsequent discussion of the firing focused on the discrimination claim and Nunavut's Inuit-first hiring practices (Boparai was apparently replaced by a non-Inuk person). Moreover, the case drew claims that the premier's office had interfered in the process, raising questions about the use of political power in the territory.

Federal Auditor General Sheila Fraser generated considerable debate with her department's exposure of major managerial and financial problems with Nunavut Power Corporation, and the continued inability of the federal and territorial governments to ensure adequate housing for northern residents remained a major shortcoming of public administration in the north. Also, the near collapse of municipal administration in Kugluktuk, a problem with both administrative and financial roots, revealed the still substantial cracks in local governance and infrastructure funding in Nunavut.

There was continued evidence of the deeply entrenched culture of violence in Nunavut and of the inability of the justice system to respond to the challenges. In September 2004 a violent offender just released from prison sexually assaulted four women in Cambridge Bay. Neither the local RCMP detachment nor the local probation officer, who was already carrying a staggering caseload, was told that the man had come back to the community. Health, likewise, remained a prominent issue in the region, with the implementation of aggressive anti-smoking legislation offset by continuingly distressing news about the shortcomings of territorial health services.

While the general economic scene in Nunavut remained grim, dominated by extremely high levels of unemployment and widespread government and individual dependence on federal transfers, there was growing evidence of commercial activity taking root in the territory. The Baffin Fisheries Coalition, established to improve Nunavut's opportunities in the commercial fishery, continued to press the federal Department of Fisheries and Oceans for an enhanced quota, especially for turbot. Together with extensive training, business development, and fisheries oversight, the quota discussions formed the basis of a gradually expanding Inuit presence in the fisheries and an expanded economic basis for the territory.

Even more promising was the development of the mining sector. In 2004 the government of Canada announced preliminary approval of Tahera Diamond Corporation's Jericho mine. In the past, Nunavut had relied almost exclusively on enterprises funded either in whole or in part by government. The prospect of an independent, commercially viable mine in Nunavut, this one with an anticipated cost of construction alone of some $100 million, raised the possibility of long-term, sustainable economic growth based on natural-resource development. Although the mine was expected to be in operation for only a decade or so, it promised to spur additional exploration and development and provided Nunavut with an entrée into the high-value diamond-mining sector.

Yet, even with the promising development of the diamond mine, Nunavut's financial woes continued without any quick resolution in sight. Put simply, the government of Nunanvut saw no easy way of escaping its dependency on massive federal government transfer payments, which amounted to more than $700 million, or 90 per cent of the territorial government's budget, in 2004. In the first years after the creation of Nunavut, the government actually had surplus funds, simply because it took some time to build up the staffing of the new territory. By 2004, with the euphoria of the creation of the territory worn off, with increasing expectations for government action, and with capital in short supply, the government and the territory found themselves in a financial dilemma. Forecasts predicted an operating deficit at the territorial level of close to $50 million by the end of 2004.

The north in 2004

For much of the previous decade, the territorial north had been locked in a seemingly endless struggle against southern forces and the government of Canada. The year 2004 was emblematic of the 'new' north, a region empowered to care for its own affairs but still financially dependent on the federal government. This was a year of optimism and increasing territorial confidence. The economic boom in the NWT spread in 2004 to Nunavut, with the start of work on the latest of Canada's diamond mines. The possibility of a major natural gas pipeline seemed greater than before – and the prospect remained that there could be two and not just one connections between Arctic carbon reserves and southern markets. Indigenous organizations, no doubt exhausted from a generation-long struggle over land claims, self-government rights, and compensation, gradually settled into the equally difficult task of administering local affairs and rebuilding harmed communities. Among the most promising developments in the territorial north were the steadily improving relations between Indigenous and other northerners. Tensions of the past had largely dissipated – although not entirely. In their place, the north had developed one of the most collaborative and interconnected social environments in the country. There were signs, however, of major changes in the offing, including a markedly different relationship with the government of Canada, growing international interest in Arctic climate change, and the gradual realization that Indigenous influence over territorial affairs had become a dominant theme in the evolution of Canada's three northern territories.

ROBERT DRUMMOND

Ontario

For much of the first part of 2004, the Liberal government of Dalton McGuinty that had taken office in October 2003 seemed to be continuing the election campaign. While it announced several planned reforms (the end of mandatory retirement, abolition of the sixty-hour work week, red-light cameras at intersections, etc.), it was able to do very little to advance them until the legislature reconvened in March, and it continued to express concerns about constraints that would result from the budget deficit it had inherited from the previous government. There was considerable attention paid to the allegations of profligate spending by prominent Conservatives appointed to positions of authority in the energy sector, and the public inquiry into the Ipperwash incident in which protestor Dudley George had been killed got under way. The budget was presented to the legislature in mid-May, but it was preceded and followed by promises of increased funding for hospitals and health-care personnel, highways and infrastructure, shelters for abused women, and better processing of family-support orders. The government took the position that it could not fund necessary improvements in health and education, and balance the budget, while upholding the premier's campaign commitment not to raise taxes. When it introduced a new health levy, to be collected along with the income tax, and projected a budget deficit for fiscal year 2004, the opposition eagerly took it to task for breaking campaign promises. The premier's defence was that the people of the province would prefer, when they knew all the facts, to see quality restored to public services. They would, he believed, accept the health levy and the delay in balancing the budget as necessary compromises.

For the first half of the year, the government was also bedevilled by a continuing dispute with the owners of the 407 toll highway in the northern part of the Greater Toronto Area. The government insisted that its agreement with the highway owners required government approval for toll increases – an assertion the owners denied. The government banked on the political goodwill to be gained from voters if it resisted the unpopular increases, even if in the end it might be unable to sustain its position with regard to the need for government approval.

On the opposition side, the Progressive Conservatives were forced to seek new leadership when former Premier Ernie Eves announced his intention to step down. After a somewhat subdued campaign through the spring and summer, the party selected its new leader in September, choosing the relatively moderate John Tory in preference to more conservative candidates Frank Klees and Jim Flaherty. The NDP, in the meantime, regained official party status in the legislature when its candidate, Andrea Horvath, won a 13 May by-election in Hamilton East, taking a Liberal seat made vacant by the untimely death of MPP Dominic Agostino.

Perhaps the most significant matters of attention for the government and opposition during the year, however, were the long-standing policy issues of health-care delivery and the cost and supply of energy, particularly electricity.

Early events

The government began the year by announcing some reforms of varying significance. Almost its first action in the new year was the announcement of a new traffic rule – henceforth traffic on urban streets would be expected to yield the right-of-way to buses (for example, as they exited roadside stop areas). The government mused about the possibility of bringing back the photo-radar system (to address speeding) cancelled by the previous government. A move that was perhaps more consequential (though with narrower impact) was the announcement of an end to the lifetime ban on the receipt of social assistance levied on those who were found to have cheated the welfare system. In the matter of the government's plan to end the sixty-hour work week, there was an undertaking to consult employers and workers before taking action.

On another labour-relations matter, Labour Minister Chris Bentley indicated at the end of January that the government would not undertake to ban replacement workers during strikes but would not itself use them. In November the government finally tabled a comprehensive labour-relations reform bill, repealing many of the changes in labour law that had been introduced by the Harris government. The Liberals presented their bill as restoring a balance in labour relations, somewhere between the pro-union provisions of the NDP's labour laws and the anti-union actions of the Harris Conservatives. Not surprisingly, critics from the

NDP and the unions did not believe that the measures went far enough in the direction of encouraging organization for collective bargaining, while the Conservatives and representatives of business saw them as going too far.

A judicial inquiry into the safety of the meat industry was announced in January; the 'tainted meat' scandal of the previous year had led to call for a public inquiry, but the government elected to appoint Superior Court Justice Roland Haines to conduct the probe without necessarily holding public hearings. Preliminary work was begun on the promised inquiry into the Ipperwash incident, as interested parties posed questions about who would be called as witnesses and who would have standing to make representations.

The continuing issue of the potential use of the Adams mine in northern Ontario as a garbage site for southern Ontario (mainly Toronto) waste returned to the news in January as the province talked of plans to drain water from the site to make it usable for landfill. Local residents and others objected, and the project was delayed; in April the government determined that it would not proceed and instead introduced legislation to ban the use of the mine as a dump site. At about the same time, the province's brewers sought to contribute to reducing solid waste by urging the Liquor Control Board and other businesses to pursue a deposit-and-return system for bottles like the one operated by Brewers Retail.

When the government speculated about seeking a full ban on smoking in all workplaces and public places, a coalition of pub and bar owners argued that there would then be a need for them to be compensated for anticipated loss of business.

Energy

In mid-January, the government announced that the Task Force on Electricity Conservation and Supply would soon report with recommendations. However, much of the attention paid to the energy sector in the news was related to allegations about lavish spending by executives of the successor companies to Ontario Hydro. On 17 January, Canadian Press cited a *Globe and Mail* story that suggested former Mike Harris senior adviser Deb Hutton had, while a vice-president of Hydro One, run up lavish expenses, including 'thousands for meals.' Government spokespersons wondered if Hutton could be compelled to repay the money. Three days later, Canadian Press reported allegations that Glen Wright, former chairman of Hydro One, had billed thousands of dollars for hunting trips. Accusers suggested the trips had been seen as a good way to 'mend relations with Tory insiders' while the Progressive Conservatives were still in office. A second of the firms generated by the break-up of Ontario Hydro was similarly discussed at the end of January, when it was alleged that two former executives of Ontario Power Generation (OPG), William Farlinger and Ron Osborne, had billed some $800,000 in foreign travel costs, including concert tickets and golf fees, over a five-year period. Farlinger, a former Conservative candidate, had been released from OPG in December. He denied knowledge of missing receipts for claims he had made and asserted that all his claims were legitimate, having been reviewed by the company's internal audit staff and reported properly to the OPG board.

At the end of February, the energy minister, Dwight Duncan, sought to turn public attention to the contracts for services issued by former executives of Hydro One to prominent Conservative advisers and activists. According to Duncan, untendered contracts worth $5.6 million had been issued to prominent Conservatives, including Leslie Noble, co-chair of the PC election campaign, Paul Rhodes, election campaign communications director, and Michael Gourley, a close adviser of Ernie Eves. Long-time Conservative strategist Tom Long was a senior official of a 'headhunting' firm that had been paid over $80,000 to recruit Deb Hutton to serve as vice-president of Hydro One. Recipients of the contracts defended them as good deals for the corporation and normal business practices. Minister Duncan described them as cronyism and corruption and promised that nothing similar would happen with the Liberals in office.

In mid-March, the substance of energy policy was more directly addressed when former federal minister John Manley issued his report on the future of Ontario Power Generation. He recommended that the province rely on nuclear power to address a power shortage that might emerge as early as 2007. That reliance would lead to the restoration to service of the Pickering A nuclear station at a cost of some $600 million. Manley recommended more joint ventures with private-sector firms but urged that OPG itself remain under government ownership and retain ownership of the main power-generating assets. He further recommended a new structure for the corporation, separating nuclear and hydro/fossil generation into separate divisions, and he called for government to appoint up to twelve members with power-sector experience to the board of the corporation. He recommended that OPG withdraw from smaller operations, including wind, solar, and biomass projects. Reaction to the report was mixed, but criticisms predominated. Canadian Press (18 March) quoted Jack Gibbons of the Ontario Clean Air Alliance as saying that nuclear power was a very high-cost, high-risk option: 'Nuclear power is the most expensive way to try to keep the lights on in this province.' Similarly, John Wilson, a former Hydro One board member and then with the Ontario Electricity Coalition, expressed concern about the high cost of repairing and building nuclear reactors. Opposition response was predictably partisan, with former Conservative energy minister John Baird saying the report showed the premier had made a promise he knew he could not keep – to close coal-fired generating plants by 2007 – purely for political gain. NDP Leader Howard Hampton saw the report as demonstrating that the transition from Conservatives to Liberals had simply produced more of the same. Ken Ogilvie, executive director of Energy Probe, was quoted in the Canadian Press story as regretting the recommendation to move away from low-impact renewable energy, while the CEO of the Ontario Chamber of Commerce described the report as the 'first positive, proactive step taken in quite some time.'

After the legislature reconvened in late March, the government continued to pursue changes in the electricity sector. The high cost of energy was highlighted in early April by the announcement that the percentage of those earning over $100,000 at OPG and Hydro One had skyrocketed since 1999. At Hydro One the percentage had gone from 7 per cent to 35 per cent, while at OPG it had gone from 12 per cent to 36 per cent. In mid-April, Energy Minister Duncan announced (in a speech to the Empire Club) the plan to create a new power-management agency – the Ontario Power Authority – partly to deal with conservation initiatives but also to sign long-term contracts with private electricity generators. The Liberals had raised the price cap on electricity on 1 April, but the minister now announced that the price of electricity would be a blend of the rate set by the Ontario Energy Board for OPG-produced energy combined with the market cost of electricity. The legislation was to be introduced in June. In the meantime, the government in early May invited private-sector firms to propose new renewable-energy projects. Such projects took time to emerge, but in October Suncor, Enbridge, and Spanish-owned EHN WindPower Canada submitted a proposal for a seventy-five-megawatt wind-power project east of Lake Huron, near Ripley, Ontario. The consortium already had wind-power projects in Alberta and Saskatchewan. In November, Canadian Press reported some nine or ten contracts that firms had signed with the province to produce electricity through renewable means – five wind-generation sites ranging from thirty-nine to ninety-nine megawatts of capacity; two small water-powered projects with a total of thirty-one megawatts of capacity; and two biogas/landfill projects at 7.5 megawatts, with a third awaiting municipal approval. These projects represented something of a drop in the bucket when compared with the province's need for power.

When the energy restructuring bill was introduced in June, it followed the broad outline of Duncan's April speech, creating the Ontario Power Authority, which would include a Conservation Secretariat to promote energy conservation by government, businesses, and homeowners. One conservation measure proposed was the introduction of so-called smart meters which could allow different rates to be charged depending on time of use. The government hoped to have such meters in all Ontario homes by 2010, following the introduction of a more flexible pricing structure by the spring of 2005.

At committee hearings on the bill in August, Steven Thomas of the University of Greenwich in the United Kingdom testified at the invitation of the Society of Energy Professionals. He warned against reliance on a competitive private market for electricity, since that would result in much higher prices for residential consumers who lacked the market power of large corporations. He cast doubt as well on the likelihood that foreign firms would want to invest in creating generating capacity in Ontario. Energy Minister Duncan dismissed the testimony, saying he believed that Professor Thomas was wrong and that investors would certainly be unlikely to come into the province if a public monopoly were restored.

The continued importance of nuclear power was evident in early August as Jim Blyth, formerly of the Canadian Nuclear Safety Commission, was appointed to OPG as the director general of Power Reactor Regulation. He was charged with the task of managing the aging and life extension of nuclear plants. Producing some 40 per cent of Ontario's electricity, many such plants would need refurbishing by 2009. Observers noted the long delays and significant cost overruns in the restoration of the Pickering A station. In September the government began negotiations with Bruce Power to restart the Bruce nuclear power plants that had been closed for repair.

The unusual range and complexity of matters falling within the scope of energy policy was evident in October, when the government introduced legislation to allow power distributors to cut electricity to locations suspected of being marijuana-growing operations.

Health

In January the province announced that Dr Sheela Basrur would be appointed as Ontario's chief medical officer of health. Basrur had performed with distinction as Toronto's medical officer of health during the SARS crisis of the previous year and the appointment was greeted with general approbation. However, the impact of the SARS epidemic continued to be felt. In February, Andrea Williams, a nurse who had been a hospital patient and had contracted SARS two weeks after officials said the outbreak was over, filed suit against the city, the province, and the federal government seeking compensation for her ordeal. In March a group of thirty nurses who had contracted SARS also filed suit against the Ontario government, asserting that more protection should have been provided and that they should be compensated for suffering and hardship. In April reports were issued by Mr Justice Archie Campbell and Queen's University Dean of Medicine Dr David Walker reviewing the SARS epidemic and making recommendations for reform of the public-health system.

Justice Campbell's report, issued 20 April (and summarized in a Canadian Press story by reporter James McCarten), praised the 'heroic' efforts of the front-line health workers in eventually containing the outbreak but was severely critical of the system within which they had to work. Recognizing that it was easier to spot the problems in hindsight than it could have been for those who were dealing with the epidemic at the time, Justice Campbell nevertheless cited twenty-three problems that exacerbated the crisis. Inadequate laboratory capacity, the absence of a public-health communications strategy, and the lack of a plan to deal with a pandemic were all symptoms of the decline in public-health funding. Poor coordination with federal authorities was also cited, as well as confusion about liability and responsibilities. There was some criticism of the leadership provided by Ontario's then chief medical officer of health, Dr Colin D'Cunha, though there were no allegations of misconduct or wrongdoing. The twenty-one principles Campbell cited for reform of the system included a new mandate, new leadership, and new resources for public health, as well as the uploading to the provincial level of certain municipal public-health services.

Former Premier Ernie Eves acknowledged that there were things that could have been done better but argued that governments of all stripes had been in office over the period in which the public-health system had declined in effectiveness. It was only when the SARS crisis brought the problems to the surface that they became generally visible. Health Minister George Smitherman gave his assurances that a comprehensive public-health reform plan would be unveiled over the next two months.

The day after Justice Campbell's report, the expert panel headed by Dr David Walker released its own. That report called for an investment of almost $200 million in the public-health system over a five-year period, and the chairman called that a 'down payment.' Much of the money would go towards the creation of a new health protection and promotion agency, including a revitalized provincial laboratory. The report called as well for more training to be given to front-line health workers and for an electronic network linking health-care providers across the province. In all there were 103 recommendations, including 53 that had been contained in an interim report issued in December 2003. Medical professionals generally welcomed the recommendations, but some were nervous about how long the report would keep public attention. Canadian Press quoted Dr Richard Schabas, chief of staff at York Central Hospital north of Toronto: 'I've seen public health have these moments of attention before, and then seen it dissipate ... I just hope that we really get some change' (21 April).

The Walker panel insisted on an agency that had considerable autonomy from the political system, calling for an independent governing board nominated by experts and stakeholders. It also called for greater autonomy for the province's chief medical officer of health. The newly appointed incumbent, Basrur, indicated that she was working with Health Minister Smitherman on legislation to govern the role and independence of her office.

The government had made several announcements concerning funding for the health-care system in general throughout the late winter – money for hospital equipment such as patient lifts and electric beds in early February, more money for hospitals' general budgets later that month, and a promise of funds in early March to improve hospital safety through training to reduce medication errors and surgical mistakes. Near the end of February, Monique Smith, parliamentary assistant to the health minister, complained of some wealthy patients seeking to 'jump the queue' to receive early treatment. The Ontario Medical Association (OMA) decried her comments, saying that the problem was underfunding of the system and resultant long waits for care.

When the budget came down in May, a significant element of the spending priorities was a promise of an extra $4.8 billion over four years for health. Plans included 150 family-health teams to improve primary care, 8,000 new nursing positions, a 20 per cent increase in hospital operating funds, and over $400 million for public health over the four-year period. A vaccination program for chickenpox and meningitis, several new MRI and CAT scan sites, and major increases in the capacity to perform needed surgeries in areas with the longest wait times filled out the list. Home care and long-term care were also targeted for increased support. The expenditures were seen by government supporters as justification for the new health levy, and perhaps also for increases in the tax on cigarettes, beer, and wine.

Despite the promise of added support for hospitals, however, the province found itself facing a shortfall in hospital budgets (approximately $600 million) in the late summer and a difficult round of negotiations with physicians over the fee schedule in the latter part of the year. The province eventually gave hospitals until 1 November to produce plans for eliminating their deficits, but critics suggested that there was no prospect of their doing so by administrative savings alone. They feared that some loss of service (and/or greater wait times) would be inevitable, though Health Minister Smitherman urged people not to be worried about service cuts, saying that the government would be reviewing hospital plans with an eye on maintaining the quality of health-care delivery.

In the early spring, the province faced considerable criticism over its decision not to cancel public-private hospital partnerships that had been agreed to by the previous government. Provincial health-sector unions organized a march on 3 April to protest the policy, saying that the Liberals had promised to cancel such agreements during the election campaign. While some could understand the reluctance to scuttle plans that were already well under way, they were not happy about the government's unwillingness to promise that it would not enter into such agreements in the future. The degree of private provision in the health-care system continued to be an issue of controversy, and in July the government took action in one area of such concern when it bought five private CT/MRI clinics to bring them back into the public sector.

One of the highlights of the government's efforts to reduce wait times for medical care and problems for patients seeking a family doctor was a plan to speed up entry of foreign-trained physicians to the health-care delivery system. As early as March, the health minister, the College of Physicians and Surgeons, and the province's medical schools combined to provide a new program doubling the residency places for foreign-trained doctors. In May, however, the college was still calling for more international medical graduates to be hired, claiming that thousands of physicians from medical schools outside Canada and the United States were not being permitted to practice. And in August the government was still announcing the doubling of residency places it had begun to discuss in March. Then in October, the province appointed former judge George Thomson to review the regulatory community's appeal processes for accrediting foreign (especially health) professionals. Training, Colleges and Universities Minister Mary Ann Chambers, quoted on 6 October by Canadian Press, described the procedures as 'confusing and arbitrary.' There seemed to be little progress in an area that had appeared in the spring to have a certain urgency.

In September the government moved a little on another of its urgent priorities when it appointed Alan Hudson of Cancer Care Ontario to head a seven-person team to work on reducing wait times for surgery. In November, the province announced that $107 million would be coming to the province through a deal with the federal government, and that money was earmarked for reduction of wait times.

In October the government tackled the difficult task of renegotiating a fee schedule for Ontario physicians, after a tentative deal with a focus on primary care physicians had not been accepted. Maria Babbage of Canadian Press reported an agreement between Health Minister Smitherman and OMA President Dr John Rapin by which a reduction on Ontario Drug Benefit costs could contribute to doctors' incomes. If the drug costs could be reduced by $200 million, $50 million could be devoted to physicians' services. The aim, according to the health minister, was to reduce 'over-medication' but without risking the health of the poor and elderly who used the Ontario Drug Benefit program. The plan was not, Smitherman said, a 'bribe to doctors.' The negotiations were coming a long time after the province had sought to calm anger among some physicians about the process by which their billings were audited. The province had asked former Supreme Court of Canada justice Peter Cory to conduct a review of the audit procedures and he proposed suspending audits until he had reported. Cory held hearings in the late fall and his report was expected in early 2005.

By 13 October, a deal with doctors on the fee schedule was awaiting ratification, but the health minister refused to indicate the cost. On 20 November it was revealed that the doctors had rejected the deal, and the minister talked of the prospect of imposing the fee schedule unilaterally. On 2 December the doctors asked for binding arbitration on six changes proposed to the original agreement, but the province would not agree. The doctors then called for a resumption of negotiations, and on 7 December the province declared itself ready to bargain. The next day the OMA asked the federal health minister, Ujjal Dosanjh, to prevent the province from imposing the fee schedule unilaterally, but Dosanjh refused to get involved. On 17 December, talks between the parties resumed, but at year's end no deal had been reached.

In a related area, the government had moved in February to create a Workplace Health and Safety Action Group to advise on best practices for improving health and safety on the job. It had earlier appointed twenty-five new health-and-safety inspectors and had conducted some five hundred inspections of Toronto-area construction sites and eleven hospitals since December 2003. In June, Labour Minister Chris Bentley expressed concern about an audit of the Workplace Safety and Insurance Board that showed a lack of accountability by the agency, despite the appointment of a new interim head of the board (Jill Hutcheon, former deputy minister of labour) in March. In July the province announced plans to appoint another 200 health-and-safety inspectors.

Although issues of workplace safety continued to arise during the year, they were sometimes overshadowed by other safety concerns that originated in agricultural settings but had consequences beyond that venue. The spectre of another Walkerton-like water-quality crisis continued to alarm some observers. In early May, the government refused to review the regulation of wells in the province, though critics complained that the new rules did not solve old problems and had created new ones. NDP critic Marilyn Churley raised the issue in the legislature, accusing the government of ignoring the experts. The following day (11 May) the government announced that it might give trailer parks and community centres a six-month extension on a deadline to comply with new water-safety regulations. Some such organizations had complained of the extraordinary costs they would bear revamping their water supplies to comply with the new Safe Drinking Water Act. The government went so far as to suggest that churches and town halls might receive an indefinite extension if they were prepared to post warning signs indicating their water had not been tested. Critics decried this apparent laxity in ensuring public safety. Environment Ministry spokesman John Steele was quoted by Canadian Press on 4 May as saying there had been 100 boil-water advisories or other actions taken by health officials over water safety to that point in the year. On 14 May, Rick Lindgren, a lawyer for the Canadian Environmental Law Association, filed a request with Environmental Commissioner Gord Miller to review the regulations governing well water. In November, the province extended the deadline for rural communities to meet clean water standards – most to 1 July or 31 December 2006.

Government funding for the treatment of autism was a matter of controversy for much of the year. While it was seen as a health issue in some quarters, in others it was treated as a matter of education policy, with attention centred on the willingness of the provincial government and local school boards to pay for behavioural therapy in the schools after the age of six. In January there were reports of parents lobbying the government to extend funding for treatment beyond age six, and lawsuits had been filed in the hope of compelling government to provide funding for treatment as a necessary medical procedure. At the end of January, and again on 15 March, the judge hearing one such case awarded costs to the plaintiffs for the analysis of data that the government was accused of having withheld – assessments of the effectiveness of intensive behavioural intervention, charts, correspondence, and policy papers. The amounts awarded were $10,000 in the first instance and $300,000 in the second. On 26 March, the government announced an increase in funding for autism treatments of $120 million over three years, but the lawsuits persisted. On 9 August, an Ontario court ordered the province to pay for the treatment of a seven-year-old autistic child, but the court distinguished the case from other similar actions and the ruling had no general applicability. Later in August, a court heard final arguments in another case in which the decision to be made had the potential to affect dozens of other court cases, as well as approximately 160 complaints before the Ontario Human Rights Commission. On 10 November, the Supreme Court of Canada overturned the decision of a British Columbia court that had required government payment for autism therapy (Applied Behavioural Analysis). The Supreme Court loss in the B.C. case discouraged some in Ontario, but since the parents in British Columbia had sought unsuccessfully to have the treatment declared a necessary medical service, the Ontario parents argued instead that it was a matter of equitable access to education. Two days after the Supreme Court decision, the acting provincial auditor in Ontario (Jim McCarter) issued the results of a special audit that showed considerable sums were being misspent by the province's Intensive Behavioural Intervention program for children under six, while other funds remained unspent despite the fact that many affected children remained on waiting lists and some received fewer hours of treatment than desirable. As the Canadian Press reported on 12 November: 'While the total budget climbed to $44 million from $4 million over the past five years, the number of children receiving funding has barely budged.' In early December, four Ontario families filed suit to compel provincial payment for Applied Behavioural Analysis, not as a core medical treatment but as a requirement of the Education Act. Several families had earlier received injunctions to force partial payment of their costs while the case proceeded. The obligation to provide all students with a public education, the suits argued, was not honoured if autistic children were not in school because there was no treatment provided to make their attendance possible. The case remained unresolved at year's end.

Funding for the mental-health sector had been an issue at several points during the year – for example, in February, when health workers urged the province to end the closure of psychiatric beds, and again in April, when the Ontario Public Service Employees Union (OPSEU) complained that unstable funding was leading to cuts in services for the mentally ill.

Controversy also attended the government's decision in September to close the last three provincial institutions housing people with developmental disabilities by 2009. The move to place the residents in community housing was praised in some quarters, but critics emphasized the need to monitor residents leaving the facilities to ensure that they were not left without care. Leah Casselman, president of OPSEU, was concerned at the loss of some 2,200 jobs in the facilities but also with the possibility that the residents involved might in some cases need round-the-clock care that would be hard to provide in the community. Finally, she expressed concern about the potential economic impact on the communities – Orillia, Smith Falls, and Chatham – that were losing the employment the facilities provided. Community and Social Services Minister Sandra Pupatello pointed out that the government was doing a full review of services to the developmentally disabled to ensure that they met people's needs and were fair, accessible, and sustainable.

Before leaving office, the previous government had put in place a system of competitive bidding for contracts to provide home-care services to local Community Care Access Centres (CCACs). The result of the process was that some agencies with a long history of serving particular communities found themselves supplanted by new providers who underbid them. Concern was expressed that for-profit firms with a focus on cost containment were replacing non-profit agencies with a focus on the quality of patient care. In September the issue came to a head when the Ontario Community Support Association (an organization representing non-profit home- and community-care agencies) complained of three large contract changes that had, in its opinion, left communities without the services of experienced providers. Although the Health Ministry sought to divert criticism by observing that it was local CCACs which were responsible for the contracts, there was sufficient unrest that the government moved in October to appoint former health minister Elinor Caplan to review the home-care contract process. She was to report in six months, and in the meantime the government asked CCACs to extend existing contracts. It did not, however, put a halt to bidding on contracts already under way, nor did it authorize the review to overturn or change signed contracts. Opposition critics, especially

Shelley Martel of the NDP and Leah Casselman of OPSEU, argued that the recently signed contracts should have been reviewed and possibly cancelled. Whatever the results of the review, they would not be known until 2005.

Education

In the areas of primary and secondary education, the government was faced with issues of class sizes, funding formulae, safety in schools, and criticism of the previous government's requirements for teacher recertification. In the post-secondary sector, concerns with rising tuition and student debt, as well as anxiety about the maintenance of quality in the face of rising costs, led the government to create a special inquiry into post-secondary education under the direction of former NDP premier Bob Rae.

In April, a blue-ribbon panel on education chaired by University of Toronto Dean of Law Ron Daniels called on the government to commit $2.5 billion per year in additional funding for education. A few days later, the government introduced a 'plan for education' which had as its centrepiece a commitment of lower average class sizes. The promise of smaller classes, especially at the elementary level, had figured in the Liberals' election platform and was argued to be a valuable contributor to early student success. Smaller classes implied more teachers and some additional cost. More funding was promised for the system, and by September the premier was claiming that there were more classes of smaller size and more teachers in the system since his government had come to power.

School funding remained a matter of controversy, however. In early June, the advocacy group People for Education issued a report calling on the government to change the formula for funding schools from a per-pupil basis to something more directly related to needs. The per-pupil method, it said, led to two-tier education, because of the differential in fund-raising capacity between rich and poor neighbourhoods. The top 15 per cent of schools had raised as much money as the bottom 50 per cent. As long as schools received provincial funds in relation only to the number of students, that fund-raising differential could not be offset. A different approach to school funding appeared in the leadership campaign of Jim Flaherty, as he promised (if elected Conservative leader and returned to power) to introduce charter schools (with more local autonomy) and to restore the tax-credit for parents of private-school pupils.

Despite the increases of funds provided to the elementary and second-ary system, by late October Canadian Press was reporting that schools were facing a $1.5-billion shortfall. Nevertheless, in general the rela-tionship of the government to the schools was a congenial one, in con-trast to the acrimony that had characterized interactions between teach-ers and the Harris government. In March, the English Catholic Teachers Association had given Ontario Education Minister Gerard Kennedy a standing ovation at its convention. However, the honeymoon may have been short-lived; by December, the Ontario Secondary School Teachers Federation was complaining that Kennedy had 'interfered' in bargain-ing by communicating directly with local district presidents rather than going through the federation (Canadian Press, 15 Dec.).

One of the key education actions of the previous government had been the Safe Schools Act, with its zero-tolerance approach to school violence. Critics had charged that the act targeted minorities, treating fights and bullying by students of colour more harshly than the same ac-tivities committed by white students. They further argued that suspen-sion or expulsion from school was not likely to change the behaviour of the offenders, and would only serve to mask the problems and their causes. The Liberals had been critical of the act in opposition, and some supporters expected that they would repeal it when they came to power. Instead, Minister Kennedy indicated in May that the McGuinty govern-ment would probably not repeal the act but would strive to amend it to correct many of its failings.

In the area of pupils' health, the government considered early in the spring how it might address the problem of obesity and poor nutrition among school-age children. It noted the availability of 'junk' food for sale in the schools and suggested that it might ban such snacks. How-ever, the government disappointed observers who thought that it might remove the sales-tax exemption for meals costing less than four dollars. That exemption was seen as contributing to the attraction of fast food with little nutritional value (and with excesses of salt and sugar). The government finally got around in October to promising a list of fast foods to be banned from schools. But, by then, critics saw the measure as a means to distract voters from what they said were the real problems of the school system – the scarcity and cost of books and classroom supplies.

Another area on which the Liberals had campaigned during the elec-tion was the system of teacher testing for recertification introduced by the previous government. The system – which required recertification of teachers every five years – was widely criticized by teachers and educational experts as an unnecessary and ultimately ineffective way of assuring teaching quality. The government introduced a bill in May to end the practice, and in December the bill was passed.

In the post-secondary system, the main focus of public attention was on the rising cost of tuition in colleges and universities. The government had promised a tuition freeze during the election campaign (with offsetting increases in grants to the institutions). By late winter, the financial situation of the province had led to speculation that the government might renege on its promise. In February it denied such reports, and in April the minister of training, colleges and universities, Mary Ann Chambers, announced a two-year freeze. Critics suggested that the universities were not going to receive increases in grants from the government sufficient to cover the projected loss of tuition foregone. By August, the minister was discussing the probable rise in tuition that would come after the two-year freeze had ended, but she said that it would occur in an environment of more generous and flexible student loans. The Canadian Federation of Students – long a crusader for lower, or even zero, tuition – was concerned at the announcement, arguing that tuition had increased 137 per cent during the Harris/Eves years, along with increases in class sizes and other reductions in quality. The issue of student grants had come to the fore in May as well, when the minister asked students to return student grant overpayments, observing that the limits (and the request for repayment) were necessary to ensure that more of those in need would have grants available.

Costs of post-secondary education were highlighted in February when the faculty at colleges of applied arts and technology voted 74.5 per cent in favour of strike action. They set a deadline of 3 March for a walkout. Talks continued and job action was averted by a settlement that provided for wage increases of 7.5 per cent over two years.

The government's plan for the post-secondary sector involved, as we have seen, the establishment (13 May) of a commission of inquiry into the system, headed by former premier Bob Rae. The scope of the inquiry included both universities and colleges of applied arts and technology. The main focus was to be on the costs borne by students and the needs of the system if it was to maintain and enhance quality. Rae's appointment was accompanied by that of seven stakeholders and experts who formed an advisory panel. They began to hold meetings around the province to compile data and recommendations for a final report that would, Rae hoped, help to direct the government's policy for improvement of quality and access in the post-secondary system.

All aspects of post-secondary policy were presumed to be on the table, and the Ontario Confederation of University Faculty Associations called on Rae to recommend reconstituting a buffer body between the ministry and post-secondary institutions, similar to the Ontario Council on University Affairs that had been abolished by the Harris government. Most of the messages conveyed to the panel in its visits around the province, however, were in relation to the level of government investment in post-secondary education and the impact of rising tuition on the access to the system for students from varied economic backgrounds. The panel members were urged to think about reforms to the student-loan system, as well as tuition rates and government grants to students and institutions. By early October, when Rae spoke to the Toronto Board of Trade, he was already calling on the government to invest more in the system, and Minister Chambers was quick to assure voters that investment in improving education was high on the government's list of priorities.

The economy and the budget

The government began in January to prepare voters for the prospect of a budget that would be at odds with the promises made during the 2003 campaign. It had long complained of the unexpectedly large shortfall in funds left by the previous government, and it predicted in January that the deficit might be in the order of $5.6 billion. It warned that such a deficit might necessitate a reduction in services and the sale of provincial assets. Near the end of the month, it was reported that the provincial GDP had declined in 2003 but was projected to rise in 2004, and Finance Minister Greg Sorbara suggested he might thus be enabled to roll back tax credits and raise some fees in order to achieve a balanced budget. As citizens awaited the recall of the legislature, the premier announced that there would be a series of 'town hall' meetings leading up to the presentation of the provincial budget. Eight such meetings were scheduled in various Ontario towns and cities between 9 February and 11 March, ostensibly to gather input from Ontarians on the appropriate financial direction to be pursued but with the important additional aim of conveying a message from the government – that times were tough and hard choices were on the horizon. At the same time, the minister of economic development and trade, Joseph Cordiano, acknowledged that the government would still be making what he called 'strategic investments' in sectors such as automobile production that were critical to the province's employment and economic well-being. The premier wondered, on the other hand, about the possibility of more toll highways, with predictable opposition from the Canadian Automobile Association.

The premier continued the belt-tightening message to employees in the public sector, calling on them to accept wage restraint, and when members of the legislature were scheduled to receive a wage increase of 2.7 per cent in March, he asked them to forego the increase for a year. When the bill to enforce the delay was introduced, opposition Conservative critic Bob Runciman called it 'window-dressing' (Canadian Press, 29 March) In the meantime, the premier mused about the possibility of opening more casinos as a source of revenue. The instability of that source was made clear in early April, when the Windsor casino employees went on strike and revenue from the casino declined substantially as a result. Just two weeks before the provincial budget was to be tabled, there was a tentative settlement of the strike, but the casino reported losses of $1.6 million a day during the dispute, 20 per cent of which was lost revenue to the provincial government.

As the town hall meetings were progressing, Finance Minister Sorbara sought to accommodate voters to the prospect of a budget deficit. Balancing the budget immediately was not necessary, he said. Taxpayers expect good money management, but they also want improvements in services. Back-to-back deficits were a realistic possibility. The tension between service improvement and expenditure restraint was evident the same week as social-service agencies combined to call on government for a $500-million increase in additional funds for aid to their clients. Such a move might mean tax increases, they conceded. However, Community and Social Services Minister Sandra Pupatello suggested that the economic circumstances might mean that welfare recipients would have to wait a further year for promised increases in payment rates. Yet, when the budget appeared, it did include welfare-rate increases – the first in eleven years.

The finance minister faced a significant distraction from the provincial budget in late February when the RCMP and the federal Canada Customs and Revenue Agency began a probe into a company – Royal Group Technologies – of which Sorbara had once been a director. The opposition called on him to resign, but he denied any wrongdoing and determined to stay on. The premier supported his decision, but, given the nature of the allegations involving Royal Group share transactions, he sifted responsibility for the Ontario Securities Commission from Sorbara to Management Board Chairman Gerry Philips. In mid-March, the integrity commissioner cleared Sorbara and he proceeded with the preparation and presentation of the budget, tabled in the legislature on

18 May. In the week before the budget was to come down, the premier asked the television networks if they would provide him five minutes of air time to discuss the budget. Perhaps sensing the probability of a partisan, rather than public-service, announcement, the networks refused.

Highlights of the budget, when it appeared, included significant investments in health care, education, and social services, as well as some $3.3 billion for public transit, roads, and bridges. However, health-expenditure increases were accompanied by a decision that most eye examinations, physiotherapy, and chiropractic services would no longer be covered by the provincial health-insurance system. In addition to the new health levy and increases in the taxes on cigarettes, beer, and wine, the fee for a driver's licence would also increase. The deficit, which Minister Sorbara now estimated to be $6.2 billion for fiscal year 2003, would be cut to $2.2 billion in 2004 and would be expected to be eliminated by 2008. When final figures were compiled for fiscal year 2003, the shortfall was seen to be $5.5 billion.

Anticipating opposition criticism, the finance minister acknowledged in his budget speech that he had made choices that were 'inconsistent with our election commitments.' However, he said it would have been impossible to deliver a balanced budget 'without destabilizing public services and perhaps even the economy itself.' Not surprisingly, those whose sectors were the beneficiaries of public investment were generally pleased, while those whose services were de-listed from Medicare (such as chiropractors) and others (such as tobacco farmers) who had hoped for assistance that was not forthcoming were generally more critical. Conservative members objected to the 'tax and spend' agenda they discerned in the document, while NDP leader Howard Hampton decried the 'regressive' nature of the new health premium. The government remained hopeful that more voters would applaud the investment in public services than would regret the tax increases or service reductions. The Canadian Taxpayers Federation announced two days after the budget speech that it would file suit against the government for having brought in a budget that proposed to violate the Taxpayer Protection Act by levying a new tax for health, but Sorbara indicated the government planned to introduce amendments to the act to make it possible to proceed with the new health levy.

In June, Moody's Investors Service maintained Ontario's Aa2 credit rating and pronounced the outlook for the province 'stable.' If a deficit was inevitable, at least the province's borrowing conditions would not be worsening.

The message of spending restraint surfaced again in July, as the government announced a wage freeze for its senior civil servants. Sid Ryan of the Canadian Union of Public Employees was quoted by Steve Fairbairn of Canadian Press as saying that the freeze was 'designed to send a chill out from there to the bargaining climate across the province,' but an anonymous government spokesperson denied it was planning a wage freeze in the broader public sector (5 July).

With all the attention that had been paid to election promises and budget deficits, it was perhaps not surprising when the Office of Information and Privacy Commissioner ordered the Liberals in September to release a secret sixty-page report costing their election promises in the 2003 campaign. The thirst for transparency was further addressed in November when the provincial auditor was given authority to examine the accounts of school boards, universities, and so on in the broader public sector. In December, the government passed a law requiring that the provincial auditor review the government accounts immediately prior to a provincial election.

When the province's acting auditor, James McCarter, issued his customary report in November, there were findings of fraud in the Drive Clean automobile emissions program, poor management of assets in the hands of the Public Guardian and Trustee, and poor accounting for civil-service expenditures on meals and travel costs. Somewhat more troubling were the findings of lax enforcement of the Labour Standards Act and poor management of water and air quality. The auditor also found that the province had inadequate records of bridge inspections and insufficient funds for the bridge and road maintenance required for safety. Finally, the 20 per cent cuts in the public service that had taken place under the Harris and Eves governments appeared to have resulted in a doubling of overtime paid to full-time employees.

Public safety

Over the course of the year, the government took action in several disparate areas – family law, traffic rules, social services, public entertainment – with the aim of providing greater protection for vulnerable persons and for the public at large.

In February, the government introduced new measures to crack down on parents who were violating child-support orders. The measures were mainly intended to make enforcement easier through installation of a new computer system and hiring of more Family Responsibility Office staff, as well as a toll-free line for clients to request help with pressing issues. However, in June, Provincial Ombudsman Clare Lewis reported that the Family Responsibility Office was still failing properly to enforce child-support orders and that people were consequently being forced onto welfare. Clearly, further improvement of the system was needed.

In February as well, Children's Services Minister Maria Bountrogianni announced plans to revamp the Children's Aid Societies system to allow for more adoptions and more abuse-prevention programs. In May the minister announced that the government was also considering increasing the power of Children's Aid Societies to take sixteen- to eighteen-year-olds out of prostitution. The previous government had passed, but not proclaimed, a bill that would have allowed the Children's Aid Societies to hold such teenagers for thirty days, but the minister expressed her view that a more sustainable, longer-term system was needed. According to a ministry spokesperson, the very reason the Conservatives' bill had not been proclaimed was the need for more time to develop a system of safe houses.

In March the government announced its plan to introduce legislation that would allow a worker up to eight weeks' leave to care for a sick or dying family member without risking the loss of his/her job. In June the legislation was passed; indeed, the government extended the spring sitting one day longer than planned in order to pass the bill.

At the end of May, a court ruled that the province's movie-rating system was unconstitutional because of the quasi-censorship aspect of 'prior restraint' (the request that films be submitted for rating before screening) and the implied impediment to freedom of speech. The court allowed the province twelve months to distinguish the classification system from censorship. In December the government introduced legislation to remove censorship elements from the film-classification system; however, the Canadian Civil Liberties Association complained that the bill still allowed censorship since it proposed that a person could be named to review films and approve or refuse to approve them. At year's end, the bill had not yet been passed or amended. In the meantime, the province had in August announced a plan to extend its rating authority to adult and violent video games, seeking to establish a classification system and also to require proof of age from those hoping to rent or buy such products.

In July, Keith Norton, head of the Ontario Human Rights Commission, suggested that the Ontarians with Disabilities Act should be extended to the private sector. In October the government announced its intention to make Ontario fully accessible to those with disabilities within twenty years, beginning with a revision of the Ontarians with Disabilities Act. Business applauded the 'phase-in' approach, while critics complained that the pace was too slow. The NDP described the announcement as little more than a public-relations exercise.

Another matter of some controversy was the decision by the government, following a series of attacks on children by vicious dogs, to ban the breeding and ownership of pit bulls in the province. Owners could keep existing pets but could not acquire new ones. Owners of such dogs were quick to brand the law as ill-informed and discriminatory, arguing that many pit bulls were perfectly harmless while other breeds also included individual vicious dogs. The legislation proceeded, however, and seemed to have widespread appeal, given the publicity the attacks had engendered.

In the area of legal protection, the province had for some time had a system of informal faith-based arbitration, to be used for the settlement of disputes in family and property law when parties mutually agreed, within the boundaries of provincial and federal legislation. The system allowed parties to apply religious law, so long as it did not violate Canadian legal standards. With a growing Muslim population in the province, there was discussion of the extent to which sharia-based law could be used in such tribunals. The Muslim community was divided; some members believed that it would be discrimination if they were denied the right to use religious law where other groups had the right, while other Muslims argued that vulnerable persons might be pressed into using faith-based arbitration that would not be in their best interests. Some feared that the introduction of Islamic faith-based arbitration would be used by fundamentalists to make social conservatism dominant in the Muslim community. Still others objected mainly to the use of the word 'sharia,' since it normally encompasses not only civil but also criminal law and criminal matters were never intended to be included in the arbitration system. The government appointed former NDP attorney general Marion Boyd to review the issue and make recommendations. When she reported in December, she recommended that Muslims be given access to faith-based arbitration for family law, but she reaffirmed the expectation that participation in the system would have to be voluntary and that all decisions would have to be within the context of Canadian law. Nevertheless, the issue remained somewhat unsettled, as those who opposed the introduction of sharia into the system accused her of promoting it and the government entered 2005 still facing the issue of the extent to which Muslim religious law could be used in processes whose decisions were then enforceable in Canadian law.

Other reforms came in the area of traffic safety. A requirement that all drivers use child seats in their cars when transporting children, or face demerit points, was introduced. An existing requirement applied only to parents. The proposed legislation was to include exemptions for taxis, emergency vehicles, and out-of-province drivers. In December the government passed a series of new highway rules, including the child-seats provision but also a provision to allow charging the owner, not just the driver, of a car that passes a stopped school bus, as well as limits on passengers in cars driven by newly licensed G-2 drivers. The province also moved to extend the right to municipalities to instal red-light cameras, and undertook a $400,000-pilot project to put digital cameras in forty-four Ontario Provincial Police cruisers (twenty-two in the Greater Toronto Area and twelve in Kenora).

Conclusion

In June, the government had moved to establish a fixed date for the next provincial election – 4 October 2007. However, it had also speculated about investigating a wholesale reform of the electoral system. The government had introduced a series of small reforms (and some large ones) that were no doubt intended to convey the image of an active, concerned government, but it had spent much of the year wrestling with economic problems and looking backward to their predecessors in office. The government acted on its promise to reinvest in public services, but it did so with a conservative eye on the budget and a gradual pace that frustrated critics who had hoped for more rapid and radical change. After the upheavals (as the Liberals would have said) of the Rae and Harris/Eves years, the government believed that it had found an appropriate middle ground which it hoped to occupy and till successfully in anticipation of re-election in 2007.

DANIEL SALÉE

Quebec

It was literally unheard of. Never had a newly elected government fallen out of favour so quickly. In January 2004, barely ten months into its first term in office, the Liberal government of Jean Charest reached new lows in voters' satisfaction. Three public-opinion polls conducted by separate polling companies and taken at different times in the month all pointed to a sharp decline in popular support for the Liberals.[1] The party lost over ten percentage points between the April 2003 election and the beginning of 2004; two in three voters admitted to being dissatisfied with the government's management of public affairs. In fact, the rate of dissatisfaction had been rising at a disturbingly fast pace, going from an already quite high 45 per cent in mid-September 2003 to 63 per cent four months later. The public confrontations with the labour movement and community groups over controversial amendments to the Quebec labour code, the rewriting of the rules of collective bargaining in the public sector, and the modifications to childcare services undoubtedly played a key role in the government's descent.

The New Year brought no reprieve. The holiday celebrations were barely over when two other public-management crises emerged and compounded the government's unpopularity even further. The government first appeared incompetent in dealing with civil disturbances that went on for a few weeks in January in the Mohawk community of Kanesatake, fifty kilometres northwest of Montreal, the very site of the 1990 three-month summer stand-off between Mohawk warriors and Canadian forces. Unhappy with the decision of the band chief, James Gabriel, to fire and replace the reserve's head of police services, politi-

---

1 The first poll was conducted between 7 and 12 January by SOM and commissioned by Radio-Canada. The second one was done by Léger Marketing for *Le Devoir*, CKAC (AM radio station), and the *Globe and Mail* between 14 and 18 January. The last one was done by CROP on behalf of *La Presse* between 15 and 24 January.

cal opponents of Gabriel, intent on forcing him to step down, took to the streets, kept police officers hostage in their precinct, and burned down his house. Fearing another Oka crisis, the government tried to appease the rioters and meet some of their demands rather than clamp down on them, much to the dismay of large segments of the public that felt the government was unjustifiably kowtowing to criminal elements within the First Nation community (some of the people involved in the riots and in the opposition against Chief Gabriel were known to the police as drug dealers and for their association with biker gangs).

At the same time as these events in Kanesatake were unfolding, the government announced its decision to approve the construction of the Suroît, a new natural gas power plant to be built southwest of Montreal by 2007, at the cost of $550 million. This announcement made an additional dent in the government's quickly dwindling capital of political sympathy. The new project, spearheaded by Hydro-Québec and the minister of natural resources in spite of the recommendations of the government's own environmental review agency against it, raised the ire of environmentalists and other citizens groups who promptly mobilized to take the government to task. They denounced the government for championing a power-generating system that, in all likelihood, would not only increase the level of greenhouse-gas emissions and fail to meet the objectives of the Kyoto Accord (which Quebec officially embraced) but also contradict its own commitments to environmental protection. The Suroît file would continue to haunt the government through the year as the opposition to the project grew relentlessly.

The disapproving and at times contemptuous public reaction to the government's handling of both the Kanesatake incidents and the Suroît project came as a harsh reminder to Jean Charest's Liberals that the political truce of the holiday season was over and that they had fewer and fewer friends in the Quebec public. Something had to be done; the government spent the better part of the year trying to save face.

Damage control

In order to regain the esteem of the population, the government essentially pursued two strategies. The first one consisted of literally buying social peace. At the end of March, Yves Séguin, the minister of finance, introduced a budget that, in some ways, was quite removed from the neo-liberal tack of the government's early policies. Several political observers commented that it looked strangely like the kind of budget that the more social-democratically inclined Parti Québécois would put forward. Unlike the stringent budget Minister Séguin presented in 2003 (which was marked by significant reductions in state expenditures and a clear intent to lessen state interventions), the new budget emphasized the social mission of the state and catered to the poorest segments of the population by pouring more money into social housing, child support, and income supplements for low-income households. Right-wing critics claimed that the government was giving in to unions and community movements – traditionally PQ supporters – and was thus taking the risk of alienating its own electoral base.

The other strategy the government embraced was more encompassing and politically more perilous. In early February, Premier Charest launched an extensive process of public consultation with which he hoped to convince the population of the government's willingness to listen to grievances and discuss as openly as possible solutions to key public-policy concerns. Through the spring and summer months, twenty regional forums were held across Quebec. Civil-society organizations and ordinary citizens were invited to express their views on four major areas of public management considered against the backdrop of Quebec's aging population and the precarious state of the province's public finances: health and social services; education, training, and jobs; family and social development; and regional and sustainable economic development. The whole initiative culminated in mid-October with a three-day, national forum chaired by the premier, in which most major social and economic stakeholders took part.

Quebec governments have regularly resorted to broad-based public consultations to create an atmosphere of social cohesion and lend legitimacy to policy choices that might otherwise meet with popular resistance. Many believe that they are the mainstay of the so-called Quebec model and bear witness to the social consensus that undergirds Quebec society. By banking on this tradition, Charest was gambling that the positive feelings such consultations tend to elicit would replenish the political capital of his government. In truth, most participants were perplexed by the government's ultimate decision to forge ahead with its controversial plan to 're-engineer the state' and effect neo-liberal policy changes in spite of the strong reservations unrelentingly expressed by key social and economic actors. While the public-consultation strategy may have appeased some of them, it would only be temporary: critics denounced it as nothing more than a public-relations exercise designed to conceal the government's unwillingness to bring forward a general policy framework that would meet with the support of the majority. In the end, the positive spin that the government put on the consultation process and its outcome did not register with large segments of the population which continued to harbour deep-seated resentment towards the Charest administration and question whether it would ever modify its policy agenda to take into account the voice and concerns of the people.

Re-engineering the state in order to 'shine among the best'

While on the surface of things the government undoubtedly saw in the consultation process a means to convince Quebecers that it was willing to listen – thus giving the government a more flattering and more accommodating public image – it also used the process as a way to communicate more subtly and in a more conciliatory fashion than it had so far the rather unpopular policy vision that it was seeking to imprint on Quebec society since its election. In March, barely a month after announcing the consultation process, Premier Charest released a substantial document that was to serve both as a backgrounder for the regional forums held later in the year and as an official statement of the government's policy package. This document, titled *Briller parmi les meilleurs* ('Shine among the best'), revealed the government's intention to emphasize seven strategic policy priorities. They included improving the physical health of Quebecers and access to quality health and social services; focusing the public education system on the academic success of all students; achieving Quebec's full economic potential within a sustainable-development perspective; encouraging regional autonomy and development; supporting families, a higher birth rate, and social development; affirming Quebec's identity and promoting its interests and culture in Canada and throughout the world; and reviewing the role of the state and reconfiguring the delivery of its services.

These priorities were formulated in general enough terms that hardly anyone argued with the government about their importance. The underlying message carried throughout the document, though, was far from uncontroversial. According to the government, Quebec's woes are largely attributable to an inefficient state structure and an inappropriate administrative culture; because the Quebec state is directly involved in too many aspects of social and economic life, its way of doing things, of bringing services to the population, is cumbersome, ineffective, and financially draining; hence, the state needs to be modernized and 're-engineered.'

Unsurprisingly, the action plan the government put together in *Briller parmi les meilleurs* rested on a strong commitment to transform the state and do away with well-entrenched administrative practices. The guiding motif of the document was couched in terms of concerns for Quebecers' well-being and quality of life as the government claimed to seek the improvement of all those public services which were essential to the welfare of citizens, increased efficiency of state structures, and greater prosperity for Quebec as a whole. To fulfil these objectives, the government put forward a four-pronged implementation strategy, the first thrust of which centred on 'improving ways of doing things': this entailed simplifying service delivery, rationalizing and centralizing administrative-support services, increasing the number of partnerships and contractual relations with the private sector, rationalizing the management of the government's extensive real estate properties, and putting in place a new performance-management policy through the strengthening of internal audit activities. The second aspect of the implementation strategy stressed 'organizational simplification,' by which the government intended to introduce a 'culture of ongoing re-evaluation' of government agencies, amalgamate several existing entities, and reorganize various services into executive agencies. The third focal point of the implementation strategy emphasized the 're-evaluation of programs,' whereby the government would review existing programs in light of the state's missions, according to criteria of effectiveness, efficiency, subsidiarity, and financial capacity, and with a view to simplify, refocus, or, if necessary, abolish the ones that did not conform with these criteria. Finally, the last dimension of the implementation strategy called attention to the importance of human-resource planning as an opportunity to renew the workforce of the state, make it more responsive to new needs, and redesign teams in order to allocate appropriate human capital where it was needed.

Although the general objectives of *Briller parmi les meilleurs* seemed to be unobjectionable, the government's conception of their implementation implied significant structural and institutional transformation that appeared extremely worrisome to several social-advocacy groups, civil-society stakeholders, and critics for whom it spelled job losses and the disappearance of acquired rights for state workers, as well as the privatization of and ensuing diminished access to state services for the general public. Unions and community groups in particular took a strong and unequivocal stance against one of the most publicized and visible offshoots of the government's action plan, private-public partnerships (PPPs).

Building on experiments in Europe and the rest of Canada, the government brought the notion of PPP into its policy framework to involve the private sector in the production of large public-infrastructure projects and the delivery of key services in order to lighten the financial burden of the state and afford much needed social goods at a lower cost. In the mind of the government, PPPs should be seriously considered as a management tool by the whole range of public bodies, including government departments and agencies, community colleges (CEGEPs), school boards, and universities, in the establishment of education, public health, and social services; the idea held potential too, the government believed, for regional and social services boards as well as municipal agencies responsible for projects funded primarily by the province. Determined to apply the idea of PPPs to its public-management practices, the government, in June, introduced Bill 61, An Act respecting the Agence des partenariats public-privé du Québec, in the National Assembly. This new legislation set out the organizational and operational rules applicable to a new governmental agency created to advise the government on any PPP matter, provide expertise to public bodies in the evaluation of PPP projects, and oversee initiatives for which a PPP partnership was considered a possibility.

The political arena was largely given to public arguments over PPPs as the deliberations and hearings of the parliamentary committee on Bill 61 went on through the fall. Supporters of PPPs generally contended that they make good economic sense since they allow the state to share with the private sector the risks inherent in any new venture; they are a mark of fiscal responsibility and can provide access to private-sector know-how that the state simply does not have. Be that as it may, although the government remains in control and defines the parameters of any project and service-delivery mechanisms, PPPs entail the partial privatization of public goods and services that were previously available free of direct charges, and rest on the operation of the profit motive in areas of social intervention hitherto untouched by objectives of private gains. For that reason, opponents were concerned that the involvement of the private sector would signal the end of free access to essential public goods. They denounced the principle of PPP as a neo-liberal ideological chimera with a poor track record wherever it had been applied. More often than not, they argued, the private-sector partner eventually found the venture insufficiently profitable or was unable or unwilling to follow through with its financial commitments, leaving the state with a much higher tab than originally anticipated. Furthermore, the new PPP agency would create, in their view, an unnecessary, additional layer of bureaucratic intercession and foster administrative centralization, which runs counter to the very idea of a lighter, more efficient state that the government claimed to favour. Public-sector workers' unions, for their part, deplored the implication that the recourse to PPP entailed, namely, that they were unable to provide the requisite expertise and that the private sector was better equipped to deliver services in a financially sound way.

Benefiting from the advantages of power, the government won the debate. Bill 61 was passed amid relative public indifference a week before Christmas. In fact, notwithstanding its stated willingness to include the public's views in its efforts to transform the Quebec state and society, the government proceeded unflinchingly in the end with its original blueprint. Bill 61 was but one manifestation of the government's resolve to go ahead with its own ideas. It was part of a much broader and much vaunted plan to 'modernize' the Quebec state put forward in May by the minister of the Treasury Board, Monique Jerôme-Forget, a plan that included a 20 per cent reduction in the size of the public service over the next ten years and a clear realignment of the state's administrative and organizational culture according to private-sector criteria of performance and efficiency.

Bill 57, the Individual and Family Assistance Act, was another major proposal for reform that stirred considerable commotion in concerned circles. Introduced in June in the National Assembly, the bill had a dual purpose: implement measures, programs, and services designed to foster the social and economic self-sufficiency of individuals and families; and encourage individuals to engage in activities that promote their social integration, their entry into the labour market, and their active participation in society. Although the bill authorized the minister of employment and social solidarity to establish a variety of support measures such as employment-assistance, social-assistance, and direct financial-assistance programs for individuals experiencing difficulty re-entering the labour market or gaining economic self-sufficiency, it was strongly criticized by social-advocacy and anti-poverty groups. They argued in essence that the bill failed to satisfy the parameters set in the 2002 law against poverty,[2] added new constraints for individuals attempting to qualify for the assistance programs, created inappropriate categories of welfare recipients that did not correspond to the lived realities of people

2 This law was passed unanimously in the National Assembly in December 2002. Drafted by a coalition of twenty-two community groups and designed to cut poverty in half over the next ten years, it committed the government to establishing an anti-poverty action plan within two months of its adoption and to giving progress reports every three years. It also set a minimum level for social-assistance payments, created a monitoring agency, and provided funds for anti-poverty initiatives.

on the ground, gave the minister too much discretionary power, and did not properly address the insufficient level of social-assistance payments. The vast majority of briefs presented in parliamentary committee opposed the bill and a coalition of community groups strongly urged the government to withdraw it. At year's end, though the government had not succeeded in passing the bill, it was still on the order paper and likely to be resubmitted to the National Assembly in 2005.

Failing to please

In the end, the conciliatory overture of the consultation process did little to bolster the government's image in the public mind. Even as the government was desperately trying to mend fences, a number of civil-society groups stepped up their offensive against its initiatives. Unions and the community sector, still reeling from last year's suite of modifications to the labour code, labour relations, and social protection, remained unrelenting in their criticism. Protests over the Suroît project continued unabated (and eventually led to the government's decision to scrap it definitively in November). Students, unhappy with the government's unwillingness to commit unequivocally to its electoral promise of not raising tuition fees, organized demonstrations in Quebec and Montreal and stormed out of the national forum in October. Even the government's natural allies and the segments of the electorate that initially backed its policy agenda showed impatience at its seeming inability to hold fast and clarify its priorities: many among them felt that the government was not going far enough or fast enough in its reform program and appeared unprepared and indecisive on a number of key issues. At the end of 2004, nearly two-thirds of the population were still dissatisfied with Jean Charest's Liberals; the party barely succeeded in getting one candidate elected in four by-elections held in September – a telling indictment of its policies less than eighteen months into its first term. By then, commentators were unabashedly labelling the Charest government the worst in Quebec history.

A number of observers have attributed the failure of the government to garner broad-based support for its policies to the relative weakness and inexperience of Jean Charest's ministerial team. Yet, while the ability of a government to push its policy agenda forward owes much to its managerial competence and leadership, the socio-political conjuncture in which it operates can be a more definitive determinant of success. In seeking to enforce its particular policy agenda, the Charest government sparked a far-reaching social debate about the nature and role of the state, the continued affordability of extensive social protections, and the social consequences of strict fiscal responsibility, thus creating in its wake considerable insecurity among concerned socio-economic stakeholders about the effects of the government's proposed policy agenda on the future of acquired social rights, social cohesion, and relations between social actors. This insecurity and the unavoidably oppositional character of the debate largely hampered the government's capacity to forge a consensus over the policy choices it championed.

That debate, of course, is not new, nor is it unique to Quebec. Most Western democracies have confronted it. It was resolved bureaucratically in many cases by the adoption of an even more radical neo-liberal path than that favoured by Charest's Liberals, without much adverse political consequences for its proponents, and none or little of the collective soul-searching it seemed to elicit in Quebec. Things, though, are somewhat trickier in Quebec. Since the contemporary emergence of an ever-growing welfare state has been intimately tied to the political affirmation of Quebec's national identity since the 1960s, questioning the state – expressing reservations about the 'Quebec model' of social solidarity – is somehow tantamount, in the minds of many, to casting doubts on the very legitimacy of the national aspirations of Quebecers. Although the Parti Québécois, when in power, also pushed forward a number of policy changes that had an unmistakable – though usually unspoken – neo-liberal tack that irked unions and social-advocacy groups, it was generally able to contain opposition: constituencies bearing the brunt of unpopular reforms tended to be political allies within the nationalist movement, and they accepted, albeit unenthusiastically, the sacrifices involved in the implementation of neo-liberal policies in the name of the greater cause of Quebec sovereignty borne by the PQ. As anti-sovereignists, Charest's Liberals do not, for obvious reasons, enjoy that kind of political leverage: faced with a governing party that never kindled any hope for Quebec sovereignty, unions and advocacy groups have had no reason to continue to cooperate with an avowedly neo-liberal government.

Controversies about the proper management and social purpose of the welfare state have been an integral part of the Quebec political landscape for two decades. On the whole, though, they have drawn but episodic attention as the national question has tended to supersede them in public debates. Unpopular neo-liberal reforms were almost routinely delayed or watered down, first by Liberals (under Robert Bourassa) for fear of social unrest that could fan the flame of nationalist fervour, and then by Péquistes for fear of jeopardizing the social cohesion necessary for successful national affirmation. Previous governments trod very carefully on issues of social-policy changes and public-management reforms, sensing all too well the volatility of the Quebec public. By putting a decidedly neo-liberal policy package at the forefront of its agenda, the Charest government broke with this tradition of caution and brought to a head an inherently thorny social debate that its predecessors had managed to keep under wraps with varying degrees of success.

Charest's own limited familiarity with the imperatives of Quebec politics led him to underestimate the depth of the social opposition to the vision of public management and social change that he and his government thought best for Quebec. In the end, the intrinsically polarizing nature of the debate on the contemporary state, and the underlying class divisions that it entailed, essentially disqualified the Charest government as a force for social unity in the minds of social advocates: seeking, as it did, to reduce the action of existing social protection and social solidarity was to take action against the most vulnerable elements of the population. Inexperience, then, did not account for everything in the Charest government's political misfortune; there were also at play systemic realities that transcended the deeds and misdeeds of politicians. Charest and his collaborators were obviously not prepared for the politics of it all.

Federal-provincial relations: firming up the provincialist stance

Provincial premiers and the federal government breathed a sigh of relief when Jean Charest became Quebec's new premier in 2003. Quebec finally had at the helm a government that was not hostile to Canadian federalism and in fact was quite disposed to be an active and positive contributor to its success. Indeed, Charest made overtures towards the federal government and quickly took a leadership role among provincial premiers to spearhead the new Council of the Federation. Quebec, it seemed, would no longer rain on Canada's parade.

In 2004 the tone changed somewhat as the Charest government, pushing for a more decentralized federalism, faced off with a central government generally unprepared to agree to the claims of the provinces for increased financial support. Quebec's minister of finance came back from the annual meeting of finance ministers in February disappointed and frustrated with his federal counterpart, Ralph Goodale, who remained deaf to the fiscal-imbalance argument, imposed a variety of budgetary cuts and a new equalization formula without prior consultation with provincial premiers, and offered no increase in transfers to the provinces to finance health expenditures. Things seemed to brighten up later in the year with the successful, but arduous, negotiation in September of a new agreement between Ottawa and the provinces over the financing of public health. Ottawa committed to disburse $18 billion over the next six years, of which Quebec secured $4.3 billion in unconditional transfers in addition to increased equalization payments. Two months later, though, on 8 November, in a speech given on the occasion of the 40th anniversary of the Confederation Centre of the Arts in Charlottetown, Charest lashed out publicly at the federal government for its centralistic and unfair management of the Canadian federation. Ottawa is not the boss of the provinces, he argued unequivocally: 'In Canada, the provinces are not accountable to the federal government. Each government is accountable to its electorate in its own jurisdiction ... Each government must be free to act within its jurisdiction to fulfill its proper responsibilities. Membership in a federal state does not imply that we must fit a single mould ... The danger to our federation is not that Quebec wants to govern in its own way; it is the view that all provinces and territories are the same.'[3]

The notion that federal arrangements in Canada must be reviewed to allow for more flexibility, a greater degree of cooperation, and respect for each province's jurisdiction, as well provide a fair fiscal and political balance, is central to the Charest government's view of federal-provincial relations. The minister for Canadian intergovernmental affairs, Benoît Pelletier, took this message across Canada at every opportunity, using a rhetoric at times reminiscent of the sovereignist discourse to suggest in no uncertain terms that Ottawa was inappropriately hoarding money that belonged to the provinces, regularly abused its spending power, and unashamedly encroached on fields of provincial jurisdiction by making many of its transfers to the provinces conditional on the fulfillment of its own policy choices.

Still, although the Charest government harboured unambiguous resentment at Ottawa, it always stopped short of calling for Quebec secession, preferring instead to work to improve the federation. In a speech given to the Canada West Foundation on 24 March, Minister Pelletier made clear that Canadian federalism would not be able to function and evolve in a healthy manner unless essential conditions were met. They included a balanced distribution of powers between the two orders of

3 http://www.premier-ministre.gouv.qc.ca/salle-de-presse/discours/2004/novembre/2004-11-08-en.shtm (accessed 11 Aug. 2007).

government; an adequate fiscal capacity so that each order of government can fully assume its responsibilities and avoid financial dependence on the other; the possibility for the provinces to express their views on the governance of the federation and have influence on the federal legislative process; and the development of effective mechanisms to foster intergovernmental dialogue in sectors where convergence is required between initially divergent interests.[4]

The Charest government has never been known to resort to the threat of secession should Quebec's claims be overlooked. Yet in 2004 it undoubtedly surprised quite a few people by standing as a staunch defender of provincial administrative and political powers. The presence of Jean Charest, whose credentials as a strong proponent of a united Canada are unassailable, probably encouraged many to expect little or no quarrel with Quebec. In truth, internal political circumstances gave Premier Charest little choice but to put up a fuss. The precarious situation of the province's public finances, for one thing, forced him to go adamantly after an adequate share of Ottawa's accumulated surpluses in order to afford much needed public expenditures, particularly in the health sector. Ottawa's reluctance to dole out more than was strictly necessary dampened Charest's customary cheery disposition towards Canada. On the other hand, baring teeth at the federal government is a strategy that has often proven beneficial to Quebec political leaders. It is not uncommon to see the popularity of a government surge in public opinion polls following a vehement charge against Ottawa. No doubt Charest thought that banking on that approach might improve his government's poor appeal. It was improbable that his government would ever radicalize its position further on issues of intergovernmental relations, but he reminded Canada that even with a premier who feels deeply for the unity of the country, Quebec is not to be taken for granted.

Searching for their way: opposition parties and the national question

Charest's political opponents were somewhat taken aback by his ability to stand up to the federal government and push for more asymmetry in the way the Canadian federation operates. With the new federal-provincial agreement on health, he succeeded in destabilizing both the

4 http://www.saic.gouv.qc.ca/centre_de_presse/discours/2004/saic_dis20040324_en.htm
(accessed 11 Aug. 2007).

Parti Québécois and Mario Dumont's Action démocratique du Québec (ADQ) by showing that Ottawa was not all that closed to Quebec's rightful claims and that tangible benefits could be drawn from a more cooperative approach with the federal government and the other provinces. Although officially opposition parties downplayed Charest's success, expert observers and even former sovereignist politicians, like Jacques Parizeau, acknowledged that the agreement on health represented a significant departure from the traditionally centralizing behaviour of the federal government and thus a major, positive change in federal-provincial dynamics that played to Quebec's advantage (*Le Devoir*, 18 Sept.).

In a way, Charest challenged both opposition parties to redefine themselves insofar as the issue of Quebec sovereignty was concerned. The PQ, for one, essentially scrambled to clarify its perennial position and convince the population that the government's success and assertive demeanour in federal-provincial diplomacy was but a smokescreen and did not imply that Quebec's interests were better protected. The ADQ, on the other hand, opposed to Quebec secession but not quite unconditionally federalist, worked hard to spin its vision of Quebec's place within the Canadian federation in a way that seemed sufficiently different from the Liberals. In neither case were the results all that persuasive. Both parties were grappling with an internal vacuum, which weakened their ability to constitute a real political alternative to Charest. Given the population's dissatisfaction with his government, this was in fact a blessing in disguise.

Wrestling with old demons: the Parti Québécois

The electoral defeat of 2003 came as a hard blow to the PQ, and as is often the case in such situations, hints that the leadership of the party was inadequate were many and increasingly forthright. Bernard Landry had to battle vigorously all through the following months to deflect ungenerous insinuations about his ability to lead the party to the next election and discourage the jostling for position of potential successors. His decision to launch the 'season of ideas' in the fall of that year, enjoining all party members to contribute to the renewal of the party platform and vision, bought him some time and afforded the party relative internal peace through the first half of 2004, but by the end of the summer he was confronted with problems that did not bode well for his and the party's political future. In August, Pauline Marois, a high-profile former senior minister in all the PQ cabinets since René Lévesque, openly called for his resignation by requesting that a leadership race be held as soon as possible. Public-opinion polls released in early September – days before news of Charest's highly successful dealings with Ottawa over the health agreement even hit the media – showed that the PQ had lost an eight-point lead over the Liberal Party during the summer months and was now neck and neck with its rival. In addition, an internal report authored by three rising PQ MNAs, who had gone on a fact-finding mission through all the province's regions earlier in the year, revealed bluntly that Quebec youth were largely uninterested in Quebec sovereignty, which many associated with an older generation of politicians disconnected from daily reality. Finally, looming in the background was talk of the imminent creation of a new left-nationalist political party, which was unwelcome news for the PQ since it could only spell the loss of much-needed electoral support down the line.

Beleaguered, but keeping an upbeat attitude, Landry came to the mid-October meeting of the party's National Council ready to promote a new strategic plan and assert his leadership. Hoping to pre-empt grumbles from the radical elements of the party who have always insisted (albeit with little success) that sovereignty should be achieved without delay, he proposed that a vote in favour of the PQ in the next election be considered as a mandate for the party to initiate a political process unequivocally designed to lead rapidly to sovereignty. The plan included stepping up the attack against the federal government in order to bring to light the 'fundamental contradictions' between Canadian federalism and Quebec's aspirations, rallying supporters of sovereignty outside the PQ in the fight for independence, and holding a referendum on sovereignty as soon as possible after the election with a simple, clear, and direct question. To those ends, Landry further advocated that public funds be utilized to support efforts towards sovereignty; that a preliminary democratic constitution be drafted and followed by a final version which would be adopted by a national constituent assembly after a post-referendum declaration of independence; that an extensive information campaign be put in motion to explain the advantages of sovereignty to Quebecers; and that a non-binding proposal for an economic agreement with Canada be drawn up.

Landry's proposal came as a surprise, for never in the past had the PQ committed so clearly and so audaciously to tying its election to sovereignty and to such a politically exacting timetable to achieve it. Landry himself had always been a proponent of flexibility and prudence, of making sure that 'winning conditions' were well in place before setting a referendum process in motion. His new boldness was interpreted by most observers as a desperate attempt to dissipate the rumours of fratricidal conflicts, reunite the party, and, of course, preserve his own leadership. Unfortunately for him, moderates felt that his approach was a dangerous gamble which could cost the party the next election, and hard-core independentists dismissed it as nothing more than a mere overhaul of the old *étapiste* strategy that had proved so ineffective in the 1980 and 1995 referendums on sovereignty. At the end of the day, Landry's move only unleashed the party's old demons and pushed it into yet another internal, self-absorbed, and largely divisive debate on the best strategy to make Quebec sovereignty a reality. Interestingly, through all this, the party never sought to examine or deal with the fact that a majority of Quebecers had, over the past three decades, repeatedly indicated that they would not endorse its nationalistic sovereignty project; it continued to be blindly devoted to a political objective of increasingly little resonance with the Quebec public. By the end of the year, still wrestling with its internal angst, the PQ was too deep in the throes of an all-consuming process of collective soul-searching and disengaged from the broader political reality to be a truly effectual opposition or to appear as a valid alternative to the Charest government.

Political autonomy: Action démocratique du Québec

Mario Dumont's ADQ was certainly anxious to fill the political gap created by the PQ's self-inflicted torments over leadership and strategy, but, with only five MNAs and therefore very little opportunity in the National Assembly to take the government to task effectively, this goal proved difficult to achieve. Despite garnering nearly 20 per cent of the vote in the 2003 election, and winning an additional seat in the September by-elections, the ADQ also had to come to grips with an image problem. Dumont's positions on a number of policy issues clearly located the party on the right of the political spectrum, but his high-profile, public opposition to a CRTC decision suspending the broadcasting licence of a Quebec City radio station, whose controversial but highly popular talk show hosts are well known for their often outrageous and offensive rants against public figures, identified the party as a magnet for populists, demagogues, and unsophisticated voters. It may have won votes in Quebec City's lower-middle-class and blue-collar districts, but it did little to secure a base of support broad enough to transcend the unflattering branding of the ADQ as a party that 'panders to the yahoos' (*Gazette*, 28 Sept.). In fact, with the exception of its victory in the Quebec City riding of Vanier, the ADQ did rather poorly in the September by-elections, coming in dead last, with very low percentages of the vote (less than 5 per cent on average) in the other three ridings in contention.

In order to shake off its persistent image as a minor and inconsequential party and gain a much-needed degree of intellectual respectability, the ADQ turned to constitutional issues. At its annual convention held in late September, the party ratified with much fanfare a document detailing its vision of Quebec's role and position in the Canadian federation. It proposed in essence to make Quebec into an autonomous state within Canada. Though remaining an integral part of Canada, an autonomous Quebec would enjoy full and undivided authority in areas where its jurisdiction is already constitutionally acknowledged, obtain additional powers, have its own constitution, and be the only government authorized to collect income tax. The ADQ argued that its approach offered Quebecers a third way between the all-out sovereignty propounded by the PQ and the Liberals' ready acceptance of existing constitutional parameters and jurisdictional boundaries – a third way that would enable them to enjoy total control over their collective destiny without breaking Canada apart.

The irony of Dumont's presentation of his party's new constitutional package was not lost on political observers who were quick to recall his speech before the Canadian Club in Toronto two years earlier when he had declared that the ADQ intended to leave constitutional questions alone. Commentators also found very little that was 'new' in the ADQ's proposal: not only did most of it draw inspiration from the Allaire Report,[5] it basically resuscitated the same constitutional position that the ADQ had put forward at its General Council in 2001 but that was then swept under the rug in Dumont's Canadian Club speech a year later. In the end, the ADQ's move to re-enter the field of constitutional policy failed to strengthen its political appeal. Far from appearing as an innovative and credible alternative to the main parties, the party looked amateurish and ill-prepared. Many saw in Dumont's rekindling of constitutional questions nothing more than an improvised and whimsical manoeuvre to muster some political capital. If that was

5 The Allaire Report was adopted in 1991 as the basis of the constitutional policy of the Liberal Party. Its mainstay was the claim of twenty-two exclusive powers for Quebec. Premier Robert Bourassa eventually pushed for the party to move away from the report in favour of the less demanding 1992 Charlottetown Accord. Mario Dumont, who was then the president of the Liberals' youth wing, disagreed with Bourassa, stood against the Charlottetown Accord, and eventually left the Liberal Party to found the ADQ in 1994 with Jean Allaire, the author of the Allaire Report.

indeed his objective, reopening the unity question could not have been a more poorly chosen approach. As the Charest government was showing on the ground, the notion that Quebec should strive to exercise fully its constitutionally recognized powers was not exclusive to the ADQ: the party's claim to originality on that score thus seemed quite meaningless and unlikely to attract larger segments of the electorate. And, as the PQ was discovering, matters pertaining to Quebec's political status within the Canadian federation roused little interest among the population. Dumont and his party were, in all likelihood, barking up the wrong tree.

Quebec: a blocked society?

Jean Charest stated with pride in an end-of-the-year review that his government had amply demonstrated in 2004 its commitment to Quebec's long-term development. The changes that had been initiated under his watch, he claimed, notably with respect to the management practices of the state, the health and education sectors, and federal-provincial relations, would benefit all Quebecers and provide Quebec with a stronger footing to ensure sustainable social and economic development in the years ahead: 'Quebec changes, Quebec is on the move. Quebec is renewing its capacity to prosper, honour its social mission and stand its ground both in Canada and abroad. Quebec is responding to the challenges of the 21st century. The government is thinking forward to develop in partnership with all Quebecers a society based on equity for all generations.'[6] From her vantage point as president of the Confederation of National Trade Unions (CSN), Claudette Carbonneau offered a much less buoyant assessment of the year that had just passed. In her view, despite a massive rejection of its policy package by the population, the Charest government stubbornly went ahead with changes that did not in any way serve the interests of the majority of Quebecers but translated instead into less state support for key sectors, reduced state services, the incapacity to tackle the fiscal imbalance, higher prices for electricity, daycare, and drug and car insurance, and a growing salary gap between underpaid state employees and the rest of the Quebec workforce. Far

6 http://www.premier-ministre.gouv.qc.ca/salle-de-presse/communiques/2004/decembre/ 2004-12-17.shtm (accessed 8 Aug. 2007). Translated from French by the author.

from promoting equity and social justice, she concluded, the government had widened the social divide.[7]

The contrast between these two appraisals of the social and political situation in 2004 could not be starker. It was hardly a surprise, of course, but it did illustrate the significant distance that separates two very distinct visions of public management and socio-economic priorities, each vying for dominance in policy making. It also signalled a new turn in the dynamics of governance in Quebec. Since the mid-1980s the business of running Quebec has proceeded for the most part through a system of informal cooperation between the government, business, labour, and a variety of civil-society socio-economic actors. Although consensus has never been perfect or easy to achieve, final decisions on key policy issues have often reflected choices agreed upon by a fairly wide and varied spectrum of stakeholders. As the situation has evolved since the election of the Charest government, this may no longer be possible. While the Charest government benefited from a disorganized and weak opposition from mainstream political parties to remain relatively unscathed in the National Assembly, the vehement resistance from civil society to its policy package pointed to the existence of deep social fault lines. The tendency of past governments to govern through consensus kept the divisions largely concealed; as things stood at the end of 2004, it was unlikely that these divisions would be easily mended in the years to come.

7 http://www.csn.qc.ca/Communiques/CommDec04/Comm29-12-04.html (accessed 8 Aug. 2007).

RICHARD WILBUR

New Brunswick

Faced with a one-seat majority after the 2003 general election, the Progressive Conservative government of Bernard Lord knew it was in for a rough year both politically and financially. The premier acknowledged this on 29 January in a 'State of the Province' address delivered to a $125-a-plate dinner attended by about six hundred at a Fredericton hotel. He identified New Brunswick's 2004 priorities as sustainable health and senior care, quality education, job creation, lower automobile insurance, and balancing the budget (*Telegraph Journal*, 30 Jan.). In addition, he promised that his government would decide the future of the Point Lepreau Nuclear Generating Station, make a decision on the future of crown lands, and update the Municipalities Act to provide a stable funding formula. For the current budget year ending 31 March, he predicted a balance of $5.5 billion for both expenditures and revenues but warned that next fiscal year could see a deficit of $300 million, due mainly to mounting health-care spending and a federal government that, he claimed, was not sharing its health-care burden while sticking with an inadequate equalization formula. Lord warned that 'the government has no choice but to cut, reduce or outsource to the private sector some government services to erase the looming deficit' (*Times Transcript*, 30 Jan.).

Other views of the financial picture

'Save Millions. Just cancel the new regional hospital' (*Telegraph Journal*, 23 Feb.). That was the main message that 350 Woodstock area citizens presented to Finance Minister Jeannot Volpe, who had been criss-crossing the province to get ideas on how to balance the budget and avoid a projected $300-million deficit for the fiscal year ending 31 March. Commenting on the minister's earlier statement that he could not guarantee unconditional grants to municipalities, Woodstock mayor Randy Leonard said that his community 'couldn't afford to have any more money clawed back from us' (*Telegraph Journal*, 13 Feb.). A licensed practical nurse said it was not fair that New Brunswick seniors were paying the highest daily fees in Canada for nursing-home care, $118 per day, when neighbouring provinces like Quebec charged $27.76. Volpe agreed but said that 'overall tax rates, such as Quebec's, are higher so everyone pays for the service.' A few days earlier, the minister expressed his frustration at hearing suggestions for more spending rather than ideas on where he should make cuts. 'If people continue to call for more spending,' he warned, he would seriously consider raising taxes (ibid.). This prompted Premier Lord to do some damage control via a conference call from Atlanta, where he was participating in a trade mission: 'We've been very clear in our position. For us, raising taxes is a last option. We have no intention of raising the income tax, or HST or gas tax or tobacco tax' (*Telegraph Journal*, 5 Feb.). Two weeks later, a report by the auditor general, Daryl Wilson, accused the Lord government of using 'accounting semantics' for its use of the so-called rainy day fund of $100 million, set up three years earlier, 'as a means of obscuring the actual financial results ... To say it is a surplus is wrong; they had a deficit [for 2003–4] of $109.4 million' (*Times Transcript*, 19 Feb.). A respected expert in public finance, Donald Savoie of the Université de Moncton, agreed: 'Transferring money into or out of the fund does not increase or decrease the finances of the province as a whole ... This is creative accounting' (ibid.).

On 23 February, just before heading off to Vancouver for a premier's meeting, Lord told a news conference that it would be 'very, very difficult' to keep his promise of a balanced budget this year after learning that the federal equalization payments to New Brunswick would be $100 million less than expected (*Telegraph Journal*, 24 Feb.). (Under legislation introduced and passed by the Lord government, New Brunswick must balance its books over a four-year period.) 'Unless something unforeseen happens, I think we can expect a deficit, for fiscal purposes, this year,' the premier informed the media (ibid.). He added that, until the federal government agreed to transfer more of its surplus to the provinces, every province except Alberta would suffer.

A month later, Volpe introduced his 2004–5 budget, and in contrast to earlier predictions of a deficit of as much as $350 million, he forecast a surplus of $2.4 million to be achieved largely by the elimination of public-service-sector positions plus a reorganization and consolidation of departments. Of the 750 positions that would be abolished over the next few months, he said that 130 were already vacant. On the revenue side, he expected that the province would receive an additional $23.4

million from the new federal health grants promised by the federal government of Jean Chrétien. He also predicted that higher service fees and the doubling of fines for traffic violations would bring in another $23 million.

The overall expenditures for the 2004–5 fiscal year were forecast at $5.7 billion, or 2.3 per cent higher than the previous period, with the largest sums going as usual to health ($2.06 billion) and education ($1.15 billion). Volpe said that the municipal grants would remain at the same level ($60.4 million) until 2007. On 14 April, the budget was approved in principle, with all twenty-seven government members on hand to defeat the twenty-six negative votes cast by the opposition. The vote was clearly the highlight of what was another dull spring session of the legislature, which dragged on until adjournment in the first week of July.

During the evening of the last Friday in June, Volpe introduced An Act Respecting Fines for Provincial Offences, which would double the minimum fines and increase the maximum fines on a long list of minor offences (*Telegraph Journal*, 1 July). For example, minimum speeding fines would be increased to $288 while those driving without a licence or insurance would pay a minimum $1,200. Volpe said that the fine increases 'will help the government recoup some administrative costs' (ibid.) In October, through orders-in-council, the Lord government authorized fee increases for vehicle inspection ($25 from $15) and increased the driver licence fee to $15 from $7, effective 1 November (*Telegraph Journal*, 18 Oct.).

Government rejects no-fault public auto insurance

Few were surprised when the Lord administration turned down the no-fault public auto-insurance model recommended by a legislative committee chaired by NDP leader Elizabeth Weir. Nearly four months after she presented her report, Lord unveiled in the legislature his plan, which would have an average annual cost of $869 and a $1,000 deductible while cutting in half the accident benefits for medical and death expenses, income replacement, and home-care support (*Telegraph Journal*, 30 June). Under what he called the 'no-frills option,' where people can pay less for insurance if they are willing to accept a lower level of coverage, medical coverage would be limited to $25,000. Replying to his statement that 'New Brunswickers have a choice to buy it or not,' Weir said that poor people 'don't have the luxury of choice … The only people who will buy this plan are people who have no money' (ibid.)

She thought the plan would allow insurance companies to offload medical and rehabilitative expenses on the already overburdened Medicare system. Lord said that he rejected a public system because he believed it would be too costly to set up and run. He noted that the new plan was expected to cost on average 15 per cent less than what people generally paid for a standard package, which, he said, currently cost $1,011 a year. Also, he cited an actuarial report by PricewaterhouseCoopers which concluded that rates would not be lower under a public system. Another factor was protecting the jobs of those working in the insurance industry in New Brunswick. The leader of the Liberal opposition, Shawn Graham, who supported a public-insurance model, accused Lord of 'being in the pocket of the insurance industry' and agreed with Weir's view that the new plan 'is doomed to fail' (ibid.) The new measures would go into effect on 1 January 2005.

In September, the justice minister, Brad Green, appointed eleven people to a new agency that would approve automobile-insurance rates, a role that had been the responsibility of the Public Utilities Board. The majority, including former Tory MP Elsie Wayne, had close ties with the New Brunswick Conservative Party, a point raised by T.J. Burke, the Liberal justice critic. He added: 'By naming well-known Tories to a board that will somehow regulate automobile insurance rates and have the power to investigate classes of automobile insurance ... it goes to show that the government isn't doing anything serious to resolve auto insurance rates for New Brunswickers' (*Telegraph Journal*, 24 Sept.). Considering that auto insurance was the major issue in the 2003 general election – a contest that saw a healthy government majority reduced to one – it remained to be seen how the electorate would respond to the Lord government's solution.

Contrasting responses to civil-service cuts

A pre-budget meeting that Premier Lord and Finance Minister Volpe held in late March with forty-five union officials representing 20,000 public-sector employees seemed to have positive results. Tom Mann, executive director of the New Brunswick Public Employees Association, said that 'it marked a victory for us' because of the premier's pledge to respect the unions' collective agreements and not freeze or roll back wages, noting: 'Given the financial challenges the government is up against, it's welcome news that it isn't planning layoffs' (*Telegraph Journal*, 25 March). Two weeks later, Mann revealed that union leaders had reached a deal to protect current contracts and reduce the number of displaced workers (*Telegraph Journal*, 9 April). A spokes-man for the Canadian Union of Public Employees, Danny Légère, said that, of the 750 positions being eliminated, about 588 were unionized while 222 were classified as management positions. Also, about 475 of the 588 unionized positions were currently unstaffed, so that fewer than 100 workers were actually losing their jobs. Three weeks later, 106 people in the Department of Health and Wellness were told their positions were being eliminated (*Telegraph Journal*, 29 April). Deb-bie McGraw, president of the 5,000-member New Brunswick Nurses Union, who had learned of the impending cuts a few days earlier, said that while no nurses, social workers, or psychologists had been cut, her biggest concern 'is the co-ordination of the programs delivered with the regional directors and supervisors eliminated' (ibid.). In September, her members voted overwhelmingly to accept a contract giving them a 24 per cent raise over the next four years and making them competitive with their colleagues in the other Atlantic provinces (*Telegraph Journal*, 24 Sept.).

It was a different story when about 650 support workers, members of CUPE local 1212 at the francophone Georges L. Dumont and the Moncton General hospitals, in the premier's home riding, began a bit-ter three-week strike in mid-October to back demands for a wage hike and job security. The same local had held a three-day strike in 2001 and signed an agreement only when the Lord government passed but did not proclaim back-to-work legislation. This time, the longer walkout forced the two hospitals to make drastic service cuts. After a settlement was reached, the government announced that doctors affected by the dispute would receive up to 80 per cent of the average lost income, with the money coming from the Income Stabilization Fund. Nurses employed on a casual basis were also affected: when many were not called in dur-ing the walkout, they also lost wages but were not compensated. The health minister, Elvy Robichaud, denied nurses' charges that the doc-tors were double-dipping: 'It was making sure those people who were needed in New Brunswick would be here when we need them' (*Times Transcript*, 24 Nov.). He understood some people were upset but argued that 'it was worth the risk.'

The perennial problem: financing and staffing health care

Early in January, a government-commissioned study by Fujitsu Consult-ing, completed in 2002 but never made public, was leaked to the media (*Telegraph Journal*, 12 Jan.). Throughout its 265 pages, it warned the

Department of Health and Wellness to take immediate action to head off a massive physician shortfall, including sixty-one family-practice positions. In the new era of health-care delivery, the report said that it would take three new doctors to fill the gap left by 'an old school doctor who carried a patient list of 5,000 and worked 100 hours a week.' Minister Robichaud said that, while the report had not been officially released, the government had been working on a recruitment strategy since the report's completion. He revealed no details but said that the strategy would update the government's last attempt to lure doctors, nurses, and other health practitioners to New Brunswick. A second Fujitsu study on doctor staffing, completed in the fall of 2003, was also being kept under wraps, despite a call for its release by Dr Paul Cloutier, president of the New Brunswick Medical Society. He said that the taxpayers 'who have footed the $800,000 bill for the report deserve to get a chance to see it now, before the province releases its plan for health care ...There's more than one way to read a report' (*Telegraph Journal*, 13 Jan.). Robichaud acknowledged that New Brunswickers would be involved 'but when you want to plan you don't want 700,000 people' doing it (ibid.). Three weeks later, the government released its version of the report, which differed significantly from the leaked version, notably in the absence of any reference to the need for 150 more doctors (*Times Transcript*, 5 Feb.).

On 2 March, Robichaud was in the heart of the Acadian peninsula to announce reduced services for the Caraquet and Tracadie hospitals. The former would become a community health centre offering services twelve hours a day with a walk-in clinic but would no longer have an emergency department. The hospital's thirty-nine beds would be closed (*Times Transcript*, 3 March). The hospital in Tracadie-Sheila (Robichaud's home riding) would offer emergency medicine but all surgeries requiring general anaesthetic would be moved to the Bathurst hospital, 100 kilometres away. 'I'm conscious ... that my announcement will cause some discontentment,' Robichaud told about 200 constituents, 'but this decision is necessary because ... of the difficulty in covering emergency room hours and the difficulty in attracting young doctors here' (ibid.). A short time before his announcement, members of the Strategic Committee to Save Health Care on the Acadian Peninsula held a news conference to release the results of a recent survey. It showed that the majority favoured the construction of a single centralized hospital at Pokemouche, which is an equal distance from Shippaga, Caraquet, and Tracadie-Sheila, the three main centres on the peninsula. Robichaud favoured the idea of a centralized hospital 'but there is just no funding available for such a venture at the moment.' Caraquet's mayor, Antoine Landry, said that the battle over the town's hospital was only beginning. 'We're going to keep fighting. If we have to go to court, we'll go to court' (*Times Transcript*, 3 March).

On 3 June, in what proved to be a preview of the long-awaited health plan, Premier Lord announced that about 300 hospital beds would be cut across the province, including less than thirty beds at the Miramichi hospital which had been rumoured to lose one hundred (*Telegraph Journal*, 4 June). He said that the cuts were 'part of a sweeping attempt to slash costs ... The government will redirect the money ... into the health-care priorities ... There will be some re-configuration and consolidation in non-clinical services ... administration, HR services, payroll services, IT services – the same things that we've been doing here in government' (ibid.) The money saved would be spent to improve immunization for children, increase drug coverage for seniors and working families with catastrophic health problems, provide more doctors, nurse practitioners, and nursing homes, improve ambulances services and strategies to fight cancer and heart disease, and reduce wait times for surgery.

A week later, over 3,000 gathered in front of the legislature to protest the government's new four-year health plan. Most had come from the Miramichi area but some, representing the Upper St John River valley, objected to the planned loss and/or downgrading of their local hospital facilities (*Telegraph Journal*, 10 June). The lone Conservative MLA who ventured beyond the metal barricades placed in front of the legislature's front steps was Tanker Malley of Miramichi-Bay du Vin, who braved the pushing, shouting, and verbal abuse to say that 'Miramichi hasn't lost services yet. I haven't let you down yet' (ibid.). Another to address the increasing unruly crowd was Clem Tremblay, mayor of Dalhousie, who revealed he had not learned that his town hospital was being downgraded to a community health centre until he was driving down to Fredericton. 'This government took the heart and soul of our community' (ibid.). He had already contacted other mayors in his region, including the mayor of St Quentin, whose hospital would also be reduced to a community health centre, and they all agreed to form a coalition to try to reverse the plan.

Inside the legislature, Premier Lord was revealing the details of his government's health-care plan, entitled 'Investments in Care and Services.' The Premier repeated his earlier views that the plan was 'a necessary step to resuscitate the ailing health-care system' (*Times Transcript*, 10 June). The department would be investing $125 million over the next four years, which would include enhanced ambulance services to meet national standards, the establishment of four new community health centres, recruitment and retention strategies for allied health personnel, seventy new physicians, ninety-five new university nursing seats, a new provincial cancer-care network, enhanced home-based palliative care, acute care, and mental-health services, and smoke-free legislation. The plan also focused on New Brunswickers' deplorable health habits, which had resulted in higher than average rates of obesity, smoking, high blood pressure, diabetes, and cardiovascular diseases.

Premier Lord asked New Brunswickers to look past unpopular measures, a comment that prompted Liberal leader Shawn Graham's response that it was 'ludicrous for the government to start ripping beds out of hospitals when there's no place for people occupying them to go' (ibid.). Elizabeth Weir, the NDP leader, told the House she was shocked by the lack of detail on the plan. 'From what I can see, it is a prescription for privatization and hallway medicine' (ibid.). The New Brunswick Medical Society called for the health plan to be sent to the legislature's Select Committee on Health for public consultation. On 1 July, in the reader's forum section of the *Telegraph-Journal* addressed to the health minister, the president and vice-president of the General Practice Section of the New Brunswick Medical Society, Drs Michel Landry and Jane Touchie, indicated their support for some of the new plan's recommendations, including smoke-free legislation and enhanced home-based care, but expressed concern about the impact on patients of cuts in acute-care services (*Telegraph Journal*, 1 July). They also wondered what had happened to the Fujitsu report, which 'clearly showed that the province needs many more nurses and between 40 to 100 family physicians every year for the next 10 years ...This government's answer ... seems to be: "Let's cut the number of nurses and physicians by closing hospital beds."' Over the next few weeks, the minister and the president of the New Brunswick Medical Society exchanged views via the daily newspapers (*Times Transcript*, 9 July; *Telegraph Journal*, 24 Sept. and 18 Oct.), indicating that while both sides agreed on the need to reduce New Brunswick's per capita hospital-bed ratio (one of the highest in Canada), they disagreed on the timing of the cuts and whether they were based solely on medical rather than political factors. Meanwhile, communities facing the severest cutbacks continued their opposition with some apparent success. When the New Brunswick Community Health Care Coalition announced plans to demonstrate in Fredericton at the fall opening of the legislature, Health Minister Robichaud announced that he 'is now studying a proposal' from St Quentin to reduce

the beds by six instead of the original twelve (*Daily Gleaner*, 30 Nov.),
but he reaffirmed the government's decision to go ahead with the other
hospital downsizings as well as its controversial plan to build a new
regional hospital in the upper St John valley. The Woodstock hospital
would be closed, a decision that, if carried out, brought the threat that
fourteen of its present medical staff would refuse to provide services at
the new facility (*Times Transcript*, 31 Dec.). The government position
was defended when the House reconvened on 2 December amid a protest outside from about 200 citizens who had journeyed down from the
northern regions despite the bitter cold and windy weather (*Telegraph
Journal*, 3 Dec.). About the only good news in this bitter controversy
came from proposals enabling students at the Université de Moncton
to remain on their own campus while taking the first and their final
years of medical training for a degree granted by the Université de Sherbrooke. Commenting on the ongoing negotiations, Robichaud said that
he hoped the plan would be operating by September 2006 (*L'Acadie-
Nouvelle*, 18 Dec.).

New Brunswick Power's Orimulsion fiasco

The biggest political question remained unanswered at the end of the
year. Why did New Brunswick Power, with the approval of the Lord
government, proceed with a $750-million upgrade to the Coleson Cove
power plant near Saint John so it could burn Orimulsion when there
was no signed contract with the state-owned Venezuelan company, the
world's only source for this kind of fuel? Negotiations began in 2003
and New Brunswick Power officials thought the signing was a formality
until they learned that the Venezuelan government had been considering
ignoring any Orimulsion deals not backed by a signed contract (*Times
Transcript*, 20 Feb.). For the past ten years, the same firm had been sup-
plying Orimulsion fuel to the power plant at Dalhousie, and when New
Brunswick Power began looking for a cheaper fuel for Coleson Cove, it
turned again to Venezuela. On 26 February, the power commission filed
a lawsuit seeking $2 billion in damages if the Venezuelan firm did not
sign an agreement (*Times Transcript*, 26 Feb.). This figure is based on
the estimate of twenty years to recover the $750-million refurbishment
costs compared to the six to seven years it would take with Orimulsion.
In addition, using bunker fuel over the same period would add another
$100 million.

Two weeks later, Premier Lord announced that David Hay, an investment banker, who had co-authored a special government report on New

Brunswick Power in 1998, would be its new president and CEO (*Times Transcript*, 4 March). He was asked to review the Orimulsion deal and report by the end of March. Instead, the Standing Committee on Crown Corporations held four days of meetings in April, hearing from New Brunswick Power and Energy Department representatives. In his testimony, Hay said that senior New Brunswick Power officials did not tell their board of directors or the government that the deal was in trouble. This was contradicted by Hay's predecessor, Stewart MacPherson (*Times Transcript*, 29 March) but was corroborated by Bill Thompson, the deputy minister of energy, who also revealed that the government had not been told about the cost overruns involving the fuel-delivery system, a figure that jumped from $40 million to $242 million (*Times Transcript*, 30 March). On 7 April, Jim Brogan, vice-president of generation for New Brunswick Power, who had been strongly criticized by Hay for his handling of the delivery-system contract, suddenly resigned (*Times Transcript*, 7 April). The Crown Corporation Committee's report on the hearings, prepared by a former Tory organizer, contained several spelling errors and no conclusions (*Times Transcript*, 31 Dec.), and it was left to Auditor General Daryl Wilson to decide whether he would study the issue.

Meanwhile, on 1 October, New Brunswick Power became a holding company overseeing four subsidiaries: New Brunswick Power Generation, New Brunswick Power Nuclear, New Brunswick Power Transmission, and New Brunswick Power Distribution and Customer Service. Derek Burney, a former Canadian ambassador to the United States, became chairman and his new board of directors included Graham Brown, former chief operating officer of Ontario Power Generation and an expert on nuclear energy, and Shirley Mears, senior vice-president and chief financial officer of Hydro Ottawa Holding Inc. Their biggest decisions over the next year would be whether to refurbish the Point Lepreau nuclear station and how much to increase hydro rates. On 31 March Premier Lord predicted that New Brunswick Power would have to increase electricity rates by as much as 6 per cent if Lepreau was to be refurbished without federal help (*Daily Gleaner*, 1 April). He added that 'they have provided interest-reduced loans in the past. We are asking for [one] now. We just want the interest to be zero' (ibid.) In August, Irving Oil received approval to build a Liquified Natural Gas (LNG) plant near Saint John and in October it announced it would definitely go ahead with the project, which would involve partnering with the Madrid-based petroleum giant Reposol. In a year-end interview, David Hay said that one of the ways to lessen New Brunswick Power's cost pressure was the early retirement program announced in December, which could save the corporation $40 million by offering packages to as many as 500 senior employees (*Times Tran*script, 31 Dec.).

Other economic developments and responses

While New Brunswick Power had been from its inception a crown agency, there seemed few other economic sectors that did not have government ties or cash infusions, despite mediocre to poor records in returns. Early in January, Finance Minister Volpe revealed that the government had been forced to write off $29 million in bad loans offered to companies that subsequently went bankrupt. He added that 'we are taking more security now in our loans but there is still a risk' (*Times Transcript*, 5 Jan.). Six weeks later, the New Brunswick Innovation Foundation, which had been set up by the Lord government in 2002, invested $450,000 in Ensemble Collaboration Corporation, a fifteen-month-old firm dealing in computer-based training (*Telegraph Journal*, 21 Feb.). So far, it had no products, customers, or revenue, but, in announcing the grant, Lord said that the foundation's investment was not a government handout. 'This is an equity position, and therefore the money, if everything goes well, could come back' (ibid.). On 23 March, during a media conference call, Lord declared that after its first year, the Restigouche-Chaleur Initiative, established in October 2002 with a $25-million fund to be spent over five years, 'is producing the desired results in northern New Brunswick (*Times Transcript*, 24 April). After his party lost all the seats in the region in the 2003 election, there was talk that the plan would be scrapped, but he promised it would continue. To date it had funded sixty projects, including a new call centre in Campbellton and a $500,000-tourist initiative, as well as giving several expansion grants to existing businesses. In May, Lord visited Campbellton, Dalhousie, and Bathurst and announced more grants totalling $6 million, including funds for a Bathurst-area firm making rubber products and grants to improve the water systems in Campbellton and Dalhousie (*Times Transcript*, 19 May). In November the call centre that had opened in Campbellton less than a year earlier closed its doors, to the surprise of its sixty employees. Meanwhile, the government funds continued to flow, with Premier Lord on hand to make the announcements. A $25-million Miramichi Regional Economic Development Fund was unveiled in late April. In July the city of Miramichi received $1.6 million 'toward making the city's newest retail centre a reality' (*Telegraph Journal*, 6 July). In September, the premier was in Edmundston to announce a provincial grant of $1.219 million to renovate and upgrade the city's Convention Centre. In November, with Lord at his side, Dan O'Neil, CEO of Canada's second-oldest company, Molson's, announced that it would spend $35 million on a new facility in Moncton, which would open in 2007. The provincial government would provide $3.5 million in the form of a non-refundable loan guarantee, a move destined to raise strong objections from Molson's biggest local competitor, Moosehead Breweries of Saint John.

The minister of agriculture, fisheries, and aquaculture, David Alward, received support from all sides of the House with his motion opposing his federal counterpart's decision to transfer 320 tonnes of New Brunswick's snow-crab quota to Prince Edward Island fishermen. In a second dispute a few months later, Island lobster fishermen clashed with New Brunswick herring seiners, claiming that they were dragging too close to shore in violation of existing regulations. When the seiners docked in Souris, PEI, to take on supplies, they were prevented from going ashore. In response, Alward loaded his car with food supplies intended for the seiner crews. His arrival at the Souris wharf was met by an angry crowd, and, upon the advice of the RCMP, he left the scene without accomplishing his mission.

Events in the provincial forestry sector revealed much deeper problems. Private woodlot owners learned early in March that they would lose $800,000 in silvaculture funding for 2004–5; crown land leaseholders faced similar cuts as part of a $5.5-million reduction in the department's budget. In September, the legislature's Select Committee on Wood Supply made twenty-five recommendations after province-wide public hearings in response to the Jaako Poyry Report on Forestry. Financed by the private sector and released in December 2002, the Poyry study called for a doubling of the softwood harvest on crown lands over the next fifty years. While not endorsing that specific approach, the legislators' key recommendation was for the industry to focus on diversification.

One week later, the St Anne-Nackawic pulp mill, about an hour's drive above Fredericton, abruptly closed its doors with the loss of 400 jobs. The next day, the mill's New York owners filed for bankruptcy. It was not long before the broader effects of the closure became apparent. It was town's only employer and soon commercial outlets began to close and For Sale signs appeared before scores of homes. Hundreds of non-mill workers, including truck drivers and wood cutters, also lost their jobs. Each year for the past thirty-five years, the mill's output, over 200,000 tonnes of pulp product, mostly in the form of high-quality photo paper, had been shipped out of the port of Saint John. The Lord government immediately named a former deputy minister of natural resources, Georges Bouchard, to head a task force to find a buyer. Despite recurring rumours that one had been found, by year's end there was no confirming announcement. Lord said that his government 'hopes to ink a deal ... before Christmas' with an unnamed company (*Telegraph Journal*, 4 Dec.). It proved to be Tembec, a huge Quebec-based firm, which admitted it was interested but wanted an agreement with the former Nackawic workers' union, the Canadian Auto Workers. In fact, they reached a tentative five-year agreement on labour issues but this only made possible continued negotiations. What made the closure even more serious was news that the bankrupt firm owed an estimated $30 million in pensions to about 250 unionized workers and an undisclosed number of management staff. This issue sparked an angry response to the Throne Speech of 2 December by Elizabeth Weir, the NDP leader and MLA for Saint John, in what would be her final major speech in the legislature (the previous October, Weir had announced that she was resigning as party leader). She said that the pension situation 'puts into clear focus the injustice of our current bankruptcy laws and the need for reform' (*Telegraph Journal*, 14 Dec.). Rather than agreeing to her request for an independent commission of inquiry, the Lord government introduced an amendment to the Pensions Benefits Act to include a sunset clause and restricting the bill solely to the Nackawic pensioners (*Times Transcript*, 18 Dec.).

In November, Fraser Paper Nexfor announced the elimination of seventy-eight jobs at its mills at Edmundston and across the river in Madawaska, Maine. The Finnish owners of the UPM Miramichi mill announced on 29 September that they would be permanently closing their kraft mill at the end of January, but when a strike threatened in mid-December, they moved the date ahead, affecting 400 jobs and reducing the area's economy by $100 million (*Times Transcript*, 10 Dec.). The future of the rest of the mill remained uncertain.

Another brief pre-Christmas legislative session

A lead editorial in the *Telegraph-Journal* on the Throne Speech underscored its late appearance: 'The document has been 18 months in the making – far too long for any jurisdiction to go without a priority blueprint' (*Telegraph Journal*, 3 Dec.). It promised to reduce both personal income taxes and the small business tax, to be implemented over the next three years. Starting immediately, low-income citizens on social assistance would see their heating-fuel subsidy increase from $70 per month to $90, a move that would cost an additional $350,000 annually. Childcare workers were promised better wages and benefits and rural roads would be improved. Lord said that recent deals with the federal government involving health care and equalization payments 'have helped loosen the purse strings,' but he added that his administration 'is not embarking on a spending spree.' The *Telegraph-Journal* editorial, while admitting that the premier had had to make some 'tough decisions' since the general election, zeroed in on the two biggest issues for most citizens: auto insurance, 'a file that needs stronger resolve,' and 'the energy file – an element too lightly addressed' (ibid.)

Judging by his adroit handling of his one-seat majority since the 2003 general election, Premier Lord learned under fire, especially with his delaying tactics. But some issues, notably relating to the energy and the forest sectors, remained political time bombs the longer they went unresolved.

PETER E. BUKER

Prince Edward Island

The year 2004 was one of slowed economic growth for Prince Edward Island compared both to the previous year and to the Canadian economy. A significant number of public-infrastructure and publicly supported private-sector investments were made through joint provincial-federal programs. The provincial net debt reached $1.25 billion at the end of the 2003–4 fiscal year, an increase of 11.7 per cent from 2003. In total, twenty-six bills were passed in 2004, including the Renewable Energy Act, which laid out a strategy and set targets for PEI's future energy requirements. In February the Island's largest seafood processor, Polar Foods, went into receivership for reasons variously attributed to market slumps and poor management, leaving a debt of $53 million and threatening 1,200 jobs. It was described by many as the 'largest business failure in P.E.I. history' (*The Guardian*, 14 April 2007). A state of emergency was declared in mid-February owing to heavy snowfall. All of the Island's four Liberal incumbents were returned to the Canadian Parliament in the federal election of 28 June; three were given cabinet posts.

The economy

Prince Edward Island's population as of 1 July 2004 was estimated by Statistics Canada to be 137,864, an increase of 598 people or 0.4 per cent from a year earlier. Of this increase, 7 per cent was a natural increase of the existing population, 43 per cent was from international migration, and 50 per cent was from net interprovincial migration – mostly from Ontario, Nova Scotia, New Brunswick, Alberta, and Newfoundland and Labrador. Most emigration was to the provinces of Ontario, Nova Scotia, Alberta, and New Brunswick. Population-distribution statistics showed a continual long-term aging of PEI's population; the median age increased from 24.8 years in 1971 to 39.1 years in 2004.

GDP expanded from 2003 by 1.8 per cent in constant dollars to $4,023 million at 2004 market prices. Strong residential construction, a jump in interprovincial exports, and increased manufacturing accounted for much of the growth. Economic performance was moderated by weak retail sales and continuing lower tourist numbers. There was positive employment growth, increases in labour income, and strong residential-construction activity. Labour productivity increased 2.9 per cent. The Consumer Price Index was 2.1 per cent, reflecting, in part, the 8.7 per cent rise in energy costs and the 8.2 per cent increase in tobacco and alcohol prices.

The average unemployment rate was 11.3 per cent, with an all-time historic high of 66,700 people employed; the reported 2003 statistics were revised downwards. Labour-force participation increased marginally to 67.8 per cent. Gains in employment occurred in the health, education, and public-administration sectors, the primary resources sector, and the trade sector; there were employment losses, however, in the sectors of accommodations and food services, transportation and warehousing, construction, and other services. Personal income increased by 3.8 per cent; federal government transfers to persons increased an estimated 4.0 per cent, despite a 1.9 per cent decrease in employment-insurance benefits.

Manufacturing shipments increased 4.3 per cent to $1,414.3 million, mostly attributable to growth in aerospace and processed-food exports; frozen potato exports increased substantially, although fish processing was significantly down by 20.7 per cent. Aerospace products accounted for 11.4 per cent of manufacturing shipments in 2004 compared to almost none in 2000. While the total volume of exported goods grew, the value increased by only 2.4 per cent. Total farm cash receipts were 2 per cent lower than in 2003; an oversupply of potatoes in North America led to a significant 17.8 per cent drop in potato receipts to $152.3 million from the previous year, being part of a longer-term trend that saw the potato price index fall 40.5 per cent since 2002. The value of total fish landings fell by 3.5 per cent. In the tourism sector, visitor numbers were down by 11.1 per cent from the previous year, to an estimated 350,000 people, with total tourism expenditure down 15.6 per cent. November's throne speech described tourism as 'a challenge,' saying: 'Prince Edward Island felt the effects of a soft travel market, in part due to inclement weather, global events and higher fuel prices.' Housing construction increased 17 per cent to a level not seen for over a decade, and was attributable to historically low mortgage rates. The public-service sector accounted for $839.1 million or 27 per cent of provincial GDP, and 29.7 per cent of total Island employment.

Island businesses continued to expand in 2004. Cabinetmaster Architectural Woodwork of Charlottetown was awarded a $1-million contract to supply architectural woodwork for the new United States embassy in Barbados. AgraWest Investments of Souris, a manufacturer of dehydrated potato granules for food processors around the world, expanded its facility with a building addition, more equipment, and twenty-two more employees; all this added up to an investment of $2.5 million, including a $2-million repayable loan from the PEI Century 2000 Fund. An Atlantic Beef Products facility in Borden-Carleton, in which the PEI government invested almost $6 million as well as loan guarantees of up to $1 million a year to cover the construction costs of the plant, also received $1.4 million for the purchase of traceability equipment and training from the federal government. The aerospace company Testori Americas expanded its Slemon Park and Bloomfield operations, adding 40 new positions to the 245 already at Slemon Park, and received $2.7 million in a 'Forgivable Performance Loan' through PEI Business Development. Also at Slemon Park, Tronos Canada, a London-based aircraft-leasing company, established a maintenance, repair, and overhaul facility with spare-parts administration and aircraft-leasing administration to service the North American market. It received a $400,000-forgivable-performance incentive through PEI Business Development. The Island's aerospace industry employed more than 700 employees and had $180 million in annual sales. A new company, Sandwich Factory Foods, was opened in Bloomfield; approximately $1 million in equipment was invested in the 9,000-square-foot plant, which was intended to produce sandwiches for three distribution centres across the Maritimes. Norseboat Limited, located in Belfast, began manufacturing and marketing the Norseboat 17.5, an innovative sailing and rowing micro-cruising boat. In July, Sears announced plans to open a PEI department store.

Two new crops were evaluated in 2004. Four hundred acres of flax, a basis for cereal foods and a health additive, was planted by eleven PEI farmers in an extensive field trial to determine whether Island growing conditions could produce a crop of sufficient yield and quality after a smaller flax crop grown in 2003 had proven to be promising. The Island Grains and Protein Council commissioned a consulting firm to conduct a feasibility study for a malt brewery plant on PEI, targeting micro and home breweries and avoiding shipping costs that had previously prevented profitable malt barley crops on the Island.

The provincial government worked to dispose of the assets of seafood processor Polar Foods, which collapsed in February. This entailed an agreement between Ocean Choice PEI and the provincial government whereby the company committed itself to the continued operation of the processing plants in Souris and Beach Point, to the processing of all lobster on PEI and to employing 600 PEI workers in the 2004 lobster season, and to investing a minimum of $10 million in PEI over the next five years. In March the provincial government announced an assistance program specifically for fish-plant workers displaced by the sale of Polar Foods. The provincial government bought Polar Foods' outstanding debts of $53 million and PEI Auditor General Colin Younker was asked to investigate the company's collapse after the opposition Liberals demanded a public inquiry into the province's former support of the firm. Younker's report was due in 2006.

A number of public infrastructure projects were initiated in 2004. In March it was announced that Alberton was to receive $240,000 in funding for downtown streetscape enhancements. In April a newly constructed Observation Site at North Lake – 'Tuna Capital of the World' – was opened to provide a platform to view the tuna catch. Cardigan had its official launch for a waterfront-development project featuring a marina and an interpretive centre, on 10 July. On 12 August, Summerside's 'Shipyard Market,' part of the city's waterfront-improvement project, was officially opened. Work began on the St Peters Estuary Interpretive Centre, a tourism development. As well, plans were made to construct a promenade boardwalk along Covehead Bay adjacent to Route 25. All six initiatives were joint projects involving federal, provincial, and local levels of government. The Three Rivers Roma Group received provincial support for the development of a forty-hectare historic site; Jean Pierre Roma established the Compagnie de l'Est de l'Isle St Jean at what was known in 1732 as the community of Trois Rivières; the site had been excavated from 1968 to 1971. An $8-million expansion, begun in 2000, of Bluefield High School in Hampshire was officially opened in October. In December the $6-million 'new' addition and renovation of Summerside Intermediate School was officially opened; the first stage of construction had begun in 2001 and the second phase in 2003. The PEI Food Technology Centre, Holland College's Culinary Institute of Canada, and PEI Development created a partnership to develop value-added food products using Prince Edward Island ingredients.

From 23 April to 13 September, 278 Aliant workers were on strike; the strike was settled after agreement was reached on issues that included benefits, job security, pensions, and eliminating contracting-out work that jeopardized employment of regular employees. PEI's National Park was also subject to national rotating strikes by the Union of Parks Canada Employees, with a tentative deal reached on 11 October.

Media attention on the bizarre saga of gas-exploration company Meteor Creek's questionable operations continued; on 24 February the CBC television program *Disclosure* aired an investigative report.

Fiscal events

Total revenue for the province of Prince Edward Island for the fiscal year 2003–4 was up 4.9 per cent to $996.3 million compared to the previous fiscal year; provincial tax revenues remained the same at $597.6 million, equalization payments increased by 9.6 per cent, and Canada Health and Social Transfer payments increased by 15.9 per cent. Total provincial expenditure in the 2003–4 fiscal year was $1,126.7 million, an annual increase of 12 per cent. Total federal transfers accounted for 39 per cent of provincial revenue, up from 35 per cent the previous fiscal year.

Only minor changes were made in provincial taxation in 2004. A cost-recovery fee to maintain the PEI 911 emergency service of fifty cents a month on telephone bills was announced in the spring budget, effective in early 2005. In December, the Progressive Tax Rebate Program, providing tax incentives to companies and individuals who invest in innovation, growth, and development of targeted sectors across the province, was introduced.

A report by the Legislative Assembly's Standing Committee on Agriculture, Forestry and Environment recommended a fundamental shift from the existing industrialized, commodity-based model to a model founded on product differentiation and branding. This, the committee claimed, would build on the Island's pastoral image, geographic isolation, healthy environment, and tradition of family farming.

On 30 April five Access PEI sites (Crapaud, Kinkora, North Rustico, Stratford, and Morell), offering Islanders access to a range of government services, were closed, in favour of the more frequently used sites that remained. Also in 2004, the PEI Online Reservation System allowing visitors to book accommodations on the Island year-round was introduced.

In August it was announced that, with help from the Atlantic Lottery Corporation, the Charlottetown Driving Park would be transformed into a 'racino,' with 225 electronic gambling machines to provide revenue to subsidize horse racing. The project cost $25 million and was anticipated to give the province $5 million a year in revenues and double the racing purses. This sparked a public debate centring on the danger of increased gambling addiction.

The 'tough' budget of March 2004 forecast a $33.1-million deficit for the coming year; Provincial Treasurer Mitch Murphy claimed that the deficit would have been much higher without $46 million in expenditure cuts and without the budget's tax increases; in the fall sitting of the legislature, Murphy said that the deficit might reach $116 million because of a $40-million equalization adjustment, a $33-million pension adjustment, and a $23-million loss from the collapse of Polar Foods. Health and social-services expenditures accounted for the largest share of the provincial budget at $428 million or 40.2 per cent of the total expenditure; education accounted for $222.6 million or 20.9 per cent of the total.

Politics and the legislature

In total, the provincial legislature passed twenty-six bills in 2004, including the Renewable Energy Act, laws to eliminate bootlegging, legislation to remove cigarettes from pharmacies, and an act that anticipated nurse practitioners.

In June the PEI Energy Framework and Renewable Energy Strategy was announced, setting targets for the implementation of renewable energy on the Island. Among the goals, PEI committed to a renewable portfolio standard for electricity of at least 15 per cent by 2010. As of 2004, about 5 per cent of the Island's electricity came from wind power. In September, Natural Resources Canada announced funding to Stuart Energy Systems for the preliminary engineering phase of a hydrogen fuelling station to support demonstration projects involving hydrogen-powered shuttle buses in Charlottetown. 'Renewal' was also key within the provincial public administration itself; the provincial executive began a 'Program Renewal' process in June that created twenty committees to examine all provincial departments, agencies, boards, and commissions with specific regard to public interest, effectiveness and efficiency, affordability, accountability, and emerging trends, with an expected completion date of 15 January 2005.

Peter McQuaid, chief of staff to Premier Pat Binns, and deputy minister, resigned, effective 6 April 2004. Subsequently, McQuaid ran for the Conservative Party of Canada but lost by a wide margin to Liberal incumbent Lawrence MacAulay in the riding of Cardigan in the federal election of 28 June. On 19 July, McQuaid rejoined government in his old position. All four Island federal seats went with decisive majorities to the Liberal Party; the other three seats went to Shawn Murphy (Charlottetown District), Joe McGuire (Egmont District), and Wayne Easter

(Malpeque District). In July, McGuire was appointed minister of the Atlantic Canada Opportunities Agency, Murphy was made parliamentary secretary to the minister of fisheries and oceans, and Easter became parliamentary secretary to the minister of agriculture and agri-food, with special emphasis on rural development, by the Martin government.

In February, Premier Pat Binns attended the Atlantic Canada Premiers Meeting in Corner Brook, Newfoundland. PEI's Legislative Assembly hosted the 30th Session of the Assemblée parlementaire de la Francophonie (APF) on 4–7 July; the APF serves as a democratic link between francophones among seventy-three parliaments worldwide, and over 250 French-speaking parliamentarians and officials attended the meeting on the Island.

The Legislative Assembly resumed its 62nd session on 30 March and adjourned on 20 May 2004. The first session was prorogued on 2 November 2004, unusual for being in an adjournment period, after forty-seven sitting days. The House did not prorogue following the spring session to allow legislative committees to continue to meet and give flexibility in the event that members needed to reconvene on short notice. The legislature was recalled on 18 November, and proceedings began with the Speech from the Throne read by Lieutenant Governor J. Léonce Bernard. It adjourned on 16 December after seventeen sitting days.

In March the PEI government announced a moratorium of up to one year on new construction- and demolition-disposal sites while a comprehensive review of the Environmental Protection Act Waste Resource Management Regulations governing them was conducted. In May, the report *Recommendations for the Regulation of Pesticides in Prince Edward Island* was released, containing many recommendations to modify existing legislation and practices. In June a major review by an interdepartmental steering committee of the 1987 provincial forestry policy was announced, responding to a call to change the focus towards non-timber forest products and non-commodity values, including landscape and water quality; policy change was sought because the Island's forest had decreased in area, volume, age, and complexity between 1990 and 2000. In December the province released the *Forest Policy Discussion Paper*. On 24 August a report presented to the provincial government by the Public Forest Council warned that issues surrounding sustainability, theft, trespass, and inconsistent harvest standards endangered the ground hemlock harvest; the council offered specific recommendations to remedy these problems. On 30 June the P.E.I. Electoral Boundaries Commission released an interim report on proposed changes to the area, boundaries, and names of the province's twenty-seven electoral districts. Nine of the electoral districts were at variance with the Electoral Boundaries Act because of population changes. A notable change was that of increasing urbanization; the urban electorate of PEI comprised 44.27 per cent of the 99,252 electors. The commission held four public hearings in September to receive submissions on the proposals contained in the interim report, and its final report was submitted on 5 October. Also on 30 June the first comprehensive report on the provincial government's French-language services was released, following upon the French Language Service Act of 1 April 2000. The Premier's Council on Healthy Child Development released the *Third Annual Report on Children 2002–2003* in July; it indicated that PEI children are generally doing well based on national indicators, although some indicators showed poor performance. The *Second Report on Common Health Indicators*, which measured and tracked citizen health status and the health-care system's performance, was released in November.

In terms of the workings of the provincial government itself, an Act to Amend the Legislative Assembly Act was passed; it effectively exercised parliamentary privilege by clarifying that any committee of the Legislative Assembly may command and compel attendance before the committee and the production of documents. The Standing Committee on Community Affairs was asked to review of the Freedom of Information and Protection of Privacy Act. A motion in the legislature established a Special Committee on Climate Change on 20 May to create a provincial climate-change strategy.

In 2004 there were continued problems associated with the previous year's protest by Island fishers against New Brunswick herring seiners unloading their catch on the Souris wharf. In March PEI Minister of Fisheries Kevin MacAdam expressed reservations concerning some of the options outlined in a report on the conflict in the herring fishery, submitted by 'a qualified and independent third party' appointed by federal Department of Fisheries and Oceans (DFO), Allister Surette, to the federal minister of fisheries and oceans; the provincial government wanted to return to the 1983 exclusion zone, which included a twenty-five fathom line, to protect fish stocks. In December, MacAdam accused the province's federal MPs of blackmail for trying to convince fishermen not to support legal actions against the DFO because such actions could bring fisheries negotiations to a halt. As well, MacAdam obtained a legal opinion with respect to the payment and deployment of the RCMP in the previous year's legal protest at the federal government wharf in Souris. Based on that opinion, he said that these matters were the responsibility of the federal government. There were other conflicts between DFO and the provincial minister as well. On 11 August, MacAdam expressed concern over DFO's changes to the Management Plan for Lobster Fishing Area 25 in the Northumberland Strait, where catches had steadily declined for twenty years. The cause of the enormous decline was variously attributed to poaching, herring seining, and scallop draggers, as well as to catching egg-laying females in August. MacAdam criticized the DFO's decision to change the five-year management plan agreed to the preceding year; that plan specifically sought to conserve productive female lobsters. In June, DFO announced that 2004 would be the last year for an allocation of the Gulf snow crab quota to PEI's groundfishing fleet. In November the provincial government decided to pursue legal action against the government of Canada to seek a resolution to a number of outstanding fisheries disputes, including the herring seiner boundary line and the unfair and inequitable allocation of several fisheries species including Bluefin tuna, snow crab, and gulf and northern shrimp. During the year, to streamline departmental management, the forestry portfolio was removed from Department of Agriculture, Fisheries, Aquaculture, and Forestry and became part of the new Department of Energy, Environment and Forestry.

Island fisheries and aquaculture were threatened on another front; the provincial Department of Agriculture, Fisheries, Aquaculture, and Forestry undertook a summertime awareness campaign for boaters to help prevent the spread of aquatic invasive species in Island waters. Green crab, clubbed tunicate, and oyster thief, all abundantly present in PEI waters since the late 1990s, were threatening existing aquatic plants and animals as well as the shellfish industry.

In the health-and-safety sector, the PEI government placed a total ban on tobacco use in provincial adult correctional facilities by 30 September. The twenty-four-hour emergency department services at the Stewart Memorial Hospital in the Tyne valley closed on 7 October following a critical accreditation report, but there was a partial reinstatement of services following local outcry. Amendments to Occupational Health and Safety Act Regulations were extended to workplaces where fewer than three persons are employed and to farm operations. The new Registered Nurses Act received royal assent in December 2004, paving the way for regulations to be drafted in anticipation of advanced nursing practice in PEI by nurse practitioners. As well, a three-year Master Agreement with Island physicians promised an additional $2.1-million investment over three years to foster the recruitment and retention of physicians. The new $55-million Prince County Hospital began operation on 4 April. After years of pleading by the city of Charlottetown, the provincial government gave police increased powers to seize the assets of illegal bars as of 1 January 2005, raising the penalties for bootleggers to a point where the crime no longer would have an economic payoff. In April 2004 it was announced that the Alberton and Souris courthouses were slated to close.

In April, Prince Edward Island statutes and regulations became available on the provincial government website, and in November the proceedings of PEI's Legislative Assembly were webcast in their entirety for the first time; the permanency of this latter service was to be reviewed at the end of the spring 2005 session. Prince Edward Island Energy Corporation entered into a contract with Investco Inc. of Calgary, Alberta, to scan and digitize various sets of oil and natural gas exploratory well data; under the terms of the agreement, Investco became the exclusive distributor of PEI's well logs and drilling reports.

Other events

On 29 January, the 2003–4 school calendar was revised to make up for school days lost because of poor weather; nine school days had been cancelled to that date. Shortly afterwards, on 19–20 February, the Emergency Measures Organization declared a state of emergency for PEI in response to a severe snowstorm that dumped seventy-five centimetres of snow on the Island and was dubbed 'White Juan,' alluding to Hurricane Juan of September 2003. Some 12,000 homes were without power, and all access to the Island was cut off. In June, PEI experienced a forest tent caterpillar outbreak as part of the insect's natural cycle; however, only unhealthy or stressed trees were at risk from the defoliation caused by the caterpillar. The Department of Environment and Energy investigated an incident of fish mortality discovered on 3 September in Middleton.

An appeal of a 2003 jail sentence in the high-profile case of Cass Rhynes led to the overturning of the conviction by the provincial Supreme Court and Rhynes's acquittal. The crown appealed that decision, but the decision was upheld.

The Lobster Science Centre at the Atlantic Veterinary College and the PEI Department of Agriculture, Fisheries, Aquaculture and Forestry co-hosted the 8th International Conference and Workshop on Lobster Biology and Management in Charlottetown in September 2007.

PEI won distinction in 2004 through the performances of a number of sports figures and by hosting several national sports events. Contessa Scott and Frank MacIntyre won gold medals with the Canadian goalball team in the Paralympics in Athens, Greece, in September. Island participants in the National Seniors Games held in the Yukon captured twenty-eight medals. PEI hosted the National Dart Tournament, the Cavendish Farms National Pee Wee Baseball Championships, the National Midget Softball Championships, the Senior Women's Canadian Fastpitch Championship, and the National Senior Men's and Women's Soccer Championships. The University of Prince Edward Island's woman's soccer team won its first ever Atlantic University Sport title. 'Brad Richards Day' was held in Murray Harbour on 3 August. Richards was a winger for the Stanley Cup-winning Tampa Bay Lightning; he won the Conn Smythe Trophy for the team's most valuable player in the Stanley Cup playoffs and the Lady Byng trophy as professional hockey's most gentlemanly player.

The province honoured other achievements and hosted other events in 2004. An innovative project designed by Isle@sk to link libraries across the province received the 2004 National Innovation Achievement Award sponsored by Micromedia ProQuest and presented by the Canadian Association of Colleges and University Libraries. PEI hosted the National Music Festival in August at the University of Prince Edward Island and the Confederation Centre of the Arts. The PEI Food Technology Centre in Charlottetown received an award from the American Association of Cereal Chemists for the accuracy of its analysis; it was the most accurate of all the laboratories in the world participating in the check-sample program for fat, fatty acids, and cholesterol. The centre successfully completed the required transition audit to the ISO 9001:2000 quality standard in 2004, a rigorous international standard emphasizing process management in monitoring and optimizing tasks and activities rather than just looking to the final product.

Several Island individuals received public recognition for their achievements. John and Bea Keaveny received the Helen Allen Award for exemplary promotion of adoption by the Adoption Council of Canada. In September the Order of PEI was awarded to Father Éloi Arsenault of Egmont Bay, the Reverend Dr Francis W.P. Bolger of Charlottetown, and Barbara McNeill of Summerside. The third annual Institute of Public Administration Canada–P.E.I. Lieutenant Governor's Award for Excellence in Public Administration was given to Kay Lewis, executive director of Prince County Hospital, in December. As well, the provincial attorney general granted the title of Queen's Counsel to M. Jane Ralling, Ronald J. Profit, and Brian L. Waddell. In December, Frank

Ledwell was appointed PEI's second poet laureate, for a two-year term, by the provincial government.

Several initiatives were of note. In February a joint federal-provincial agreement to create a new Bachelor's Degree in Education with a specialization in French immersion at the University of Prince Edward Island, in collaboration with the Université de Moncton, was announced. In the spring, students in sixty-nine Island schools planted red oak trees to celebrate 2004 as the Year of Learning and Innovation. In June the Archives PEI website – a provincially sponsored searchable database – was launched, linking over 1,100 collections in six provincial institutions. Also in June, Province House, completed in 1847, was designated under the provincial Heritage Places Protection Act in recognition of its historical importance to Canada.

Notably as well, 2004 was the 400th Anniversary of the Acadians' arrival on PEI; it was celebrated with events held throughout the year and sponsored by public funds totalling over $1.2 million. Leading travel magazine *Condé Nast Traveler* released its '17th Annual Readers' Choice Awards' and listed PEI as number three in the top ten North American islands, and, in a *Travel & Leisure Magazine* readers' survey, PEI was designated the highest-ranking island in the continental United States and Canada. The Norseboat 17.5 was named by *Sail Magazine* as one of the 'Best Boats of 2004' and placed first in the sailboat division in the 480-kilometre 'WaterTribe Everglades Challenge' in southwest Florida in March 2004.

ROBERT G. FINBOW

Nova Scotia

The year 2004 in Nova Scotia was marked by cooperation between government and opposition, as all parties sought to avoid any confrontation which could bring down the minority government of Conservative Premier John Hamm. With an election possible in the minority situation in Ottawa, with all three parties short on resources, and with the public weary of campaigns, no political leader wanted to be responsible for forcing another vote. The premier denied rumours he would try for an election soon, despite the Tories' rising poll numbers at year's end. The two opposition parties were forced to tread carefully to provide a credible alternative without triggering a confidence vote which would require an election. Despite some rancour and rhetoric, the legislative sessions were uneventful and compromise bills enacted both government and opposition measures.

Nova Scotia played host to the Congrès mondial acadien (World Acadian Congress), which featured multiple family reunions among this dispersed populace and moving closing ceremonies at Grand Pré, site of commemorative icons from the tragic deportation of 1755. Premier Hamm welcomed the congress as an opportunity to highlight an important element of Nova Scotia's history and culture and to renew links with kindred communities outside Canada. The province joined with Ottawa to officially recognize Acadian Day on 15 August. Despite this high-profile event and a popular tour by tall ships from around the world, several factors – a higher value for the Canadian dollar, continued U.S. economic slowdown, and border-security concerns – hampered tourism and contributed to a modest economic performance, furthering political uncertainty. Ongoing battles with Ottawa over equalization, health care, and other transfers made sustaining a budget surplus a continuing challenge, which complicated inter-party cooperation.

Politics

Notwithstanding a sluggish economy, the Conservative minority government managed to maintain the reins in the legislature and increase popular support. There were no major scandals to undermine confidence in the Hamm regime. The government was criticized for deciding to place a new MRI machine in the premier's riding, even though it rated lower on need than other communities. The NDP attacked Nova Scotia Business Inc. for buying Christmas presents from an Austrian crystal maker instead of a local firm it had subsidized. Late in the year, the opposition decried a budget update which earmarked $60 million for roads and bridges, which was designed to permit strategic pre-election spending without legislative approval; the poor state of roads was a hot-button political issue in rural regions. Reliance on gambling revenues to make such commitments was also criticized given the social costs of addiction to video-lottery terminals (VLTs) and other games of chance. The premier denied election rumours and promised a moderate course into the spring of 2005, to avoid courting a non-confidence vote despite polls showing high satisfaction with his government: 35 per cent expressed intention to vote for the Conservatives, with government approval ratings over 60 per cent. Hamm boasted of increased university and college funding and better health-care delivery, contrary to opposition claims of funding shortfalls. In spite of painful back problems and persistent rumours of his departure, the premier refused to clarify his future plans by year's end.

The NDP was now seen as a government in waiting, with acknowledgment from political foes that the party no longer 'scared' voters. Low-key leader Darrell Dexter appeared to connect with voters and won praise from formerly hostile columnists and activists, who felt he could now credibly form a government. His pragmatic policy choices and strong advance organization seemed to put the party in good position to succeed in a future election. The party prepared moderate economic-policy positions, emphasized core issues like auto insurance, and highlighted new candidates in public appearances to increase public familiarity and comfort with the NDP team. One sign of the party's new moderation was a decision to accept political donations from publicly traded companies which were deemed to follow 'ethical' practices, even though party policy simultaneously, and confusingly, called for only contributions from individuals for all parties in future. The party hoped its stance on seniors' health coverage, no-fault auto insurance, gas price regulation, and elimination of the Harmonized Sales Tax (HST) on heating costs would win favour with the province's pragmatic voters. But fall polls put the NDP at only 28 per cent support, and its leaders lamented the government's rising popularity, gained by implementing NDP ideas (*Chronicle-Herald*, 29 Dec.).

The Liberals tried to boost their waning fortunes but were forced to delay their leadership convention until the fall to focus on the federal election campaign. Liberals selected businessman Francis Mackenzie as leader in a lacklustre contest which did not generate much excitement or interest. All three candidates were originally from Cape Breton. Former cabinet minister Russell MacKinnon withdrew for lack of caucus support; he had angered many of his fellow MLAs by supporting the Hamm government's spring budget. Mackenzie beat out another former cabinet minister, Richie Mann. The party appeared tired by the divisive federal leadership battle, by federal and provincial elections, and by the loss of their promising young leader, Danny Graham, who had resigned to care for his ill wife. Prominent candidates withdrew early on and the online remote-voting system could not match the excitement of a live convention. Some insiders conceded that the party needed to generate new policies to re-engage with the voters, a tough task in the climate of cross-party cooperation needed to avoid a premature election. The party was in no shape for an electoral contest, but its poll numbers stayed competitive, even exceeding the NDP in the fall at 31 per cent support. This created hope the Liberals could return to a prominent role in future elections if Mackenzie could revitalize its platform and increase its effectiveness in the assembly.

The legislature

The minority government survived the brief spring session of the legislature, with support from the NDP. The opposition party backed legislation to rescind planned tax cuts, roll back a generous pay hike for MLAs, set up a modest debt-retirement fund of $6 million, limit property-tax assessments, and provide a $2.6-million tax break for an oil refinery. Other laws governed quarantine for pandemics like SARS, created a health-promotion office, and required proof of age for sale or rental of violent video games. The proposed Petroleum Pricing Act, which would require two days' notice of planned oil price hikes by retailers, was not passed before the session concluded; MLAs opted to wait while an all-party committee examined fuel pricing. The Liberals, who opposed the budget and other bills, expressed disappointment with the session, which they considered a 'bust.' But the NDP suggested that its support had helped make the minority government function in the citizen's interest (*Daily News*, 21 May). The calm was broken by one incident: MLAs were upset after a man was arrested in the legislature for carrying a concealed knife. This episode highlighted growing concerns about security at the legislature, where tumultuous protests by students, public-sector workers, and others remained commonplace.

The three parties agreed on the key priority of a balanced budget to avoid past pitfalls of deficits and spiralling debt. Negotiations over specific tax increases or spending cuts to achieve this goal remained more contentious. A proposed 39 per cent pay raise for MLAs was nixed by the premier. The April budget was heavy on fee increases and tax-cut rollbacks but did not incorporate significant new spending. It projected a surplus of $2.1 million on a total budget of $5.5 billion. Only those earning less than $29,590 a year would get the promised 10 per cent tax cut. Fees for motor- vehicle registration, court processes, and ambulances went up along with some 500 other fees. Tobacco taxes were increased by $5 a carton, and corporate taxes also rose. Business complained about the increases, which would undermine its already precarious competitive position. It also condemned a decision to defer action on reducing or eliminating the business-occupancy tax, which was a major source of municipal revenue but harmed the province's competitiveness.

As Official Opposition, the NDP influenced the budget's provisions rolling back tax cuts, which had threatened to force a deficit, and increasing taxes on the largest firms and wealthier taxpayers. The party also secured full coverage for health care for seniors in nursing homes and insisted on funds to reduce health-care wait times. The government resisted calls to exempt heating oil from the HST and instead provided a one-time low-income energy-assistance rebate of $200. The government also did not act on the NDP proposal for gas price regulation (*Daily News*, 3 Dec.). The opposition assailed a $1-million contract to a marketing agency to find a new 'brand' for promoting Nova Scotia to investors and tourists. The spending was considered wasteful at a time when user fees were rising and funding for the arts and other programs was shrinking.

Low-spending commitments for education were criticized. School boards scrambled to make cuts, and university tuition rose again to compensate for funding which remained at 1994 levels. The government pointed to funding for schools for special-needs education, math instruction, Black student support, and small classes at the primary levels. Nova Scotia ranked last among provinces in funding per student even before the budget. Universities also had to adjust to the lowest per-capita student funding in Canada; tuition, soaring to record levels, was now the highest in the country. Tuition rose 7.7 per cent in the fall and now averaged almost $6,000 per year for full-time university students.

Student leaders complained that the Conservatives rejected tuition roll-backs or freezes and removed loan remissions, leading to increased student debt and denying access to low-income residents (*Chronicle Herald*, 3 Sept.).

The NDP supported the budget after getting the government to cover full costs for health care for seniors in nursing homes; the party had criticized the policy whereby seniors had to liquidate assets, including residences, before health costs would be covered. With a majority as-sured, the Liberals were free to vote against the budget, even though it met their demand for a reduction in planned income-tax cuts to avoid a deficit. Some Liberals cited a shortfall in education and rural-develop-ment funding and failure to include a clear plan to address health-care costs; interim Liberal leader Wayne Gaudet noted that the balanced-budget projection was based on an optimistic economic scenario (*Cape Breton Post*, 18 May). Liberal MLA Russell MacKinnon broke ranks to support the budget, which may have undermined caucus support of his leadership bid later in the year. The premier blamed Ottawa for the province's austere position, pointing to the federal government's failure to deliver on promised health-care funding and equalization renewal.

The fall session was low key, with mostly housekeeping measures passed, thereby avoiding potential confrontation which could spark the government's defeat. The government went so far as to review draft legislation with opposition members in advance. Bills passed includ-ed measures to provide computerized monitoring of prescriptions, to help custodial parents gain child support, and to provide more French-language services in the public sector. A Tory backbencher succeeded with a private member's bill providing for binding arbitration instead of strikes for police. An NDP proposal mandating reporting for nursing-home abuse also passed. Liberal MLAs successfully moved a measure requiring use of booster seats for children between four and nine years old. A private member's bill to elect senators (modelled on Alberta's new practice) stalled. Partly reversing the premier's spring decision, MLAs quietly approved increases to their salaries, per diem rates, and housing allowances, which did not require receipts.

The opposition sought changes to provincial whistleblower policies which currently prohibited public servants from reporting suspected wrongdoing to the media, unions, or police; the policy was termed 'Or-wellian' and prevented the public from learning of wrongdoing (*Cape Breton Post*, 15 Dec.). Changes to workmen's compensation, and re-vised plans to cover unfunded liabilities, were required after a court ruling that chronic pain had to be covered in the plan; the Workmen's

Compensation Board sought to add sectors like banking and insurance to the system, to spread the costs. The government was forced to delay a measure allowing health-care professionals to make decisions for mental-health patients who were not competent to decide on essential care; it also delayed standards for ambulance services because of fears that some rural providers would be forced to close. Although the Liberals did attempt to paint the NDP as too soft as the Official Opposition, none of the parties had an interest in forcing an early election, and so, despite rancour, cooperation prevailed (*Chronicle-Herald*, 20 Oct.).

Economy

The provincial economy trailed Canada in growth in personal income and domestic provincial product. Lack of good employment opportunities sent young people elsewhere or mired them in service-sector jobs, with low wages and limited benefits, which had replaced employment in declining primary sectors. The province began touting immigration to provide a boost in population and taxable income in a region faced with an aging population and continued loss of its youth to other regions. Young people experienced mounting debts in a province with the highest tuition fees in Canada and could not afford to wait for good jobs at home. More promisingly, an international survey of business climate suggested that, in all of the countries of the Organisation for Economic Co-operation and Development (OECD), Nova Scotia communities, notably Pictou, Truro, Halifax, and Sydney, were among the most competitive places to operate. Provincial voters rejected Sunday shopping in a plebiscite held during municipal elections in October. The vote total, 53 per cent to 47 per cent, was viewed by government ministers as decisive. But some retail outlets planned to challenge the ban, citing an uneven playing field with smaller stores which were allowed to open (*Chronicle-Herald*, 7 Oct., 31 Dec.).

Projections for the offshore were mixed, after several years of stagnant royalties. Exploratory drilling came up empty in promising areas. Estimates for reserves in the Sable region were cut by 30 per cent following previous cuts in the past two years as existing facilities suffered from uneven gas flows. Encana and its partners delayed development plans for the Deep Panuke project and abandoned the Crimson well for lack of potential. Several prominent firms let drilling licences lapse and turned their attention elsewhere, such as the Arctic. After years of promises about a development windfall, political leaders now called for 'realistic' attitudes to the ups and downs of the offshore energy industry, which would take time to develop (*Chronicle-Herald*, 29 Dec.). Royalties from Sable gas were expected to drop from $27 million to $23 million, though the province hoped to retain more of this revenue under a deal to end equalization clawbacks. Despite uncertain production, the government estimated that it would reap between $600 million and $1.1 billion in royalties over the life of the Sable project.

Meanwhile, commercial distribution of natural gas in the province inched forward very modestly. Heritage Gas signed up some 125 customers, barely one-quarter of its estimate for the year. Fifty businesses were among the first to sign on as the pipeline expanded to thirty kilometres. Nova Scotia gas was being used by local consumers for the first time, since all previous production had been exported. The company still aimed to bring gas to towns like Amherst and expand in Dartmouth and elsewhere; some 20,000 homes and 6,500 businesses should, it claimed, have access by 2010. Expansion in alternative energy such as wind farms only partially compensated for decreased offshore fossil fuel activity. While alternative sources would supply some energy to Nova Scotia Power (NSP), the energy giant continued upgrades to coal-handling facilities and natural-gas conversion to meet its primary production requirements.

Nova Scotia Power was criticized for frequent and prolonged blackouts which critics blamed on degraded infrastructure. The company attributed its problems to adverse weather, including repairs from extensive damage caused by Hurricane Juan in 2003, a record-setting blizzard which dumped ninety centimetres of snow in February, and major fall storms. The mayor of Halifax and opposition leaders sought an independent review of whether Nova Scotia Power had undermined its maintenance services since privatization to boost profits. Untimely power outages coincided with NSP's application for a rate increase to cover $150 million in past taxes after courts rejected company claims to capital-cost-allowance deductions on borrowing costs of the crown corporation prior to privatization. Critics suggested that hefty bonuses for senior management made high rate claims unseemly and that costs to consumers for past taxes should be minimized (*Chronicle-Herald*, 24 Nov.). Eventually, somewhat lower rate increases were approved after negotiations with some of the company's largest clients; a consumer advocate was also brought in to represent the public in hearings on electricity rates. In another sector, the province's major telecom utility, Aliant, was hit with a prolonged strike which reduced company revenues and caused some customers to defect to competitors.

Despite pledges to end wasteful business subsidies, the government promised $4 million for Michelin's $41-million retooling of its three plants. The plants employed 3,400 people in otherwise distressed rural areas, making support for the firm politically significant. The opposition also criticized a $2.5-million loan guarantee to a lumber firm as a 'bailout.' The NDP pursued a freedom-of-information request on a payroll rebate to grocery giant Sobeys, claiming that the government was blocking the full release of details. Maritime Life was taken over by national giant Manulife but avoided some local job cuts when it attracted CGI from Montreal to partner on its information-technology needs. The move was assisted by a $7.9-million payroll rebate from Nova Scotia Business Inc. (NSBI), but CGI promised to attract other clients to create more high-paid jobs (*Chronicle-Herald*, 31 Dec.). The legislature adopted a motion opposing efforts by Clifford Frame, former operator of the ill-fated Westray coal mine, to reopen a zinc mine; after he retired as head of the company, the plan to reopen the Gay's River mine was reconsidered and the company examined the cost-effectiveness of the proposal.

NSBI announced that it would focus less on low-wage job creation in call centres, which had been the primary focus for the past decade. Instead, attention would shift to information technology, energy alternatives, manufacturing, and life sciences to generate better-paying jobs. Labour leaders suggested that other sectors might fit better with local markets and resources and be less likely to leave on short notice. Call centres were now often departing to seek cheaper labour in places like India, despite receiving NSBI salary rebates (*Daily News*, 23 April). Christmas tree producers faced a setback when U.S. inspectors held up shipments because of suspected infestation. Cattle producers were also faced with closure of the U.S. border because of fears of mad cow disease. Construction activity was high, especially in Metro Halifax, where several large-scale projects were under way. These included construction on the Halifax harbour clean-up project, airport expansion, and construction of a new community college campus, new university buildings, and several condominium complexes. Construction employment was up 20–25 per cent from 1999 levels. Several downtown tower proposals were slowed by public opposition. A rural development moratorium in the Halifax region helped boost residential growth in surrounding counties; the freeze was to be lifted once the regional planning process was complete (*Chronicle-Herald*, 21 Dec.).

Intergovernmental affairs

Nova Scotia was able to use the close federal election campaign of 28 June to get all parties to pay attention to its concerns about offshore energy revenues. The province had long complained that Ottawa had not delivered on royalty payments promised under the Atlantic Accord, signed in the 1980s with the Brian Mulroney government, which came due now that federal infrastructure costs for the offshore had been fully repaid. While this issue was deferred, Prime Minister Paul Martin was forced to consider ending the clawback which saw the province lose equalization funds as royalties rose, negating most of the revenues from offshore development. After a federal promise to Premier Danny Williams of Newfoundland and Labrador, Hamm applied pressure for a comparable deal. On the eve of the tight election race, Martin agreed to negotiate to improve the provincial share of royalties. Despite an agreement to raise federal equalization by up to $2 billion, Hamm was later angered by what he considered Martin's flip-flop on his promise to exempt Nova Scotia from equalization clawbacks after the election.

Under pressure from the resurgent Conservative opposition in Ottawa, the Liberal minority government finally agreed to remove the clawback but insisted on an eight-year time limit. Nova Scotia did not want to sign a deal with an 'expiry date.' The federal government resisted opposition calls, backed by Nova Scotia, to move away from a five-province standard for equalization to a new formula which included all ten provinces but excluded non-renewable resource revenues, such as offshore royalties. While sharing concerns over lost revenues from the equalization clawback, Premier Hamm did not raise the same degree of tension with Ottawa as Premier Williams, who stormed out of talks and removed Canadian flags from public buildings. After supporting Williams for some months, Hamm, at year's end, negotiated a solution which extended the accord from eight to sixteen years. This continued a trend of more conservative tactics by Nova Scotia, which divided the two provinces and did not contribute to winning gains for the Atlantic region over the long term.

Health-care costs were a major focus of intergovernmental negotiations. Despite a promising federal strategy to rectify past underfunding, Hamm claimed that Ottawa fell short by some $90 million in health-care funds and pressed the federal government to implement fully the recommendations of the Romanow Commission. Cash-poor provinces were not able to rectify shortcomings such as doctor shortages, emergency-care closures, or long wait times for surgery and treatment without additional federal financial support. Nova Scotia sought information about how the HST was collected and a legislative committee asked officials of the Canada Customs and Revenue Agency (CCRA) to testify. They backed out on short notice and the legislature issued subpoenas to compel them to appear. The CCRA sought legal advice. The province and Ottawa also squabbled over how to pay for the Sydney tar ponds clean-up. Ottawa offered 50 per cent but the province insisted it required a 70 per cent federal share to allow the much anticipated clean-up of Canada's worst polluted site.

Premier Hamm had planned to back Peter MacKay for the leadership of the united Conservative Party, despite MacKay's earlier promise never to merge the Conservatives with the Canadian Alliance. But MacKay bowed out of the race early on. Despite some initial reluctance, and his rejection in most areas of the province during leadership selection, Nova Scotia Conservatives rallied around Stephen Harper, who was selected as leader of the unified new Conservative Party, notwithstanding lingering resentment over his past comments on the region's 'defeatist' culture. The federal sponsorship scandal, which rocked the Liberal government of Paul Martin, touched the province, with reports of generous funding for the maintenance and repair of *Bluenose II*, the provincial icon and tourist magnet.

Nova Scotia municipalities sought changes to revenue equalization to ensure that all communities received comparable levels of services. They also wanted guarantees against escalating costs for education, fearing that budget cuts would force them to pay more to preserve some school programs, such as supplemental funding for music or the arts. The Union of Nova Scotia Municipalities recommended exemptions from provincial sales taxes, an end to the business-occupancy tax, and property-tax levies for Nova Scotia Power installations to boost municipal revenues. Criticism of the Hamm government was led by the Cape Breton Regional Municipality, which actually threatened legal action against the province for allegedly violating the Canadian constitution's equalization clause by 'shortchanging' Cape Breton (*Cape Breton Post*, 15 April). Halifax and Cape Breton were also at odds over whether Ottawa's proposed gas-tax payments for municipalities should be distributed by population or by 'need.' Ultimately, however, the province leaned to Cape Breton's need-based proposal and also preferred joint decisions by the three levels of government over use of the projected $85 million. Ottawa preferred distribution to municipalities on a per-capita basis (*Cape Breton Post*, 6 Aug.).

MELVIN BAKER AND PETER NEARY

Newfoundland and Labrador

The year 2004 was one of financial reckoning in Newfoundland and Labrador. On 5 January, Finance Minister Loyola Sullivan released a special review of the province's finances, *Directions, Choices and Tough Choices*, by PricewaterhouseCoopers (PwC). The report was sobering and was the focus of a 'State of the Province' address given by Premier Danny Williams the same evening. The PwC findings, he said, showed 'an evolving financial crisis,' which, 'if ignored or unresolved,' threatened the entire future of the province (Executive Council, News Release, 5 Jan.). What the situation required was 'accountable and strategically minded government' and decisions made 'for the right reasons – not for political reasons' (ibid.). The mess could not be 'fixed overnight' and would 'require hard work and sacrifice by everyone' (ibid.). Accordingly, in relation to pending contract negotiations, the government had made known to public-sector union leaders earlier in the day that it had no money for salary increases. On 20 February, Williams announced a restructuring of government departments.

The Speech from the Throne read by Lieutenant Governor Edward Roberts on 18 March at the opening of the 1st session of the 45th General Assembly reiterated the themes of fiscal restraint and administrative improvement. The government's 'new approach' would highlight three priorities during the coming year: economic growth, the administration of 'low-waste, high-quality social programs,' and improvement of federal-provincial relations to bring 'real benefits to the people, economy and treasury' (Executive Council, News Release, 18 March). The government was committed to 'fiscal discipline' and to begin bringing expenditures into line with revenue (ibid.). In keeping with all of this, the legislature would be asked to adopt 'a strict code of conduct' for members, along with new procedures for auditing members' expenses (ibid.). The government now also promised to regulate lobbyists, introduce a Transparency and Accountability Act, and ensure a stronger and more independent government purchasing agency. In the interest of procedural fairness, it promised to amend the House of Assembly Act to put general elections on a fixed four-year schedule and ensure timely by-elections.

Details of the government's plans for bringing the province 'back from the brink' financially followed in the budget speech delivered by Sullivan on 30 March, which forecast revenue of $3,948 million in 2004–5 and expenditure of $4,310 million for a cash deficit of $362 million (*House of Assembly Proceedings*, 30 March, vol. 45, no. 7). This was a considerable improvement on the deficit of $602 million for the year forecast by PwC, and the government's intention was to bring revenue and expenditure into balance in 2007–8. To achieve this, it would close offices and institutions, cancel some scheduled projects and defer others, eliminate 4,000 positions from the public service through attrition and retirement, drastically reduce the number of health and school boards, and increase tobacco taxes and vehicle-registration fees. One of the sacrifices to be made was the postponement for one year of the opening of The Rooms, the newly constructed gallery, archives, and museum complex in St John's. 'We are taming the fiscal tiger,' Sullivan confidently asserted, but the immediate result of the budget was bitter and prolonged strife with organized labour (ibid.).

At midnight on 31 March the Newfoundland Association of Public and Private Employees and the Canadian Union of Public Employees began a public-sector strike across the province. The government's pay offer proposed a five-year agreement with no wage increases in the first two years and increases of 2 per cent, 3 per cent, and 3 per cent in years three, four, and five respectively. By contrast, the unions wanted a five-year deal that would deliver 5 per cent increases in each of the last three years. 'We cannot,' the premier declared, 'ask every Newfoundlander and Labradorian to be part of the solution to our fiscal challenge, and not ask the same from the unions' (Executive Council, News Release, 31 March).

The strike proved long, bitter, and, at times, decidedly personal. The premier drew national attention by wading into picket lines outside the Confederation Building to talk directly with strikers. Ultimately, however, the government could not break the impasse and decided on back-to-work legislation, introduced on 26 April. In an attempt to head this off, the strikers returned to work on 28 April, but subsequent negotiations between the two sides also proved futile. Finally, on 3 May, the back-to-work legislation, which imposed the settlement the government wanted but was opposed by both Liberal and NDP members, was passed by the House. To say the least, the new government had weathered a hard storm.

But spring was now in the air, and with it came the federal election called by Prime Minister Paul Martin for 28 June. At dissolution, five of the Newfoundland and Labrador seats were held by the Liberals and two by the Conservatives. Thirty candidates stood for election in the province and the high point of the campaign was the visit of Prime Minister Martin on 4–5 June, en route to the D-Day 60th anniversary commemoration in France. On 5 June he made a commitment to give the province a better deal on offshore oil revenue under the 1985 Atlantic Accord. By a 1984 ruling of the Supreme Court of Canada, the oil was under federal jurisdiction, but development had proceeded under a joint arrangement specified in the Atlantic Accord and on the understanding that the province would be the 'principal beneficiary.'[1] This deal had been praised all round at its inception but, from the province's point of view, had not worked out well because of its adverse effect on equalization payments. Accordingly, it had become a matter of serious contention between St John's and Ottawa and had come to rival the 1969 Churchill Falls power contract and foreign overfishing in the province's list of wrongs inflicted on it in Confederation.

With Premier Williams now campaigning hard for 100 per cent of the offshore revenue and advising voters not to support the Liberals unless this was pledged, the prime minister was quoted as follows: 'I believe that Newfoundland and Labrador ought to be the primary beneficiary of the offshore resources, and what I have said to the premier is that I believe the proposal that he has put forth certainly provides the basis of an agreement between the two of us' (*Telegram*, 6 June). The details of all this Martin left to be worked out between the premier and Natural Resources Minister John Efford, the province's representative in the federal cabinet. Based on what Martin said in the media and to him personally in a phone conversation, Williams understood his 100 per cent revenue requirement to have been met. A long-standing Newfoundland and Labrador objective had apparently been realized. What effect all this had on the election outcome can only be speculated upon, but the result in seats was the same as in the general election of 2000 – five Liberals and two Conservatives. Geographically, as in 2000, the Conservatives won the St John's seats and the Liberals won everywhere else. Percentages of valid votes by party in the province were: Liberals, 48.0 per cent; Conservatives, 32.3 per cent; NDP, 17.5 per cent; Green, 1.6 per cent; Independent, 0.6 per cent.

---

1 http://www.cnopb.nfnet.com/publicat/reglaa_mou.pdf.

During the summer, Williams and his ministers were kept busy on a variety of projects. On 29 June, Education Minister John Ottenheimer announced the details of a promised commission on public post-secondary education. From 5–9 July the premier led a delegation to Ireland. On 27 July he announced the appointment of Bill Rowe, a former provincial Liberal cabinet minister and the province's leading talk-show host (on VOCM, St John's), to head a Newfoundland and Labrador Office of Federal-Provincial Relations in Ottawa. From 28–30 July, Williams attended the meeting of the Council of the Federation at Niagara-on-the-Lake, Ontario, and enthusiastically supported the proposal for a national pharmacare program. On 1 August an act passed by the legislature in June to roll back auto-insurance rates, a political hot potato in many parts of Canada, was proclaimed. On 25 August, Williams accompanied Paul Cellucci, the United States ambassador to Canada, on a tour of CFB 5 Wing Goose Bay, Labrador, a base for which the province was seeking business.

From 13–15 September, the premier attended the First Ministers Conference on health held in Ottawa. He was a prominent player on this occasion and welcomed the resulting agreement. On 27 September, however, this success was followed by the resignation of Health and Community Services Minister (and former Auditor General) Elizabeth Marshall, who criticized the premier for acting without consulting her. On 1 October, Williams shifted Ottenheimer to the post Marshall had vacated and named Tom Hedderson (Harbour Main-Whitbourne) as the new minister of education.

In the last quarter of the year, the premier's main preoccupation was the big campaign promise Prime Minister Martin had made in St John's in June. On 8 October the finance ministers of Newfoundland and Labrador, Nova Scotia, and Prince Edward Island met in Halifax to discuss 'regional concerns' before the First Ministers Conference on equalization the prime minister had called for 26 October in Ottawa (Finance, News Release, 8 Oct.). Four days later, Williams expressed concern about a meeting held in Montreal, also on 8 October, between premiers Jean Charest of Quebec, Gary Doer of Manitoba, and Bernard Lord of New Brunswick on the subject of equalization. While 'healthy dialogue' among premiers before the First Ministers Conference was a good thing, the 'voices of all provinces' must be fully represented and 'no other province or premier' could speak for Newfoundland and Labrador (Executive Council, News Release, 12 Oct.). Williams now also expressed concern about 'any linkages' between the equalization talks and the separate negotiations (flowing from the prime minister's campaign commitment) currently in progress between the federal government and his province and Nova Scotia (which had its own understanding with Ottawa) for a better deal on revenue from offshore resources (ibid.).

The premier went to Ottawa on schedule, but on 26 October, having received a bitterly disappointing letter from Finance Minister Ralph Goodale attaching terms to the prime minister's June commitment, decided not to attend the meeting on equalization. Instead, he immediately returned to St John's, where he received a hero's welcome at the airport for his strong stand on behalf of the province. On 27 October he explained his actions, which had attracted maximum national media attention, at a news conference. Following the prime minister's promise of 5 June, he explained, he had written him three times on the issue – on 10 June and 5 and 24 August. No written replies had been forthcoming, but Martin had 'stated privately and publicly that his word was good' and the province had therefore 'trusted him to fulfill his commitment' (Executive Council, News Release, 27 Oct.). Then came the bombshell of Goodale's letter, dated 24 October. This put a time limit of eight years (2004–5 to 2011–12) on the arrangement to be made and specified that additional payments to Newfoundland and Labrador could not 'result in the fiscal capacity of the province exceeding that of the province of Ontario in any given year' (ibid.). This, the finance minister asserted, 'had always been a part of the Prime Minister's discussions with Newfoundland and Labrador on how to provide net benefits to the province equivalent to 100 per cent of its offshore revenues' (ibid.). Williams rejected this position. The commitment Martin had made 'was simple and clear' (ibid.). It 'did not include a cap or a reference to fiscal capacity. It did not include any linkage to the fiscal capacity of other provinces. And, it did not include a time frame' (ibid.). Newfoundland had been promised '100 per cent of ... provincial offshore revenues with no clawback' and this was the promise that must be kept (ibid.). In a phone call, Williams said, he had asked the prime minister 'to honour his commitment once and for all' and they had agreed to talk further (ibid.).

On 10 November, premiers Williams and John Hamm of Nova Scotia met with the prime minister in Ottawa but no agreement was forthcoming. The scene next shifted to St John's, where Goodale and Privy Council Clerk Alex Himelfarb met with the premier and other provincial officials, again without settling matters. Thereafter, negotiations continued away from the glare of media attention but without a conclusion being reached. Eventually, Williams made known that his deadline was Christmas. Against this backdrop, he and Hamm met with Goodale in Winnipeg on 22 December. The meeting led to another walkout by the Newfoundland and Labrador leader. 'They've slapped us in the face at Christmastime,' he declared, and the province was through with the talks: 'We're done ... We waited long enough ... We are not talking to the federal government on this file any more. We have had it' (*Globe and Mail*, 23 Dec.).

For his part, Premier Hamm stayed with the negotiations and looked forward to hearing from federal officials about various technical issues that had arisen. Goodale offered this explanation for the impasse with Newfoundland and Labrador: 'Newfoundland's principal concerns seemed to relate to their requirements that even [at] the point from which they would graduate from equalization, they would want to retain 100 per cent of offset benefits [under equalization]' (ibid.). According to the finance minister, what Williams had requested in Winnipeg 'moved the bottom line, moved the goalpost, raised the stakes once again' (*London Free Press*, 24 Dec.). In Goodale's view, there was 'this constant effort to redefine success,' and Williams seemed 'absolutely unprepared to accept yes for an answer' (ibid.). By contrast, Williams now claimed that, under the arrangement proposed by Ottawa, the province would lose as much as $1 billion when it no longer qualified for equalization. 'We could have come home with a big cheque,' he said, 'but we were not prepared to leave money on the table that was rightfully ours' (ibid.). Back in St John's, he ordered that the Canadian flag no longer be flown on provincial public buildings. With this, a sour and divisive episode in federal-provincial relations rolled on into 2005.

All of this put the Liberal members of Parliament from Newfoundland and Labrador, especially John Efford, in a tight political corner. Provincialism reached high tide in Newfoundland and Labrador in the fall of 2004, and defending the federal government there – never an easy task – took on a whole new dimension. On 4 November, opposition leader Stephen Harper, seconded by Norman Doyle (St John's East), moved a motion in the House of Commons deploring the prime minister's attitude at the recent First Ministers Conference and calling on the federal government to keep its promise 'to allow the provinces of Newfoundland and Labrador, and Nova Scotia to keep 100% of their provincial offshore oil and gas revenues' (House of Commons, *Journals*, 4 Nov., 198–9). On 15 November the motion lost by 157 to 110, but Liberal members Bill Matthews (Random-Burin-St George's) and Scott Simms (Bonavista-Gander-Grand Falls-Windsor) had voted for the motion, which therefore won a majority among the Newfoundland and Labrador members. In December, after the prime minister had announced the government's intention to proceed with legislation in favour of same-sex marriage, there were reports that Efford might resign from cabinet.

If politics and federal-provincial relations dominated the news in Newfoundland and Labrador in 2004, the province's sizeable and voracious media machine had much else of substance to report. In February, Elizabeth Marshall released the interim report of a task force on the serious abuse of the painkiller OxyContin in the province. In October the Supreme Court of Canada upheld a decision of the Newfoundland and Labrador Court of Appeal in favour of the 1991 decision of the provincial government, on the grounds of financial hardship, to defer from 1988 to 1991 a pay-equity settlement for 5,300 female hospital workers and extinguish the 1988–91 arrears. In November, Justice Minister Tom Marshall announced an extension of one year in the work of the commission of inquiry being conducted by retired chief justice of Canada Antonio Lamer into alleged miscarriages of justice in the cases of Gregory Parsons, Randy Druken, and Ronald Dalton. On 21 December, Chief Justice Derek Green of the Supreme Court of Newfoundland and Labrador, Trial Division, ruled in favour of an application requesting the extension of the common-law definition of marriage to same-sex unions. The provincial government did not take a position for or against on this application, but promised to respect the decision of the court.

The year 2004 brought a variety of developments in the province's evolving relationship with its Aboriginal peoples. On 5 February, based on a legal review of the 19 September 2003 Supreme Court of Canada decision in *R. v. Powley*, Williams made known the government's position that the Labrador Métis did not enjoy Aboriginal rights. On 26 May the Labrador Inuit voted in favour of the ratification of the 29 August 2003 land-claims agreement with the provincial and federal governments. Then, on 6 December, provincial legislation to ratify the agreement (given all-party support in the House of Assembly) received assent. This was historic, but the government continued to face serious problems at Natuashish, the Labrador community to which the Innu of Davis Inlet had been resettled. In September, following two teenage suicides, community leaders appealed for emergency action to deal with continuing alcohol and solvent abuse. In December a report done by David Philpott of Memorial University for Indian and Northern Affairs Canada found many shortcomings in the education available at Natuashish and called for extensive change. Also in December, self-government negotiations began between the Miawpukek First Nation of Conne River, Newfoundland, and the federal and provincial governments.

Included in the province's 2004 necrology were: Mercedes Barry (co-founder of the theatre group Sheilagh's Brush), Otto Kelland (author of the 1947 ballad *Let Me Fish off Cape St. Mary's*, a provincial talisman), Jack Marshall (prominent veteran and former MP and senator), Corporal Jamie Murphy (killed serving in Afghanistan), Fabian O'Dea (former lieutenant governor), and Harry Roberts (first Newfoundland president of the Canadian Medical Association). On 16 December, Lawrence O'Brien, the Liberal MP for Labrador, died of cancer in St John's. He was a good friend of the prime minister, who interrupted a North African trip to attend his funeral at Happy Valley-Goose Bay on 20 December. On 19 September 2004 the fishing vessel *Ryan's Commander* from St Brendan's, Bonavista Bay, capsized near Cape Bonavista in a howling autumn storm, whereupon a brave and daring rescue mission was undertaken by a Canadian Forces Cormorant helicopter from 103 Search and Rescue Squadron, Gander, piloted by Captain Scott Tromp. In the event, four crew members of the vessel survived, but brothers David and Joseph Ryan were lost. In 2004, as always, nature was never far from the news in Newfoundland and Labrador.

Obituaries

AGOSTINO, DOMINIC (24 March, age 43). Ontario Liberal MPP for Hamilton East from 1995 to 2004.

ARAFAT, YASSER (11 November, age 75). Chairman of the Palestinian Liberation Organization (PLO).

BARRIS, ALEX (15 January, age 81). Journalist, author, and television personality; member of the Order of Canada.

BERTON, PIERRE (30 November, age 84). Renowned author, newspaper columnist, and television personality; companion of the Order of Canada.

BOUEY, GERALD (9 February, age 83). Governor of the Bank of Canada between 1973 and 1987; companion of the Order of Canada.

BRADSELL, ANDY (28 March, age 33). Security contractor.

CAMPBELL, NORMAN (12 April, age 80). Composer, television producer and director, and co-writer of *Anne of Green Gables – The Musical*; officer of Order of Canada.

CANTOR, NORMAN (18 September, age 74). Canadian historian of medieval history and author.

CHAREST, MICHELINE (14 April, age 51). Television producer and co-founder of animation company Cinar Corporation.

CONDO, RAY (15 April, age 54). Musician.

COTRONI, FRANK (17 August, age 71). Reputed Montreal mobster.

CREIGHTON, DOUGLAS (7 January, age 75). Founding publisher of the *Toronto Sun*; companion of the Order of Canada.

DRYDEN, MURRAY (1 February, age 92). Father of former NHL goalie and current MP Ken Dryden.

EARLE, TOM (19 October, age 77). Journalist and first radio or TV reporter permitted access to the Parliamentary Press Gallery in Ottawa.

FAIRCLOUGH, ELLEN (13 November, age 99). First woman to serve as cabinet minister in Canada; served as secretary of state and minister of citizenship and immigration under John Diefenbaker; officer of the Order of Canada.

FIA, ALBERT (5 June, age 89). Aerospace engineer, first non-American to be awarded NASA's public service award.

GIBSON, ERNEST (20 January, age 102). Reported to be the last surviving person to have served with the Royal North West Mounted Police.

GIGANTES, PHILIPPE DEANE (9 December, age 81). Journalist, author, Liberal Senator, and former aide to Pierre Trudeau.

GLASSCO, WILLIAM (13 September, age 69). Professor of English, co-founder of Toronto's Tarragon Theatre and former artistic director of CentreStage – now Canadian Stage; officer of the Order of Canada.

GOLDSCHMIDT, NICHOLAS (8 February, age 95). Pianist, conductor, and founder of the Canadian Opera Company; officer of the Order of Canada.

HEAD, IVAN (1 November, age 74). Lawyer, professor of law, and political adviser to Pierre Trudeau; officer of the Order of Canada.

IANNUZZI, DAN (21 November, age 70). Co-founder of CityTV and OMNI television stations; member of the Order of Canada.

JEWISON, MARGARET ANN ('Dixie') (26 November, age 74). Wife of film director Norman Jewison.

JOHNSTONE, LUCILLE (31 December, age 80). Entrepreneur and social activist; appointed to the Orders of British Columbia and Canada.

KANDER, JUNE (26 December, age 73). Humanitarian and educator, died in the Asian Tsunami.

KASH, EUGENE (6 March, age 91). Violinist and former music director of the National Film Board.

KIERANS, ERIC (9 May, age 90). Former Quebec minister of revenue and health under the Liberal government of Jean Lesage; officer of the Order of Canada.

LAVOIE, SERGE (4 December, age 41). Former principal dancer with the National Ballet of Canada.

LINEHAN, BRIAN (4 June, age 58). Television personality.

MCCAIN, HARRISON (18 March, age 76). Co-founder of McCain Foods Ltd.

MCCLELLAND, JOHN ('Jack') (14 June, age 81). Former president of Canadian publishing company McClelland and Stewart; companion of the Order of Canada.

MCCLUNG, JOHN (21 October, age 69). Alberta justice and grandson of Nellie McClung.

MARSHALL, JACK (17 August, age 84). Conservative Party member of

the House of Commons for Humber-St George-St Barbe as well as
a senator; member of the Order of Canada.

MAXWELL, BRIAN (19 March, age 51). Marathoner and developer of
PowerBar energy bars.

MERRITHEW, GERALD STAIRS (5 September, age 72). Former New
Brunswick Progressive Conservative cabinet minister in the 1970s
and 1980s and federal Conservative cabinet minister in the 1980s
and 1990s.

MORGAN, JOHN (16 November, age 74). Award-wining comedian and
founding member of the Royal Canadian Air Farce.

MORTON, DOUGLAS (4 January, age 77). Painter, member of Regina
Five.

NORMAN, MOE (4 September, age 75). Professional golfer.

O'BRIEN, LAWRENCE (16 December, age 53). MP for Labrador from
1996 to 2004.

OLIPHANT, BETTY (12 July, age 85). Co-founder of the National Ballet School of Canada; companion of the Order of Canada.

ONLEY, TONI (29 February, age 75). Renowned landscape painter;
officer of the Order of Canada.

PALMER, BRUCE (1 October, age 52). Musician and co-founder of
rock group Buffalo Springfield.

PENNER, JIM (17 January, age 65). Manitoba politician, member of
provincial legislature from 1999 to 2003.

PENNER, RICHARD (13 January, age 56). Director of Afghan operations for the aid organization World Concern.

POULIOT, JEAN (8 August, age 81). Founder of Quebec television networks TVA and TQS.

REAGAN, RONALD (June 5, age 93). Fortieth president of the United
States, California governor, and Hollywood actor.

RUCK, CALVIN (19 October, age 79). Author, activist, and senator
from 1998 to 2000; member of the Order of Canada.

RUTLEDGE, MARGARET FANE (2 December, age 90). Female aviation pioneer and inductee of the British Columbia Aviation Hall of
Fame.

RYAN, CLAUDE (9 February, age 79). Quebec politician who led the
provincial Liberal Party between 1978 and 1982.

SAMSON, ANNIE (29 November, age 113). Reported to be oldest person in Canada.

SCOTT, EDWARD (21 June, age 85). Archbishop of the Anglican
Church of Canada between 1971 and 1986; recipient of the Pearson
Medal of Peace.

SEVIGNY, PIERRE (21 March, age 87). Former associate minister of defence under John Diefenbaker; officer of the Order of Canada.

SHARP, MITCHELL (19 March, age 92). Former minster of trade and commerce, finance, and external affairs under Lester B. Pearson and Pierre Trudeau; companion of the Order of Canada.

SIMPKINS, JAMES (1 February, age 93). Cartoon artist and creator of what would become the mascot for Jasper National Park.

STEWART, WALTER (14 September, age 73). Journalist, author, editor, and former Max Bell chair of journalism at the University of Regina.

STEWART, WILLIAM (13 December, age 90). War correspondent during the Second World War and former Montreal bureau chief for the Canadian Press.

STRIKE, ALICE (22 December, age 108). Reported to be the oldest surviving as well as the last surviving female veteran of the First World War in Canada.

TAYLOR, NATHAN (1 March, age 98). Co-founder of Cineplex Odeon and responsible for the building of the world's first multi-screened movie theatre.

VIENNEAU, DAVID (1 December, age 53). Print, television journalist, and former Ottawa bureau chief for Global Television.

WADDINGTON, MIRIAM (3 March, age 86). Poet, short-story writer, and translator.

WADSWORTH, MIKE (28 April, age 60). Former CFL football player, ambassador to Ireland, and athletic director at the University of Notre Dame.

WICKMAN, PERCY DWIGHT (3 July, age 63). Albertan politician who championed rights for those with disabilities.

WICKS, DOREEN (1 March, age 69). Humanitarian, citizenship judge, wife of cartoonist Ben Wicks; member of the Order of Canada.

WRAY, FAY (8 August, age 96). Female actor who starred in cinematic classic King Kong.

Election tables

Canada, Thirty-Eighth General Election, 2004

Political party	Votes received	Percentage of popular vote	Candidates elected
Bloc Québécois	1,680,109	17.5	54
Canadian Action Party	8,807	0	0
Christian Heritage Party	40,335	0	0
Communist Party of Canada	4,426	0	0
Conservative Party of Canada	4,019,498	32.1	99
Green Party of Canada	582,247	0	0
Liberal Party of Canada	4,982,220	43.8	135
Libertarian Party of Canada	1,949	0	0
Marijuana Party	33,276	0	0
Marxist-Leninist Party of Canada	8,696	0	0
New Democratic Party	2,127,403	6.2	19
Progressive Canadian Party	10,872	0	0
Independents	47,068	0	0
No affiliation	17,796	0.3	1
Rejected ballots	118,868		
Total	13,683,570 [a]	100	308

Source: Elections Canada
[a] There were 22,466,621 eligible voters; voter turnout was 60.9 per cent.

Alberta, Twenty-Sixth General Election, 22 November 2004

Political party	Votes received	Percentage of popular vote	Candidates elected
Alberta Alliance Party	77,466	8.70	1
Communist Party	98	0.01	0
Alberta Greens	24,451	2.75	0
Alberta Liberal Party	261,737	29.39	16
Alberta New Democratic Party	90,829	10.20	4
Progressive Conservative Association of Alberta	416,886	46.80	62
Separation Party of Alberta	4,695	0.53	0
Social Credit Party	10,998	1.23	0
Independents	994	0.11	0
Rejected ballots	3,956		n/a
Total	894,591[a]	100	83

Source: Elections Alberta
[a] There were 2,001,287 eligible voters; voter turnout was 44.70 per cent.

Nunavut, Second General Election, 16 February 2004[ab]

District	Votes received	Percentage of valid votes	Candidate elected	Candidates defeated
Akulliq	161	34	Steve Mapsalak	George Bohlender, Joani Kringayark, John Ningark, Roland Tungilik
Amittuq	277	40	Louis Tapardjuk	Solomon Allurut, Enoki Irqittuq, Paul Hauli, Levi Kaunak
Arviat	282	37	David Alagalak	Peter Alareak, Peter Two Aulatjut, Kevin O'Brien, Jay Saint, Kono Tattuinee
Baker Lake	352	48	David Simailak	David Askawnee, Becky Kudloo, David Toolooktook
Cambridge Bay	311	54	Keith Peterson	Harry A.M. Aknavigak, David Kaosoni, Harry Maksagak
Hudson Bay	127	43	Peter Kattuk	Moses Appaqaq Jr., Joe Arragutainaq, Kupapik Nineocheak, Johnny Tookalook,

Iqaluit Centre	263	45	Hunter Tootoo	Natsiq Alainga-Kango, Mike Courtney, Kevin MacCormack, Pauloosie Paniloo, Mary Ellen Thomas
Iqaluit East	569	70.5	Edward Walter Picco	John Amagoalik, Norman Ishulutak
Iqaluit West	415	76.99	Paul Okalik	Doug Workman
Kugluktuk	215	40	Joe Allen Evyagotailak	Donald Havioyak, Millie Kuliktana
Nanulik	154	35	Patterk Netser	Emily Beardsall, Willie Nakoolak, Bernard Putulik Sr.
Nattilik	305	43	Leona Aglukkaq	Tom Akoak, Anthony Anguttitauruq, David Irqiut, Simon Qingnaqtuq, Sonny Porter, Ruediger H. J. Rasch
Pangnirtung	305	62	Peter Kalabuk	Simeonie Keenainak
Quttiktug	174	44	Levi Barnabas	Lucas Amagoalik, Pauloosie Attagootak, Larry Audlaluk, Anthony Ullikatar, Rebekah Uql Williams
Rankin Inlet North	n/a	Acclaimed	Tagak Curley	n/a
Rankin Inlet South Whale Cove	206	38	Lavinia Brown	Jerry Ell, Percy Kabloona, Ishmael Naulalik, Solomon Voisey
South Baffin	300	58.59	Olayuk Akesuk	Malicktoo Lyta, Martha Lyta
Tunnuniq	142	31	Jobie Nutarak	Enuaraq Appitaq, Sam Omik, David Qamaniq
Uqqummiut	148	26	James Arreak	Stevie Audlakiak, Phoebe Hainu Palluq, Peter Iqualukjuak, David Iqaqrialu, Samuel Nuqungaq, Lootie Toomasie

---

Source: Elections Nunavut Reports to the Legislative Assembly by the Chief Electoral Officer.

[a] There are no political parties in Nunavut, since the territorial government functions on a consensus-building rather than on an adversarial basis.

[b] There were 11,285 eligible voters at the time the election was called but more showed up on election day to vote (final count was 13,302); voter turnout was 81.22 per cent (based on the final voting list count).

Index of names

Index of subjects